White But Not Equal

White But Not Equal

MEXICAN AMERICANS, JURY DISCRIMINATION, AND THE SUPREME COURT

Ignacio M. García

the university of arizona press | tucson

The University of Arizona Press
© 2009 The Arizona Board of Regents
All rights reserved

www.uapress.arizona.edu

Library of Congress Cataloging-in-Publication Data

García, Ignacio M.
   White but not equal : Mexican Americans, jury
discrimination, and the Supreme Court / Ignacio M.
García.
      p. cm.
   Includes bibliographical references and index.
   ISBN 978-0-8165-2750-2 (hardcover : alk. paper) –
   ISBN 978-0-8165-2751-9 (pbk. : alk. paper)
   1. Hernández, Pete—Trials, litigation, etc. 2. Jackson
County (Tex.)—Trials, litigation, etc. 3. Trials (Murder)—
Texas—Jackson County. 4. Race discrimination—
Texas—Jackson County. 5. Jury selection—United
States. I. Title.
KF224.H468G37   2008
345.73'0252309764127—dc22   2008036617

Publication of this book is made possible in part by the
proceeds of a permanent endowment created with the
assistance of a Challenge Grant from the National Endowment for the Humanities, a federal agency.

13   12   11   10   6   5   4   3

This book is dedicated to Gustavo "Gus" García, Carlos Cadena, John J. Herrera, and James De Anda for their tenacious pursuit of jury rights for their people. And to every other civil rights lawyer and reformer of the 1950s. They truly earned their stripes in the most difficult of times.

Contents

Illustrations

All photographs are from the Dr. Hector P. Garcia Papers,
Special Collections & Archives, Bell Library, Texas A&M University,
Corpus Christi.

Acknowledgments

No book is ever easy to write, although they are often very fulfilling once the hard work is done. This one was no different though I was particularly lucky to have some very fine research assistants and some very good colleagues who helped me complete the work. Dan Combs, David Wilson, Jed Rogers, and Gilbert Bradshaw were outstanding research assistants who contributed in more ways than I can acknowledge. I was lucky that two of them, Dan and Jed, are going to be very good historians in their own right, and that David and Gilbert will be outstanding lawyers. All of them got interested in the work and so they contributed ideas and asked some very hard questions about what I was doing. Brigham Young University should be very proud of these talented graduate students.

I also had the "usual suspects" in my corner. Those who have read my past books will know that Grace Charles and Tom Kreneck have been constant companions in my historical voyages. Grace (as assistant archivist) and Tom (as head of the Special Collections at Texas A&M University in Corpus Christi, Texas) both facilitated my research by providing me not only with documents but also with their own knowledge of the case and the individuals involved. They also served as sounding boards for my often unfounded ideas.

I was also lucky to meet up with two other individuals interested in the *Hernández v. Texas* case. They were Carlos Sandoval, an award-winning filmmaker, and Robert Piña, a playwright from California. Sandoval's camera opened up several doors in Edna, Texas, where the case originated, and Robert provided me with some material he found. Both were helpful and our correspondence and conversations truly helped this work along. I was particularly motivated and inspired by the several days I spent with Carlos as he and his crew filmed places and individuals in Edna. His documentary about the case is an excellent piece of work that will complement this book and provide a visual sense of the importance of the case.

I was greatly assisted in this work by several legal scholars who have written on the case. Some are quoted in this work, others are not. Yet all those whose names follow provided me the foundation upon which to build my own work. To Michael A. Olivas, Ian Haney López, Kevin R. Johnson, Juan Francisco Perea, Clare Sheridan, Richard Delgado, George A. Martínez, and to others left unmentioned, thank you. Your scholarship made mine possible, even though you might justifiably take issue with my conclusions.

Finally, I am grateful to my wife Alex and my grandson Adrian, who often accompanied me on my research trips to do this book and were quite tolerant of staying in cheap motels in small Texas rural towns, eating greasy food, and waiting in the lobby of small public libraries as I went through rolls of microfilm. They are my inspiration as are my other children and grandchildren, who proudly proclaim that one of "theirs" writes books.

White But Not Equal

Introduction

Oralia did not hear the shot, being too preoccupied with the thoughts of a twelve-year-old child, but she saw her father's foreman come out of the tavern, approach the brand new '51 pickup and blurt out, "Caetano has been shot!" When she rushed to her father's side, Joe "Caetano" Espinoza was under a tree, breathing heavily, with a small bullet hole near his heart, but still conscious enough to give her his billfold and his watch. Thirty minutes later he was dead, the victim of an argument with a young cotton picker. One more dead Mexican at a local cantina in a rural Texas town might not have been important to most people, but this particular crime ended up having constitutional and political ramifications well beyond Edna, Texas. Three years after the shooting—on May 3, 1954—Espinoza's killer's conviction would be reversed in the Supreme Court's first landmark civil rights case under Chief Justice Earl Warren, and the first dealing with the rights of Mexican Americans under the U.S. Constitution.

The high court ruled that Pete Hernández, the quick-tempered twenty-one-year-old cotton picker who shot Oralia's father, had indeed been discriminated against, and so had many other Mexican Americans before him, in the selection of the jury that convicted and sentenced him to life in prison for Espinoza's death. Speaking for the majority—two weeks before the more famous *Brown v. Board of Education*—Chief Justice Warren wrote, "It taxes our credulity to say that mere chance resulted in there being no members of this class (Mexican Americans) among the over six thousand jurors called in the past twenty-five years [in Jackson County, Texas]. The results bespeak discrimination, whether or not it was a conscious decision on the part of any individual jury commissioner."

It would take many years before Oralia fully understood what had happened to her father's killer, but for Mexican American reformers, the ruling provided them an immediate opportunity to highlight on the national stage the struggle of their people to gain full acceptance of their citizenship. Jury discrimination had been one of the most insidious forms of discrimination that Mexican Americans confronted in the pre–civil rights era. It affected them negatively in two ways: first, it meant that there were no jurors who understood the circumstances that often led many Mexican Americans to fall on the wrong side of the law; and second, being denied a seat on the jury box was a denial of one of the most fundamental of American rights— to sit in judgment of one's peers.

For Mexican Americans, being judged by a jury composed solely of those who rarely understood them and often discriminated against them was tantamount to having the legal system against them. After all, what could they expect of the same people who treated them as second-class citizens, who refused to pay them adequate wages, segregated their children in school, and saw them as "foreigners" and as racially different? Could these jurors by themselves be trusted to understand the cultural and social nuances that separated them from those whom they judged? Could they be expected to be sensitive to the accused when no one was there to silence their prejudices? And could Mexican Americans ever be seen as fully engaged citizens if they could not participate in one of the most important functions of a citizen? If Mexican Americans were not considered trustworthy to sit in judgment of their fellow Americans, could they be trusted with their vote or with their leadership? Could they be good neighbors?

Taking *Hernández v. Texas* all the way to the Supreme Court became the summit of Mexican American litigation up to that point because the outcome influenced greatly how Mexican Americans saw themselves in American society. The case itself did not create a new view of Mexican Americans but rather confirmed one that reformers had been forging for nearly a quarter century. In their minds, Mexican Americans were loyal citizens who had gone to war for their country, fed the nation with their labor, constructed its highways and public buildings, and believed firmly in the "American way." They thus believed that they deserved to be allowed to fulfill their civic obligations and to be trusted to be good citizens. Sitting in a jury, hearing the evidence, and making an informed decision represented an opportunity to prove their worthiness as Americans. Just as important was having the opportunity to counter the backroom prejudices that might creep into a final decision when the life of a Mexican hung in the balance.

For a quarter of a century, Mexican Americans had been litigating for inclusion under the nation's judicial umbrella, and during that time a number of issues dealing with Mexican American civil rights had come to the forefront. One, in particular, came to dominate the discussion among Mexican American civil rights advocates in the 1950s: Were Mexican Americans white or people of color? If of color, then precisely what color? And how were their rights to be constructed in a society that seemed to only see black and white when it came to judicial and civil rights matters? This was a critical matter for Mexican Americans through most of the twentieth century and one that continues to be debated even today in some quarters. What does it mean to be white "but not really" and to be "of color" but not black?

In essence much of the discussion and legal maneuvering of *Hernández v. Texas* would revolve around this question because being "in-between" white and black provided the foundation for rampant discrimination and exclusion of people of Mexican descent. They were not seen as able to fulfill their role as full citizens—that is of being white—but at the same time did not merit inclusion in the Equal Protection Clause of the U.S. Constitution because they were not black. To be protected, they had to be one or the other or find a way to legitimize a separateness that would integrate them into the American judicial color scheme. The challenge proved difficult for Mexican American civil rights advocates. Their own ambivalence toward their identity compounded the problem. It was easier for their working-class neighbors in the barrio to see themselves as "Mexican" or brown. Many Mexicans of the early twentieth century and especially those who were immigrants did not yet confront the issue of whiteness, nor the need to pick a color in American society. Mexican Americans—those born in the United States or naturalized as American citizens—however, were a different story. They understood well that as the "other" or "foreigners" or "greasers" or simply "Mexicans" they were being classified away from full inclusion in American society. And inclusion was, in their minds, the only way they could benefit fully from their status as citizens.

It was quite apparent to early civil rights leaders that Mexican Americans had to make a collective surge toward integration in order to acquire and safeguard their rights as citizens. This is why *Hernández v. Texas* became such an important piece of litigation. It was through this case and in the nation's courtrooms that Mexican Americans sought to present their own views of where they "fit" in American society and where they stood on the American binary of black and white. They also sought to formalize a new philosophy of what it meant to be Mexican Americans, which while recognizing their national origins spoke to their firm belief that they were Americans first and foremost. Having replaced the immigrant leaders and political leftists of the past as the new elites in the barrios of the Southwest, these more Americanized reformers saw this as their time.

To prosecutors, however, it was a simple case of one Mexican killing another in a barroom fight. There were witnesses, an initial confession of self-defense, and the murder victim had been a popular Mexican American in the area. For the defense it was also a simple case. The man had committed the crime and the extenuating circumstances were suspect. At any other time, the court proceedings would have led to a conviction and life imprisonment, which is what Pete Hernández initially received. The crime, however, occurred at an important point in Mexican American civil rights litigation and advocacy.

Mexican American civil rights activity had surged during the late 1930s and most of the 1940s and victories in the courtroom had been surprisingly frequent. Throughout the Southwest, Mexican Americans had challenged segregation and discrimination—mostly in the public schools—at an unprecedented level. Supporting this litigation were a host of advocacy organizations and individuals who challenged America's commitment to the principles it had extolled during the just-concluded Second World War. By the start of the 1950s, Mexican Americans were also beginning to participate in the electoral process more frequently. Although they did not yet form a national constituency, they were already important in some localities and even dominant in others. Anglo politicians were often disdainful of Mexican American concerns but in close races they sought to be the "least" of the competing evils.[1] Blatant discrimination was also becoming more difficult to defend in the public arena.

The changing nature of Mexican American subordination made it possible for Mexican American lawyers to challenge discrimination in other areas besides education. While their "public school" victories—of which there had been many by the 1950s—had not yet changed the status quo, they were confident that the court decisions were building a foundation for decisive victories in the future. More important, Mexican Americans now had lawyers within the community who were capable of taking a case all the way to the Supreme Court and winning. The lawyers in the *Hernández* case—Gustavo "Gus" García, Carlos Cadena, John J. Herrera, and James De Anda—were part of a small but tenacious group of lawyers challenging discrimination throughout the West and Southwest. They formed part of a new generation of veterans of both world wars who came home ready to fight for their rights. Native-born, well educated, and proud of their identity, they had no fear of taking on a society and a judicial system that discriminated against their people.

This story, then, is about how this case reflected this new attitude of reformers in the larger Mexican American civil rights effort. It is also about being white but a "class apart" and about not being black while being a "person of color." It is about understanding the historical crevices that Mexican American civil rights have occupied and about why they are important to the historical record. As the final ruling of the Court did, this work provides a space for Mexican American civil rights that is neither exclusively white nor predominantly black. In this, it goes contrary to much of the scholarship and the unofficial, but very political, interpretation of Mexican American civil rights history.

Political correctness of the conservative, liberal, and even radical persuasions argues that Mexican American civil rights history is either about joining the mainstream or about being part of the vanguard of the "people of color's" challenge to the mainstream. Neither one of those approaches accepts the reality that Mexican Americans have had to find their own niche in American society. Mexican American civil rights efforts rarely had the benefit of white liberal legal or philanthropic support and African American civil libertarians only occasionally thought of Mexican American rights in their difficult but often well-supported legal and civic crusades for their rights. In focusing on Mexican American civil rights litigation and advocacy, we see the continuing difficulty that non-black ethnic and racial groups have in fully participating in the larger society. Mexican Americans have, through their civil rights litigation, reinforced the notions of national origin, immigration status, language, and another race—neither white nor black—as part of the equation of the rights of citizenship.

Now, at a time when Latinos—a majority of whom are of Mexican descent—are the nation's largest minority and are challenging African Americans for the forefront in the battle for civil and human rights, it is time to look at civil rights history from another viewpoint, one that is almost as old as the traditional one. In doing so, we'll see how much the black/white binary of American civil rights history has distorted the history of other groups, and obfuscated the development of equal protection in American society. More important for Mexican Americans and other Latinos, a new view of civil rights history underscores the tenacity of their struggle and the difficulty of finding an identity that actually works for them in the United States. This identity is not about a traditional ethnic identity, but rather about finding a philosophical as well as judicial "self" that fully encapsulates their experience as a transnational people with very different—one could argue unique—historical antecedents. This viewpoint further demolishes the notion that American civil rights history, like its cousin—national American history—is one forged only in a process of moving from east to west, and battling slavery, black codes, Jim Crow, and legal segregation. While this book will not dwell on the larger civil rights history of Mexican Americans, it will provide a clearer picture of how we can understand it, and how we can incorporate it into American history.

This work also provides an important, though limited, glimpse of whites or Anglos and their reactions to the shifting political winds in Texas and the rest of the Southwest and West in the 1950s. Any change back then in the legal position of Mexican Americans presented new problems for the larger community, which for years had either ignored or sought to contain the influence of this community. Most Anglo politicians, policymakers, and intellectuals understood that Mexican Americans presented a major problem in maintaining a society that favored whites. Unlike African Americans (who were legally segregated) and other non-white groups (who lacked the numbers to challenge the status quo), Mexican Americans had legal status as whites—though they were treated as non-white—and were growing in number rapidly. That their labor was crucial for American postwar industries added another aspect to the dilemma.

Throughout the Southwest whites had been able to keep Mexican Americans as outsiders and second-class citizens with minimal use of legal means. De facto segregation and discrimination—that is discrimination based on tradition, customs, or cultural and racial prejudices rather than law—had been an effective method of keeping Mexican Americans from participating in the larger society. It had been effective because de facto exclusion had made class, color, gender, education, and political ties qualifiers for acceptance. This meant that only those with money, education, and political connections could participate, and even then only if they insisted. These qualifiers lay the burden of inclusion on the Mexican Americans themselves. Historian David Montejano has argued that for segregation to have been successful, many Mexican Americans had to internalize their own inferiority.[2] White supremacy could not exist as dominantly if all their efforts were constantly and energetically resisted. Thus, there were many Mexican Americans who acknowledged or who grudgingly accepted those qualifiers. The relatively few Mexican Americans who actually participated in the larger society shows that these qualifiers were difficult hurdles to overcome.

The law, which favored Anglos over African Americans in Texas and the rest of the Southwest, however, was the "Achilles heel" of segregation when it came to Mexican Americans. By the 1950s the law had recognized Mexican Americans as white for a century through the provisions of the

Treaty of Guadalupe Hidalgo that had ended the U.S.–Mexican War. The treaty had given Mexicans rights of citizenship, which at the time was reserved exclusively for whites, thus making them "white by law." While this recognition had been tenuous at best, it remained on the books and was a frequent "Exhibit A" for Mexican American lawyers in their lawsuits for equal treatment. For those who sought to continue to exclude Mexican Americans from full participation, the challenge was to maintain them in a socially subordinate state and to obfuscate the meaning of "white" for Mexican Americans. Anglo lawyers and judges used two strategies to accomplish the latter.

They first used the issue of qualifications to exclude Mexican Americans from many forms of civic participation, including jury duty. The argument went that Mexican Americans owned little property, rarely could afford to pay their poll tax, lacked English skills, were ignorant of the law, or were simply too indifferent to American values to merit full participation. But the rise of a Mexican American middle class in the 1940s and the return of many World War II veterans challenged that notion. Jury commissions continued to exclude Mexican Americans, but they could no longer defend publicly the exclusion on the basis of qualifications. Mexican American lawyers could always point to a small group of Mexican Americans who were able and willing to participate. The strategy of exclusion then shifted to the use of a form of color blindness that argued that white juries already served as juries "of their peers." That is, since Mexican Americans were white, any jury of twelve white people could pose as a fair jury.

This meant that Anglos could continue to keep Mexican Americans from jury duty without passing new laws or defending what by the 1940s was a politically unwise strategy. The realm of discrimination thus fluidly moved from a racialization of disqualification to a racialization of whiteness without benefits. Initially damned because they were not white, they were later damned as too white to be covered by the Equal Protection Clause of the Fourteenth Amendment to the U.S. Constitution. The use of color as a de facto exclusion was a dangerous game because it was based on hair-splitting explanations of how Mexican Americans were treated as equals in spite of the overwhelming evidence to the contrary. But many Anglos clung to this "white but not equal" ideology because in their minds it took the "Mexican problem" out of the realm of racial politics, and because regional courts had shown hostility to jury discrimination cases dealing with Mexican Americans or other Latinos in the first half of the twentieth century.

This exclusion, regardless of its foundation, spoke to the position of Mexican Americans in Texas and much of the Southwest. Whiteness and blackness were the political and social poles in American society. But in legal and social interpretations, Mexican Americans oscillated from white to colored, and any number of interpretations could put them on one side or the other. This made it difficult to follow one winning legal or political strategy. Whiteness, with all its inherit advantages, was always the preferred status, but because it was so difficult to attain—and maintain—and because there were many Mexican Americans who did not want to consider themselves Anglo and many Anglos who also did not want to consider them as such, the strategy of race could not be ignored. Mexican American lawyers claimed that their constituencies were treated as a different race and thus deserved protection under the Fourteenth Amendment. The competing strategies also reflected the different notions that prevailed in the barrio. Mexican Americans, but particularly *mexicanos*, were ambivalent about de-Mexicanizing themselves because they believed that this stripping away of cultural and national identity did not necessarily lead to integration into American society. After all, calls for full participation and for assimilation had been sounded ever since the U.S.–Mexican War. Numerous elite and middle-class Mexican Americans had heeded the call but the returns had rarely been seen as significant to the community as a whole.

Assimilation and the promotion of Mexican Americans as "white" also compounded the issues of identity among many Mexican Americans. Were they white? Most thought so, but what did that mean? Was being a "white" Mexican different from being a "white" Anglo? And could you be "white" when you were regarded as colored and treated as such? Were one's experiences and conditions a reflection of color and if they were, what color? Mexicans and Mexican Americans could more easily understand their "Mexicanness" because it was based on their living conditions, their labor, their limitations, their connection to the home country, and on the way that Anglos treated them. While their racialization was socially constructed, their whiteness was not. It was simply a legal notion that occasionally served them well—as in the case of naturalization—but that most often was contested, and in the case of jury duty, worked against them.

This is why *Hernández v. Texas* proved to be such an important case for Mexican Americans. It put the jury system under judicial scrutiny and allowed Mexican American lawyers to expose the de facto exclusion it fostered for what it was: racism—though the term itself never entered into the debate. The Supreme Court did not take the bait, and its ruling that Mexican Americans were white "but a separate class" left much to be desired in legal terms, but the "victory" proved extremely important for Mexican American reformers seeking recognition in the national arena.

The decision also temporarily put to rest—among middle-class civil rights advocates—the debate on whether Mexican Americans were white or not. This allowed Mexican American individuals and organizations to move aggressively for more inclusion and to demand the rights of full citizenship. The Court, and thus the law, declared them white—thus part of the mainstream—and declared them "a separate class"—thus protected by the Equal Protection Clause of the Constitution. This is a designation they would be only partly satisfied with for another ten years before the advent of the Chicano Movement again brought to the forefront the debate over ethnicity, race, and the place of Mexican Americans in American society.

The Chicano Movement was also a result of the ruling. Because many things were left unsettled and because Mexican Americans remained somewhere in between the two racial poles, the debate and the accommodation and/or redefinition remained and continues to remain an important unresolved issue. The *Hernández* case is now perceived in some Latino legal circles as a "first" step in the defining of Latinos as a "separate race." That this would occur fifty years after *Hernández v. Texas*, which sought to recognize Mexican Americans as white but a "class apart," is an indication of the complexity of the issue of discrimination and speaks to the ambivalence within the same community about its identity and the place it wants to occupy in American society. This ambivalence will be borne out in the discussion of the case and its place in the Mexican American "experience" and in the way that experience is perceived or "constructed" historically.

To understand how Mexican Americans would come to see *Hernández v. Texas*, it is important to note that civil rights history for this community is different from that of most other minority groups in the United States. One starting point might be a discussion of how little Anglo support there was for Mexican American civil rights even among traditional civil libertarians. There would never be massive funding as there was for the African American civil rights efforts, nor would countless numbers of white advocates come forward to help. No championing American newspapers, politicians, or academicians would come to the aid of the cause, and only a few journalists were willing to highlight or expose racism toward Mexican Americans. Even many who did support some form of civil rights did so within a context that tended to trap Mexican Americans into an Anglo version of what was good for them. Liberal social scientists, while deploring some of the conditions of the barrio and the treatment of its citizens, seemed to put much of the solution on the shoulders of the "Mexican-origin" population. "Learn English, mingle with your neighbors, stay in school and Americanize, then things will get better," was the usual counsel. "If you act more like

Americans, then the courts will use the 'common knowledge' approach to include you," was another common piece of advice. This "common knowledge" was the same used to classify ethnic and immigrant groups as either white or non-white. It simply meant that if the broader society considered someone white, then the courts would follow suit.

But all of this rarely favored Mexican Americans. Common knowledge did not provide a definitive answer as to their place in society. As with the courts, the common opinion was that at times they were white and at other times they were not—so much, again, depended on class, skin color, geography, labor needs, and social and cultural proximity to Anglos. Whiteness came from the needs of politicians, employers, government officials, and intellectuals. Sometimes Mexican Americans were needed as non-white workers, at other times they were needed as white voters. Their class and familial connections might make them white, but their politics and defiance might make them "others," which usually meant non-white. In the formal sense, there was never any doubt that they qualified to be white, but because Anglos rarely had to deal with Mexican Americans in a *de jure* sense, the social and cultural constructions were much more fluid and advantageous to use in discriminating against them.

Another aspect of Mexican American civil rights history is that unlike the feelings toward African American oppression, not much guilt existed then or now regarding the conditions of the Mexican or Latino. For many Anglos, the war with Mexico was not a war of aggression but rather an expansion of democracy and liberty. The marginalization of the Mexicans who remained in the territory was seen as a consequence of their inability to adjust to a new society, rather than a blatant effort by government officials and white citizens to dispossess them of land and political power. This, of course, is a complete distortion of the historical record but remains the predominant view even as greater efforts are made in historical scholarship to include them as part of the mass of "disadvantaged" minorities.

This view of *disadvantage* but not *victimization* became prevalent even among some Mexican American civil rights advocates in the late 1940s who sought to draw a line on the border to separate themselves from their southern brothers and sisters. Others like George I. Sánchez, the preeminent advocate of his generation, believed that Mexican Americans were not prepared to "live up to their American obligations." While he blamed Anglo American discrimination, he nonetheless put the problem within the context of the Mexican American's inability to resolve his or her own exploitation. Thus, American empathy was crucial as it offered to many the only manner through which issues of discrimination and segregation could be resolved. Lacking political and economic power and facing an identity crisis at the elite level, Mexican Americans could do little within the mainstream of society. While laborers organized strikes and barrio organizations protested the most blatant elements of racial discrimination, most Mexican American civil rights individuals and groups sought legal protection from their disadvantages and social inclusion to be able to participate in civic and cultural functions. Of all the aforementioned groups, they were the most adamant that Anglos would like them if they knew them better. Like civil libertarian Alonso S. Perales, they wanted to convey "the qualities and virtues of the Spanish speaking people . . . to all listeners," in the hopes that discrimination would cease.

They were not naive, however, to assume that all would change by simply changing perceptions. After all, much of the perception and public image that Mexican Americans had was based on their legal and social status as well as their situation in regards to public policy. They were seen as inferior because they had been treated as inferior for so many years. The end result of that treatment had been underemployment, limited education, and social alienation from the larger society. Still, they understood that the continuation of that inferior status resulted from their categorization as "foreigners," "lazy," "violent," and "ignorant." The perception had to change and to that end organizations such as the League of United Latin American Citizens (LULAC), Pan American Union, Alianza Hispano-Americana, the American GI Forum and a host of others, worked tirelessly to make Mexican Americans better educated and more motivated citizens. They combined this social uplift with a tenacious legal challenge to school segregation and public discrimination. In essence, *Hernández v. Texas* was not so much about one man failing to get a fair trial, but about a whole group not being allowed to "show" that they could participate. This participation was crucial in the formation of a counterimage. Mexican Americans could only shed the stigma of their "otherness" from mainstream society if they participated and proved themselves to be good citizens.

Jury duty represented the ultimate sign of citizenship. More than voting, it represented the undertaking of a civic obligation that, while open to all citizens, was bestowed on a relative few. Jury status meant that an individual had been seen by his peers and by the judicial system as capable of upholding the traditions and standards of the law of the land. If Mexican Americans could gain that trust from Anglos and from state and local governments, they would make a strong case for their equality. Both Mexican Americans and Anglo Texans understood, however, that sitting on a jury was about more than civic participation. It meant that Mexican Americans "would sit in judgment" of others, both Mexican and Anglo. For Mexican Americans, it meant that they could provide a fair hearing to their fellow barrio residents and respond to the gross injustices perpetuated on them by Anglos. Violence against Mexican Americans had been a constant in the Southwest, but more important, that violence had often been perpetuated by officers of the court. In those instances, no recourse existed in the judicial system. For Anglos, having Mexican Americans on a jury meant an acceptance that they were "qualified" and "intelligent" enough to sit in judgment of white people. This was something that few Anglos in Texas in the 1950s wanted to contemplate, much less accept. This was particularly true in rural areas where Mexican Americans were seen as second-class citizens. It was also in these rural areas that Mexican Americans were a larger part of the population. Once the legal floodgates were open, Mexican Americans would expect to participate more often and in more activities that had usually been reserved for whites only.

Here, again, Anglos saw the dubious nature of de facto discrimination. It was such a flimsy dividing line that any crack threatened to bring it all down. Jury duty represented a dramatic breach of social protocol. Mexican Americans simply could not stand in judgment over other Mexican Americans—and definitely not over Anglos. To accept this meant that there were simply no other civic duties of which they could be deprived. Seating them in juries would mean that they would decide what was discriminatory. School segregation, public discrimination, housing restrictions, and political gerrymandering could all fall by the wayside, and cause a convergence of both communities in a way that most Anglos were not ready to accept.

There was, however, another issue of importance that impacted Mexican American civil rights and their perception by Anglos. Mary L. Dudziak, in her work on Cold War civil rights argues that the conflict between the superpowers provided both a context and a restrictive framework for the development of civil rights.[3] Two historical situations influenced the view of Mexican American reformers of the 1940s and 1950s. First, Communist and other leftist organizers had played a major role in many of the Mexican American labor strikes of the 1920s and 1930s. This leftist connection went back to the early years of the twentieth century when the Mexican anarchist brothers Enrique and Ricardo Magon had been forced into exile by Mexican dictator Porfirio Diaz. While they planned their revolution, they established Partido Liberal Mexicano (PLM) clubs in the Southwest. These were meant to raise funds and recruit men for an invasion of Mexico, but many of them also became involved in the issues of discrimination and racism in the United States. A number of them became prominent in their local communities.

Eventually, other socialist groups came to believe that Mexicans would be crucial in developing a union movement in the West and Southwest and they went after them when traditional labor unions did not. They battled nationalist unions who sought to organize their fellow Mexicans to not only improve their economic situation but to battle discrimination. Though these nationalist unions were not tied to socialist groups, they were influenced by the leftist rhetoric and ideas coming from Mexican intellectuals. This unionizing coupled with other efforts to protect Mexican Americans was seen as intrusive and un-American. The disdain for Mexican American organization grew as the population grew. This massive growth resulted from the Mexican Revolution, the intense recruitment for the agricultural, mining, and railroad interests, and the economic conquest of Mexico that had occurred since the end of the U.S.–Mexican War.

Mexican American middle-class advocates were sensitive to this past organizing and past ideological politics. Many came to believe that these nationalist and socialist activities were hampering the integration of Mexican Americans into American society. Since many were war veterans or participants in home-front activities, they came to adopt their country's Cold War views. Since veteranism, or what I call "Barrio Americanism," became the prevailing ideology, it was natural that they became distrustful of leftists and socialists. While not all adopted this view and not all leftists were excluded from their civil rights activism, the anticommunist rhetoric and posture did cause Mexican American reformers of the 1950s to seek less radical alternatives. They were undoubtedly also influenced by the small openings in American society that seemed to offer the "fruits" of the world's richest and most powerful nation in the world. They were not beyond the ethnocentrism that afflicted many Americans in the postwar years.

Hernández v. Texas occurred within the context of this change in the Mexican American community. Much of the immigrant leadership and the organizations that looked south for their cultural and social cues were in decline because of deportation campaigns and the Americanization impact of the public school system and the two world wars. Most Mexican American elites now recognized and embraced their Americanism, and had created social and ideological barriers to coincide with the political boundaries that separated them from their or their parent's country of origin. They could not break all the bonds and most maintained their ties to their communities, but they searched wide and deep for crevices within the

American mosaic to find their social niche. Yet, Mexican American elites understood that they confronted a black/white binary in American society, and that they did not fit that duality; thus, they had to construct their own racial and ethnic identity within the nation.

The *Hernández* case made it rather apparent that Mexican Americans were neither African American nor completely white when it came to judicial interpretations. It also revealed that while legal challenges by African Americans were a foundation for Mexican Americans and other minorities to build on, the fact was that the black experience and conceptualization of civil rights, discrimination, and segregation simply did not fit perfectly the experiences of Mexican Americans. Mexicans and Mexican Americans were engaged in a struggle for their rights and their humanity even before the establishment of the Fourteenth Amendment and before the concept of "equal protection" came into common discussion in American society. They were citizens earlier than African Americans and they were in a position to debate the issue of whether they were white or not. African Americans never had to debate the issue of whiteness, while Mexican Americans continue that debate even today.

Discrimination toward Mexican Americans never acquired *de jure* dimensions in the same way that it did when applied to Native Americans, Asian Americans, and African Americans. Simply, lawmakers in the Southwest and California never saw it necessary or convenient to establish specific laws that singled out Mexican Americans. This does not mean that they did not exist or that there were no formal rules to discriminate against them. What it does mean, however, was that Mexican American social and class fluidity made it difficult to establish laws that covered all Mexican Americans, so most of the practices and rules that did discriminate were focused on the lower working class. The fluidity also allowed a few Mexican American elites (who had acquired their position through money, status, or ability) to move in and out of some social circles as long as they did not overreach.

This meant that there were always Mexican American elites who claimed to have not been discriminated against. Eventually, however, many of them were forced to "work for their people" for their livelihood because they had few other options. Thus, middle-class Mexican American elite status depended on their "whiteness," their economic base, and their connection to the larger society. Nonetheless, the bitter discrimination against the larger working class undermined the middle class's political, economic, and social situation. With few registered voters they could not win political office. Low wage workers could not really pay for the elites' professional services or buy from their stores, and each case of discrimination against the "meskin" signaled the precarious situation of all Mexican Americans.

Without a substantial legal foundation upon which to base their discrimination, Anglos in Texas and other parts of the Southwest depended on tradition, practice, and interpretation to make sure that Mexican Americans remained outside the protection of the law. The *Hernández* lawyers argued before the Supreme Court that the Texas law governing jury selection was actually quite fair. What was not was the way officers of the court used it against them. *Hernández v. Texas* thus calls for a legal notion of Latino civil rights. At a time when some scholars are calling for color blindness in discussion of civil rights, Latino scholars find themselves calling for a greater discussion of race in the way we write and interpret our history and in the way others write about us. Race is the great highlighter in American social discussions. The reality, however, has been that Mexican Americans, most Latinos, and other people of color, have been excluded or marginalized because most racial dialogue in American society is still framed by a black/white binary. In American scholarship there are only two major races and everyone else fits depending on their social or racial proximity to one side or the other of the racial poles. Even as many scholars promote the idea of race as a social construction, they continue to dislocate the Latino construction within the black/white binary.

This has led to a view by some that the *Hernández* case was not really a victory or a very important piece of judicial decision-making. That this assessment is seen as partly right by some is based not on the "lack of validity" of *Hernández* but on the inability of some scholars to see other people of color within their own historical context. The study of *Hernández v. Texas* faces two very serious obstacles: (1) it is obscured by the obsession over black and white in American historical and legal studies, and (2) the Supreme Court only partially dealt with the situation of Mexican Americans and refused to locate them within a larger rubric of color in American society. The hope is that this book will help us overcome those obstacles, and allow Mexican Americans and other groups of color to find their own place in U.S. history and American society.

There are, as would be expected, several limitations to this study. Because the case did not have much support from Anglo organizations and individuals, and only a limited number of Mexican Americans knew of the case nationwide, there is a very limited paper trail. Compounding this lack of sources is the fact that only one of the four lawyers involved in the case has had his papers collected, and much of the correspondence on the case has either been lost or has yet to be found. No biography exists of any of the lawyers and only one biography has been written so far on the main supporters of the case. The actual trial records—and those of the retrial— were lost and no recording or stenographer's notes exist of the arguments before the Supreme Court. Even the defendant, Pete Hernández, is almost non-existent in the public record.

Much of the secondary literature is written by legal scholars who focus on the legal ramifications of the case, and who debate its merits as legal precedence. They have, however, added very little to the historical record and most view civil rights strictly through the eyes of the law. It is also apparent that most seek to compare and contrast *Hernández v. Texas* with its more famous cousin, *Brown v. Board of Education*. By this standard, most other civil rights cases pale in comparison and *Hernández v. Texas* is no different. Also, by focusing on the *Hernández* case only as a legal case, much of Mexican American de facto history is left out of the historical record. While I do not engage much of the legal scholarship in my work, I have cited it where appropriate. Many of the elements of this scholarship are also discussed in the historical context throughout the book. I believe that legal scholars have done a masterful job in discussing the legal ramifications of *Hernández v. Texas* given the paucity of historical documents that they confronted. My belief is that this historical record will help them take the study of *Hernández v. Texas* to a higher level.

My limited knowledge of the law also hampers the study because I do not have the legal expertise needed to combine both legal and historical scholarship in the way some scholars have done with African American civil rights studies. Yet, the story of Pete Hernández and the story of his lawyers' journey through the American judicial landscape add to our knowledge of civil rights litigation in American history. They will, undoubtedly, also tell us much about Mexican American history as well.

Pete, His Lawyers, and "the Town" That Discriminated

Little is really known about Pete Hernández, his personal life, his thoughts, or what actually transpired shortly before that fateful day at the tavern. What we do know is that he was born in Jackson County in 1926, the sixth of eight children of Francisco and Leonara Hernández. His father, Francisco, according to the 1930 census, rented a farm as "a general farm worker, which likely meant that the family occupied space in or near the farm in which they worked."[1] In the late 1920s and through most of the 1930s, Jackson County was part of the central Texas cotton zone, an area that ran south to Corpus Christi and north to the southern border of Oklahoma. It stretched as far west as San Antonio and east to Houston and then became cone-shaped as it traveled north.[2] The extent to which Pete participated in the cotton industry is unclear because one newspaper account claimed he worked as a service station attendant at the time of the killing. A contemporary, however, claimed that everyone "did cotton" back then, especially if they were Mexican. We do know, however, that Francisco eventually got a truck and did some hauling within the region, though the business was not prosperous enough to provide Pete more than temporary work, and so he had several odd jobs before he was twenty-one.[3] There can be no doubt, however, that cotton was one of central Texas's primary industries, and while it is difficult from the public record to tell much with certainty about the Hernández family, there is little doubt that they were integrated into the industry at one level or another.[4]

Unlike the other rural areas of the state, the central Texas cotton industry brought Anglos, blacks, and Mexicans into direct competition for labor. Initially Mexicans and Mexican Americans were the smallest labor group and remained so for the first three decades of the twentieth century. This area claimed no Mexican past, as Spanish and Mexican settlements did not make it this far east, and so there were few Mexican families with a long tenure in the area. Much of this part of the state had been settled by southerners seeking new areas for cotton production. The area's claim to history was the part it had played in the Texas Revolution and the men it sent to support the Confederacy. History, however, was not the most important part of the area's legacy—it was cotton production and all it entailed. Harvesting that plentiful crop had made some rich but had made many others miserable.

That this area was harsh on the populations that worked the cotton fields is revealed in the census information on the Hernández family. All of Pete's five older siblings were eligible for school but only the oldest two, Juanita and Ricardo, attended, and only Juanita could read and write. Francisco, a native of Mexico, was illiterate, at least in the English language, but his wife, Leonara, a native of Texas, probably had some schooling because the census taker listed that she could read and write. Given the history of schooling for Mexicans in most of Texas during the very early years of the twentieth century, it is likely that she had only a few years of elementary schooling at best, or possibly that she learned to read and write mostly on her own. The only other thing that we learn from the census record was that all the children were born in Texas and that Francisco and Leonara were married at twenty-eight and twenty-four respectively.[5]

The Mexican-origin population of Jackson County seems to have remained stable throughout Pete's early life. A count of "Latin American scholastics" indicates that in 1928, 556 of them attended public schools. By 1942 that number had increased to only 600, which seems a rather limited increase in fourteen years. Nonetheless, in the sparsely populated county they accounted for about 21 percent of the school population. When Pete went to trial, the Mexican population made up 14 percent of the county population. Because Mexican couples were having the traditional number of children, it meant that the number of families remained constant while the school population fluctuated as the children reached school age.[6] It is important to note that most Mexican-origin children did not enter school at the earliest possible age, and rarely stayed for the full twelve years, and in fact rarely attended beyond the fifth grade. A study done in 1942 revealed that most Mexican children dropped out after the age of twelve.[7]

The 1930 census record indicates that Mexican and Mexican American families were not completely segregated in the county. It is likely that many Mexican families were scattered throughout the region, some living in the small towns and others on nearby farms where they worked, but by the time Pete entered his teens, Mexican children were already being segregated in Mexican schools and their families relegated to segregated barrios around the outskirts of town. By the 1930s, most farming was being done by Mexicans and Mexican Americans, and whatever fluidity had come with the mixture of races in the fields was being replaced with a more rigid and restrictive labor structure that kept whites, blacks, and Mexicans apart.

Whites were moving or "being moved" out of the fields as both skilled and unskilled jobs became available in the towns and cities. The situation of African Americans was more complicated. They moved on to other jobs, they dropped out of the labor force, and they were pushed out by the Mexican laborers willing to work for even lower wages. Agribusiness was seeking more and more profits by constantly reducing labor costs. In spite of their poverty, some African Americans were not willing (and many others not allowed) to follow the downward spiral of labor wages. Mexican American workers would initially take over much of the labor, but within a decade they too would lose the field employment in much of Texas to contracted labor from Mexico and to the thousands of undocumented workers who started arriving during and after World War II.

Some of these workers came to Edna, the county seat and a place writer and educator Ira Thomas Taylor described as the "Hub of the Gulf coast— Gem of the Prairie." Founded on land given to Robert Guthrie by Texas hero Stephen F. Austin, and later owned by a Mrs. Lucy Flournoy, it came into existence on July 2, 1882, when the railroad came to Jackson County, an area located in east central Texas not far from the Gulf of Mexico. By December of that year several citizens petitioned to have Edna serve as the county capital. By January 22, 1883, it became so, and in February people moved in to the new capital. Fifteen years later, the citizens petitioned for incorporation, but after one year of "having their horses, cattle, hogs, sheep and goats penned off the streets" the citizens, seeing their rural culture and livelihood threatened, held another election and abolished the "corporate existence of the City of Edna."[8]

The community was made up of old pioneer stock and German immigrants. They were agricultural people with roots back to the Texas Revolution. In fact, Texana, the oldest town in the county, served as a port of entry for volunteers from the United States who came to fight in the Texas Revolution. There they were trained and incorporated into fighting units. It was in Texana where Jim Bowie wrote one of his famous letters further fanning the flames of insurrection, and it was in Jackson County where Texans first declared their intent to free themselves from Mexican tyranny.

Taylor observed in his writings, "it seemed that all Mexican officials were tyrannical, which is a characteristic of any inferior race of people when put in a position of power."[9]

Jackson County residents would forever remember that they had to abandon their homes and live out on the prairie for several months to elude a Mexican army sent to quiet their rebellion. Their suffering is enshrined in letters depicting the hardships of the women and children and the deaths of men who joined the rebellion. For Jackson County, the war for Texas's independence was a cornerstone of their history and their personal character. They participated, suffered, and the triumph was their triumph, thus cementing their views of their superiority over the Mexicans. An interesting side note is that the town of Texana had originally been named for Mexican president Antonio Lopez de Santa Anna, when Anglo Texans still viewed him favorably.[10]

It is important to emphasize that families coming from the United States originally established Texana and Jackson County. The area had no Mexican history, unlike many other communities farther south, and its citizens never associated with elite Mexican families. Their only contact with the "Mexicans" was with army officials. The citizens of Jackson County, and those of other central Texas communities, never developed a relationship with Mexicans, nor did they ever see themselves as part of the Mexican nation. Thus, while other Texans were more ambivalent about independence, these Texans were wholeheartedly for it. And it was in areas like Jackson County that the fervor for independence spread like wildfire during the early days of the insurrection, and where animosity toward Mexicans had little opposition because of familial interests or economic needs.

After the Texas Revolution, the area developed a prosperous agricultural economy. Slaves were common in the area and after the Civil War so were free blacks, who came to comprise almost 50 percent of the Jackson County population by the turn of the century. They participated in the political process, but as with Mexicans in south Texas, they were often manipulated by corrupt political machines. When Progressivism came to the state, it did so as in the South, slightly liberal but very steeped in the culture of white supremacy. Progressivism gave Anglos in Texas an excuse to control the rights of African Americans and regulate the lives of Mexican Americans. In 1902, a mass meeting was held in the courthouse in Edna to organize the Jackson County White Man's Union Association. Its purpose was to bring the local government back under the control of the white voters and annihilate corrupt politics from the county for all time. The latter, of course, "could only" be done by adherence to the former. Simply put, only white politicians could be counted on to be civic minded, honest and incorruptible. The formation of this association represented only a small part of the move to white primaries that would become common in Texas in the first decade of the twentieth century and become codified as law in the 1920s.[11]

One south Texas office-seeker said, "We have a constituency entirely cosmopolitan and with it a vote which in its nature is purchasable, and is every year purchased."[12] Using this rhetoric, Progressives in south Texas disenfranchised Mexican voters, claiming that they were taking control back from Mexican domination. There, they confronted an entrenched Mexican American electorate that had sided at times with Anglo political machines to stave off the encroaching "New Texans" from the Midwest who were challenging the political climate in the Lone Star State. The New Texans' "purpose" was to remove corruption and inefficiency and destroy the rural old boys' monopoly in county and state government. Newcomers, attracted by an exploding agricultural economy, were dismayed by the "influence" Mexican Americans had in the local counties and towns. This influence was intended to protect Mexican American ranching elites and minimize discrimination against other Mexican Americans. In reality, the influence was limited to the elbowroom provided by the Anglos in power. Only in one or two counties were Mexican Americans really in charge and then only because they belonged to Anglo-run regional organizations.[13] In the rest of the counties, Mexicans and Mexican Americans faced segregation and blatant discrimination.

The process of removing Mexican American politicians and voters from the electoral system would last another two decades and be almost complete by 1930, when Pete Hernández was five years old. But it is in this process that we see the almost complete subjugation of the Mexican-origin population in large parts of rural Texas. It began in the one arena where Anglos had the most control—the labor sector. Historian David Montejano refers to the establishment of this control as "labor repression." It consisted of two important elements: (1) the immobilization of farm workers and sharecroppers through debt, and (2) the "dismissal or removal of wage workers for the purpose of avoiding payment."[14] The first was accomplished through the slave wages paid on the large agricultural farms and the high prices charged them for housing and/or the basic necessities by the farmer or the local communities. The second repressive action came from firings, border patrol roundups, or even vigilante action by local Anglos. Finally, the local governments had much control over where Mexican and Mexican

American laborers could work or move around. One major outcome of this unofficial strategy was that farm labor became completely Mexicanized as farmers refused to hire Anglo farm workers or sharecroppers because they were much harder to control. In Mexicanizing the farm labor population they were thus able to control a segment of society that was not likely to have many allies to turn to when conditions became unbearable.[15]

Segregated housing patterns and schools became the other methods for removing the Mexican American from full participation in the larger society. In smaller towns there were no zoning laws or specific city guidelines, but there was the usual practice of not renting or selling to Mexican workers. It is likely, however, that most Mexican families could not have afforded living outside the "Mexican" side of town even if they could have found housing. For the early laborers, housing was anything that kept the rain and sun out. Most initial housing was temporary until workers either settled permanently or moved on to follow the crops. Once stable, the families sought ways to put a more permanent roof over their heads. Once this was accomplished, Mexican workers were also interested in participating in the local community. This meant that they sent their children to school. The growth of this new student population soon presented major challenges for the public school system.

The challenges were twofold: (1) Mexican and Mexican American children did not speak the language, were extremely poor, and understood very little of American society; and (2) Anglo parents did not want their children mingling with the poor Mexican children. The first challenge created a crisis for state education officials who lacked the resources and much of the theory to educate children who were different. This "crisis" was compounded by the second problem as Anglo parents exerted fierce pressure on school officials to keep the children separate. They complained about the lack of hygiene among the Mexican American children, and about a perceived obsession with sex among the children's families. Thus, the Mexican school arose as an alternative.[16]

Ultimately, what concerned many whites was the potential "equalizing" factor of the schools. Anglos feared that once educated, Mexican Americans would begin competing for jobs other than those in agriculture and would seek political office and demand equal treatment. Not only would this disrupt the social patterns of Texas society, it would wreak havoc on the agricultural economy. This, in fact, did happen to an extent. Mexican American laborers began to demand better wages and started journeying to the Midwest and Northwest for slightly better opportunities. Growers responded by recruiting undocumented workers and pressuring the federal government to import workers from Mexico. But regardless of whether the labor force was native or foreign, it remained isolated and segregated from mainstream Texas society, and this isolation began with schoolchildren and the Mexican schools.[17]

Texas rural society saw two interconnected (but not assimilated) cultures functioning side by side. While old-time Anglos had subordinated the Mexicans, they still maintained a close relationship, often serving as mentors or patriarchs. They intermarried and selectively chose those Mexicans whom they trusted to work with them and to be part of their electoral campaigns or county and town governments. The newcomers retained and increased the subordination, but they created an even stronger cultural barrier. This came about because they feared the rise of the Mexican American population, an outcome of the growth of the agricultural industry. Like old-timers, the newcomers eventually became dependent on Mexican American labor, but by the 1940s it was impossible to control them and maintain them in one place as the old-timers had once done. Labor mobility had become the norm as farmers competed with other farmers for the much needed Mexican worker, and the automobile and the contractors' trucks allowed this labor to move around the country.[18]

Jackson County and much of central Texas experienced only part of the process described above. The Mexicanization of the region came about with the same surge of immigration that had impacted south Texas, but here in this region there was no precedent for the Mexican and Mexican American laborer. As the western edge of the Southern cotton culture region, central Texas was home to many African American and white cotton workers. When the Mexican laborers began to arrive, it caused problems for the first two groups. Racial tensions immediately grew, and it was in areas such as these that Texas politicians were the most anti-Mexican. The accommodation that revealed itself periodically in south Texas was missing in places like Jackson County. For one, there were no Mexican American elites in the area and no mutual aid organizations or other groups that sought to defend the Mexican-origin population from discrimination. Here, in this vast cotton country, Mexican immigrants and Mexican American laborers were simply beasts of burden. Initially, however, they shared this position with poor whites and blacks, but from 1910 (when they started coming in large numbers) to 1930 they slowly took over most of the sharecropping and became the predominant farm labor population.[19]

In part, this came about because Mexicans were seen as working for lower wages than the black and white sharecroppers who had been in the area longer, and who were more willing to demand better wages and take collective action. Without roots in the area, and no one to turn to for aid, Mexican workers were willing to take what they could get. One study done in 1954 found that most ranchers and farmers preferred Mexicans over other groups partly because they were willing to work for sixty to sixty-five cents per hour, a rate few whites or African Americans were willing to accept.[20] By the late 1940s, even Mexican Americans were unwilling to live off those wages, and farmers started replacing them with newer arrivals from Mexico, especially those who were in the country illegally.

Another reason for the preference for Mexicans in the fields may have been that most Anglos saw Mexicans as laborers and unskilled workers in spite of countless examples of them performing ably in other employment areas. More important, even those who might acknowledge Mexican American accomplishments distinguished the darker, poorer Mexicans as being "different" and destined for hard labor. Class differentiation allowed Anglos to befriend a few middle-class Mexican Americans, while still maintaining a harsh disdain for "all Mexicans." It also allowed middle-class Mexicans and Mexican Americans to navigate the racial boundaries, allowing them some flexibility in their lives, and thus sometimes prompting them to accept that differentiation.

It is important to reiterate that racial rigidity was far more difficult to construct against Mexicans and Mexican Americans than it was in the case of African Americans. For one, there was no legal framework to create a *de jure* Jim Crow system. The 1848 Treaty of Guadalupe Hidalgo—which ended the U.S.–Mexican War—provided Mexicans legal standing in American society no matter how tenuous it seemed to many. Also, Mexicans were acknowledged to be part of the making of Texas, and a few had served in the government dating back to the Republic of Texas. Even more significant was the U.S.–Mexico border. Regardless of how badly Mexicans were treated, there were limits to any attempt to codify that discrimination. By the 1940s, this became even more true with the signing of the Bracero Agreement between the two countries. This agreement allowed Mexican workers to come into the fields of U.S. farmers, first replacing those serving in the armed forces, and later supplanting the labor force in an expanding postwar economy. By the late 1940s and early 1950s, Texas officials had to constantly reassure both the U.S. federal government and the Mexican government that the Mexicans were being treated well in order to qualify for guest workers. While this did not eliminate the problems, it did make it difficult to legalize the unequal treatment.[21]

There was, then, a bit of fluidity in the asymmetric relationship between Anglos, Mexicans, and Mexican Americans. When the federal courts ruled de facto segregation of Mexican students was unconstitutional, both groups were forced to attend school together.[22] Mexican Americans were also able to enter the business world with their restaurants, taverns, butcher shops, bakeries, and they also became labor contractors, foremen, and skilled laborers. Their labor skills and this fluidity allowed them to occupy the available crevices. Some Anglos came to depend on their Mexican workers in ways they did not with their black or poor white workers. Mexican Americans became part of the periphery of the Anglo agricultural world because they were so indispensable to it.

One retired Edna farm worker named Fidel (who chose not to reveal his last name) remembers going to work for the same man who hired his father years earlier, and who had treated him without much antagonism. He stood next to his father and heard the old Anglo boss say, without hostility in his voice, "Tell your son to keep his mouth shut and say yes to the white man, and he'll be okay." And that is what Fidel did all of his working life. He also remembered that when desegregation for Mexican Americans came in the 1940s, he was told to sit in the back of the one-room public school and to not ask questions. He did as he was told and left school unable to read or write much English.[23] Whereas before he had been segregated physically, this time he was segregated emotionally and intellectually. Still there were others who did better in school, who befriended Anglo teachers then an Anglo boss, and saw their circumstances improve. There were always limits in communities like Edna, but the boundaries did expand with education, money, and "friendships."

Victor Rodríguez, later to become a superintendent in the area, remembers a rigidly segregated Edna in the decade before *Hernández*, where separation extended beyond the schools into the restaurants, taverns, movie houses, and public parks. Even dating was segregated as it "was prohibited to date an Anglo-American girl for the town's Mexicans."[24] But it was in the schools where young Mexican children had their first continuous encounter with a second-class life. One Anglo teacher taught the first four grades in the wooden frame building—only forty-five by sixty feet in total space—that sat outside the northwest part of town near a little creek that flooded every time it rained. Most Mexican and Mexican American students dropped out by age twelve, but if they were promoted to the fifth grade they were required to retake the fourth grade in the white school.

At the theater, Mexican patrons were relegated to the last five rows of the left section, and African Americans were placed on the balcony, where as Rodríguez remembers, they actually had a better view. Mexican Americans could not go to a restaurant after the show, though they could go to the back of the establishment and order food from the cook. If they were lucky, they got helped by a "good" cook who took their order promptly and charged them the normal price. An unlucky encounter with a "bad" cook meant waiting fifteen to twenty minutes to have their order taken by a rude individual and then being overcharged.[25] Any comfortable socializing had to be done at the local dance taverns that were run by Mexicans. There, Mexicans and Mexican Americans in Edna were able to build an internal world that strengthened their sense of community while keeping them away from conflict with the town's white population.

This segregation was pervasive and intruded itself even in places where the races mixed. On the job site, in the few integrated grocery stores, on the streets, and in governmental offices where both Mexicans and Anglos could find themselves, there was an invisible dividing line that kept them apart. There was some fluidity in and out by both groups but rarely did it break down except in the most unusual of circumstances. Even in death, segregation reared its ugly head. It was in the 1950s that the first Mexican American was allowed to be viewed in a funeral home—though the individual still had to be buried in a segregated cemetery. Not large enough to have one cemetery for whites and one for Mexican Americans, Edna had one that clearly delineated the status of each group.

Things had begun to change somewhat after World War II, particularly among the returning veterans. For Mexican American veterans it was the first time that any of them had left Jackson County and associated with others outside their community. With such experience they came back more willing to try to participate in the civic life of their communities. There were few opportunities available but these veterans bought homes, started small businesses, and joined organizations. The biggest change, according to Rodríguez, occurred among a number of returning Anglo soldiers in Edna. "You would see an Anglo-American recognizing a Hispanic in the streets, and they would stop their car and ask them if the wanted a lift."[26] It became less unusual to see Anglos inviting their Mexican acquaintances to restaurants, and becoming more concerned with those who worked with them. Rodríguez remembers the sons of the doctor for whom his mother worked coming home and building his family a home behind theirs where his family could live and Victor and his siblings could finish their schooling.[27]

This change in relationships and interaction replicated itself throughout much of Texas and the Southwest. Mexican American veterans were coming home more anxious to participate in the life of their community, to get better jobs, buy their own homes, and continue their education. The expanding economy created a more fluid labor environment and a greater dependence by Anglos on Mexican labor. By the end of the 1940s, school segregation against Mexicans and Mexican Americans had been struck down as unconstitutional, renewed organizational advocacy had caused Texas politicians to moderate their anti-Mexican rhetoric, and the small but growing Mexican American vote had helped elect moderate and liberal politicians in the state.

This softening of hostility toward Mexicans and Mexican Americans was inconsistent and unevenly distributed, and so they continued to suffer with new forms of segregation, restrictions, and harassment by law enforcement. Mexican American children were no longer sent to "Mexican schools" but they often faced segregation within the classroom—as Fidel had—and on the playground. Mexican Americans still suffered from underemployment, low wages, bad housing, and disinterest or even disdain from city, county, and state leaders, except during election season. Finally, Texans were more certain that they had established the parameters of relationships with Mexicans. These parameters allowed them to cross boundaries and occasionally allow "them" to do the same, but always with limitations. There was much more openness than in the decades before but very little came of it in places like Edna.

This is the world into which Pete Hernández was born, where he grew up, went to school, found a series of jobs, and got in trouble. Nothing really distinguished him from the countless other Mexican American youths of his time in that locality. His parents worked on a farm, he shifted from job to job in the surrounding communities and frequented the local taverns as often as he could. His family's memories depict him as a "constant" drinker but not an alcoholic, and someone who never got loud or disruptive. He was mild-mannered but explosive when people failed to respect those whom he loved. Remembered as a playful young uncle, he also was described as a sharp-shooting young man who once shot a hole in the big clock outside of one of the extended family's stores because of a personal slight. A nice dresser with a flair for the good life, he was, however, hampered by a limp from a fall. One nephew remembers the family story of Pete taking off the cast on his leg too soon because he wanted to go dancing. The limp that came after that night of dancing would make him self-conscious and often the butt of many jokes.[28] Those were difficult times when people were cruel about disabilities and limitations, especially in the male-dominated worlds of work and drink. Yet, the taverns where much of the ribbing occurred were also the places most capable of making someone forget.

Figure 1. Pete Hernández at about the time he was being sentenced to life in prison for the murder of José "Caetano" Espinoza.

On August 7, 1951, Pete Hernández's life changed forever.[29] He was out on the town with a buddy. After spending some of his hard-earned money getting slightly drunk at another bar, he and his friend went to Chico Sánchez's Tavern, a café near Sprung's Grocery on Menefee Street, which like many other such establishments in the barrio served both hot meals for traveling families and alcohol for those seeking to quench their thirst.[30] It was also a place where pickers came to wait for cotton farmers to come and select some of them for work in the fields. Like many other rural laborers in other parts of the state, they waited, hoping that their skills and tolerance for hard work and their quiet demeanor would get them work that day. Pete, himself, had been there quite often and was known as a hard worker when he chose the fields over many of his other endeavors.[31]

After he had drunk a few more beers, witnesses would later recount in court, Hernández became loud and disruptive. Sometime during his loud talking and offensive behavior, he confronted a man named Henry Cruz, probably in a clash of words. When things began to get out of hand, Joe Espinoza stepped in. Espinoza was a forty-year-old tenant farmer who was in the café on his way to a neighboring town. His daughter Oralia remembers getting ready for a visit to relatives before being told that her father had to stop over at the tavern to offer the cotton pickers twenty-five cents more an hour to avoid losing them to another farmer. It was during this time of the picking season that cotton pickers had their greatest bargaining power as they played one farmer against another for a few cents more per hour.[32]

Espinoza, a bit older and a much more respected member of the Mexican American community, rented a farm in the area and usually hired a number of the cotton pickers who congregated in that particular watering hole. His better standing in the community, his age, and probably his large physical frame gave him an air of authority that few other Mexican Americans could claim. According to witnesses, he was probably bothered by Pete's behavior or simply had issues with him from previous encounters. Whatever the reason, he and J. B. Arroyos, Pete's drinking companion—who testified Pete's behavior became disreputable—"gently" removed him from the bar and told him to go home.[33] According to one newspaper report, Sánchez, the tavern owner, had asked Arroyos to take Pete home. Espinoza must have intervened at the moment that Arroyos was trying to get Pete out of the drinking establishment or he might have taken Cruz's side in the argument. It is difficult to know for certain what happened because the court testimony went missing and no record exists of the dozen or so witnesses who testified.

Pete left to go home for a gun, returned, and told everyone to stay put and not leave. Sometime shortly after, he shot Espinoza. Sheriff Lewis Watson would later testify that Espinoza was shot once in the body with a .22 rifle when he started for the door after Hernández ordered everyone to remain in the café. The authorities would also testify that when they arrived, "Hernández and Jacinto Ramirez were scuffling over the gun in the rear of the adjacent grocery store. Taking control of the weapon, Pete made a dash with the weapon but he stopped at the call of the deputies and dropped the gun."[34]

Pete's version differs—the murder, he said, was an act of self-defense against men who could have inflicted "serious bodily injury" on him. He said that both men roughly dragged him out of the café and slammed or dropped him on the ground, after which Espinoza kicked him a few times and called him a cripple. Then his drinking buddy took two five-dollar bills from his pocket. Humiliated by being dragged out of the bar, kicked, robbed, and particularly by being called a cripple, he went for a rifle. Pete's grandparents lived near the tavern and one of his nephews remembers seeing him pass by and then return later with a rifle. Alarmed, his grandparents tried to get his attention but to no avail.[35] He came back, he said, to "scare" them and to get his money back. There is no record of the court testimony, and the only available information comes from the tidbits that came out in the newspapers. Pete recounted that as he entered the bar, Espinoza lunged at him, grabbing his leg while brandishing a knife. The other witnesses said Pete came in and started shooting. Whatever actually happened, it is clear that he shot and killed Espinoza. Perhaps because that is all he intended to do—he did not collect his money—or because the shock of what he had done stunned him, Pete then walked out of the café. He said he was going to turn himself in. The county sheriff said he arrested him just outside the establishment and gave no indication that Pete put up any resistance. Since he was armed he could have chosen to fight, but he did not.[36]

Pete's nephew, who was at his grandmother's home and followed the action outside the tavern, remembers a crowd forming outside and several people trying to take the rifle away from Pete, who was trying to escape through an alleyway. Jacinto Ramirez was one of them, and he managed to hold him up long enough for the sheriff to arrive. Pete put up no resistance from that point on, although the nephew remembers one of the arresting officers using his blackjack on one of the bystanders, probably assuming that this was another Mexican fight at a bar and that everyone was involved.[37]

The murder was news in the community, though it probably did not shock the Anglo community or possibly even the Mexican American community—except for the fact that Espinoza was dead. Mexican-on-Mexican violence was not particularly new to the barrios of Texas or any other region of working-class Mexicans. Like many other similar working-class communities, hard work, poverty, stress, machismo, and alcohol proved a very deadly combination. It was not uncommon for Mexican men to get into trouble for barroom altercations, domestic violence, and workplace conflicts. Historian Arturo Rosales argues that Mexican Americans often got into conflicts with the law because they did not understand the legal system or community standards very well. Another scholar, Max Handman, makes a similar argument—that is, Mexican Americans violate the law because many lead a "nomadic life." Even still, he wrote, "As far as I have been able to ascertain, the Mexican's nationality is no cause of delinquent behavior, and whatever variation this behavior shows is a variation due to the efforts of a human being with a different culture pattern to adjust the best he can to what seems to him the curious and capricious American system of justice."[38] That law enforcement agents were ready to use the "heavy hand" of the law against them was no secret in the barrio or among the Anglo citizenry.

It would be inaccurate, however, to imply that Pete had been the victim of unjust law enforcement, and there is no record of any mistreatment of him by the sheriff or the jailers. In many ways, Pete was what some people in both communities would have called undesirable: a young, unmarried, poorly employed man with few future prospects. With few exceptions, many Mexican American men in the area were poor, illiterate, and beaten down by hard work and harsh treatment. For the bachelors—and probably for a significant number of the family men as well—drinking and displays of "guy bravado" were a way to release tension and survive their precarious lives. Most knew how to stay within the bounds of their own barroom society, but on that August day Pete broke those bounds.

It should be noted that Pete did not represent most Mexican males in the community. The majority did not drink to excess, engage in violent behavior, or kill others. The fact that some Mexican Americans were angered by the killing reveals that this was not an acceptable form of behavior in Edna. Mexican Americans there, as in other similar towns, had established social boundaries regarding acceptable behavior in order to maintain a sense of community. While these boundaries were often stretched and broken by the typical problems of a working-class community, there was an effort to maintain them as a buffer for the hostility they often faced from the larger Anglo community. Mexican Americans understood that they had to set community standards and enforce them in order to avoid the wrath of the larger community's judicial system. It is possible that part of Espinoza and Arroyos's alleged "rough" treatment of Pete was an effort to remind him of the boundaries.

Of course, because they were unwritten and constantly evolving, these community rules were anything but refined and they were not always applied fairly across the board. Personal biases and conflicts often entered into the enforcement of the community's standards. Pete's family alleged years later that he had been a victim of constant harassment by one of the Espinoza clan, who mocked his disability whenever they encountered each other. No proof, other than family hearsay, exists to support these allegations, but there is some sense that animosity existed between Pete and the Espinozas.[39] Given his temper, it is likely that Pete fought back against the insults, even if only verbally. Or it is possible that the soft-spoken young man—when sober—had simply stored all the alleged abuses in his mind until they exploded on that day at the tavern.

It is unclear how Pete hired the lawyers who came to represent him. Attorney (and later federal judge) James De Anda remembers the Hernández family coming to John J. Herrera, a Houston attorney known for his civil rights advocacy and work with Mexican American reform organizations. Herrera was one of a few Mexican American lawyers in the region.[40] According to Ed Idar Jr., a contemporary who later to became a very well-known civil rights litigator, there were few Mexican American lawyers in the state in the 1950s, so most people went to one of them no matter where they were in the state if they wanted to be defended by a Mexican American lawyer.[41] Herrera's son, Mike, remembered years later a gentleman by the name of Cisneros bringing the case to his father's attention. Cisneros was a member of the League of United Latin American Citizens (LULAC), a civil rights organization to which Herrera belonged. He would, according to the young Herrera, often serve as the driver for the long trips back and forth from Edna during the trial.[42]

Gustavo "Gus" García, the best known of the team of lawyers who represented Hernández, remembered Pete's mother coming to him to help defend her son. In very melodramatic terms he described the encounter as one in which a grieving mother, without money and convinced that Edna officials were determined to give her son the death penalty, came and pleaded for him to take the case.[43] What is clear is that Gus—as he came to be known to fellow reformers and historians—and Herrera knew each other from their work with LULAC, and other civil rights activities.[44] In fact, the two had teamed up in 1948 to win on appeal the landmark civil rights case, *Delgado v. Bastrop Independent School District*, which declared the segregation of Texas-Mexican children on racial grounds unconstitutional. De Anda was a young lawyer at Herrera's firm and he would prove to be valuable in formulating the strategy to defend Hernández.[45]

Apart from the mother's pleading, Gus took the case, at least according to his own recollection, because he saw it as an excellent test case regarding jury exclusion. He then invited Herrera to join the defense because he was, as he put it, "the only man I knew who could possibly help me."[46] Regardless of which of them was the first to accept the case, the two men were destined to be part of a team of lawyers that would accomplish what no other Mexican American lawyer had done before. Herrera had just finished trying a case on jury discrimination the year before, and De Anda had written an extensive brief for the case. Early on, the *San Antonio Light* (October

Figure 2. Gustavo "Gus" García walking down the street, probably while he was in Washington, D.C., dressed immaculately as always.

1951) noted that Gus and Herrera "appeared certain the case would end up in the Supreme Court."

The arrival of the three lawyers—Gus, Herrera, and De Anda—in Edna created a stir in this town with few Mexican American professionals. Victor Rodríguez remembers the shining black automobile—which belonged to Herrera—arriving in town and the three distinguished looking Mexican Americans getting out to the amazed gaze of most of the Anglos and a couple of teenage Mexicanos who were playing near the courthouse. He recalled, "The one that I was impressed the most with was . . . Gus García. He was very well dressed, with a dark suit . . . white shirt . . . a beautiful tie [and] he wore a hat. And his shoes were shined so much that the shine from those shoes could almost blind you. I couldn't help but be impressed with the poise that he exhibited when he walked slowly, but very precisely, with a great deal of confidence in his gait."[47]

Rodríguez recalled saying to himself, "Someday I'm gonna own a car like that and I'm gonna dress like that."[48] Such impressions on the Edna teenager—and others who would get to know him during the trial—would lead to much hearsay and mythology concerning Gus. Rodríguez remembers hearing that when the lawyers first met the judge they were asked if they needed an interpreter, whereupon Gus responded, "No, sir, Judge, if you can't understand English or Spanish perhaps one of my colleagues can interpret for you."[49]

Years later, another story would circulate about Gus's cockiness during the first time the lawyers actually stayed in Edna for the trial, instead of making the 100-mile round-trip from Houston. The Edna hotel "discouraged" Mexican Americans from staying there but must have acquiesced to the well-dressed lawyers after the trial began. In this almost mythological rendition of the tale, Gus removed a small table and chair from the room, placed them in the middle of the parking lot, and sat there with a bottle of liquor singing, daring anyone who didn't like Mexicans to come and tell it to his face. This stunt was a reaction to numerous threats to their physical well-being the lawyers had received.[50] Gus, in his own retelling of the case, did not recount the episode, but did write, "It was necessary for us to travel . . . to and from Houston, each morning and evening to attend court because, for obvious reasons, it would have been ill advised to stay overnight in Edna, even if adequate accommodations had been available."[51]

Whatever the circumstances leading to the formation of the defense team and its ability to navigate Edna's Anglo landscape, it was clear from the start that they were going to have a hard time defending Pete as the prosecution had a solid case. There would eventually be more than a dozen witnesses, all lined up against him. The forensic evidence as well as Hernández's admission to having shot Espinoza all pointed to a quick conviction. Making things worse was the "importance" of the victim. In agricultural communities such as Edna, a few Mexican American families usually came to the forefront and became the liaison between the barrios and the Anglo neighborhoods. This proved valuable for Anglos who avoided communication with Mexican Americans except to get things done. For Mexican Americans, it was a way to have a voice and to keep abreast of the Anglo community's thoughts and actions. This role usually fell on those Mexican Americans who were better off in the community and who understood the language and had a history of successfully dealing with town leaders. Espinoza seemed to have fit that bill.

Espinoza, according to Gus, was a "popular" Mexican American in the community. Ironically, he was a more recent arrival to Edna than his killer, but he had quickly made excellent use of his time, gaining a level of economic stability unknown among most Mexican Americans in the area. His daughter Oralia remembers that her father moved the family twice so that she could go to school in a non-segregated environment. Her first two grades had been in wooden-framed buildings where she was taught with other Mexican students both below and above her grade level. By the third grade, her father had moved them to Edna, where they placed her in a "farm school" where students from "different nationalities" attended together. There, Joe Espinoza rented a farm and hired local laborers to pick the cotton and help with the chores. He quickly became good at tenant farming and within a short time he was earning enough to save a substantial amount of money and to provide his family a middle-class life.[52]

Espinoza had found his niche in a society usually closed to people like him. This allowed him to do things that few other Mexican Americans could do. Oralia remembers going to town and being able to shop and eat where they wanted. "My father would tell my mother . . . let's go eat a hamburger, and my mother would say, 'we can't go in there,' and he [would say] 'oh yes we can, I know so and so . . . who owns the place.'"[53] The same thing would happen at the bank, where the bankers were happy to see him, probably because his successful farming allowed him to deposit large amounts of money. When he died, Espinoza left nearly fifty thousand dollars in the bank, though all of it would quickly be depleted after his death.[54]

The extra resources allowed the family to hire an independent lawyer to help the state with its prosecution.[55] This was a rarity for two reasons: one is the economics of hiring a special prosecutor; and the other is the fact that an Anglo lawyer would be willing to work this case. This confirms that the family did have money and that their reputation in the community was respected even by some Anglos. This would be corroborated by Pete's family, who had known the Espinozas for years. They knew them to be better off than most Mexican Americans and as individuals who got along well with Anglos.[56] Fidel remembers them as a family who evoked both pride and distrust. Working-class Mexican Americans often depended on them to provide a buffer against Anglo hostility, but they often despised them for being closer to the Anglo community. Fidel remembers some Mexican Americans feeling that Pete was being railroaded because he had killed Espinoza.[57]

But if Joe's family was popular, as Gus argued, then there is reason to believe that there was more than one view in the community regarding the Espinozas. Families like the Espinozas were important in communities like Edna. Beyond their role as liaisons and spokespersons, the families provided a contrast to the kind of stereotypes used by Anglos to refer to Mexican Americans. The more they succeeded, the more they undermined Anglo notions that Mexicans were only "beasts of burden," uneducated, and lacking ambition. Interestingly, individuals like Joe Espinoza were the lifelines of support for reformers like Gus and Herrera and others who rallied to Pete's defense. These were the people they attracted and sought to rally to their cause. Years later, Oralia became an educator dedicated to the advancement of Mexican American school children.[58]

At the examining trial on August 8, 1951 Pete was denied bond, and on September 20 he was indicted for murder.[59] The defense team's approach was to argue for self-defense, but there seemed to be little to work with. When the trial began on October 8, they were only able to call Pete to the witness stand. No transcripts, notes, or testimony survive to shed light on the in-court strategy. Gus, an excellent trial lawyer, simply had little to work with, and as he later claimed, the prosecution had done a first-rate job. Eight witnesses testified against Pete: Mary Espinoza (Joe's wife), S.R. Mortland, Chico Sánchez, Jesús Jordan, Henry Cruz, John Tristan, Mike Peña, and J. B. Arroyo.[60]

On October 11, 1951—little more than two months after Pete had walked into Sánchez's Café—an all-Anglo jury found him guilty of "murder with malice" after only four hours of deliberation. He was then sentenced to life imprisonment even though several jurors wanted to give him the death penalty.[61] At that moment, Pete seemed destined to end up incarcerated and forgotten like many other Mexican Americans convicted of a crime in Texas. The real story, however, began before the actual murder trial and would last for more than two years, include one more lawyer, and raise the hopes of Mexican American reformers throughout the country.

Convinced they had a difficult challenge in developing a self-defense case but facing a stubborn Hernández and family who wanted "justice," Herrera and Gus elected to focus on the civil rights aspects of the case. They chose to challenge the composition of the jury, which was to their generation the last major legal barrier remaining to their incorporation into American society. While Texas, California, and much of the Southwest remained segregated societies, and discrimination was a constant for most Mexican Americans, Gus and Herrera's generation had already won a major court victory that made "separate but equal" unconstitutional as it applied to their community. Mexican Americans had been active in challenging discrimination in the courts from the earliest years of the twentieth century. Two things were certain in the minds of Pete's lawyers: (1) they had successfully struck down any notion that Mexican Americans could be segregated legally or officially, and (2) Mexican Americans were considered white by law and, thus, eligible for all rights under the constitution. The latter was, however, a much more complicated notion that served as a double-edged sword.

When Herrera and Gus chose to challenge the jury selection, they were building on several unsuccessful but important prior challenges. In fact, Herrera's firm had just finished a similar jury challenge earlier that year. *Sánchez v. Texas* was probably an even stronger case than Hernández's because the racism was more blatant, but it never made it past the appeals process, although De Anda had written what one of the appeal judges called an "exhaustive" brief. De Anda, however, was in the process of leaving Herrera's firm to form his own in south Texas, but the groundwork for the prior case served the lawyers so well that they continued to carry his name as part of the team. De Anda would go on to build a very successful legal career and become involved in some landmark decisions affecting Mexican American school children, but he would miss out on appearing before the Supreme Court on this, the first case to reach the high court on behalf of Mexican Americans.[62]

Gus filed a motion to quash the indictment and one to quash the jury panel on October 4, 1951. On the first, he argued that his client's constitutional rights had been violated on two counts: exclusion of Mexican American jurors and the selection of both the jury commission and the grand jurors before Pete's lawyers could argue the first point. These two points, said Gus, denied Hernández equal protection under the Fourteenth Amendment. On the motion to quash the jury panel, Gus provided further detail on his objections. He claimed the jury panel was "improperly selected" because all persons "belonging to a class known as 'Mexicans'" were excluded from the panel in this case and that they were "systematically, intentionally and deliberately excluded from [all] Jury Commissions and Grand Juries." He went on to add that "they had never been given an opportunity" to serve on juries. Gus then proceeded to set down the foundation for arguing racial and class discrimination of Mexican Americans as it pertained to jury selections.[63] "People of [Hernández's] national origin or class," continued Gus, "are, on the whole, of a low economic level and considered members of a distinct race, separate and apart from the other citizens of Jackson County." Exclusion was not the only problem. They were also treated as an "inferior race," denied services in many local establishments, and "for many years" segregated in the public schools, "as if they were members of an inferior class."[64]

At the start of the hearing to consider the motion to quash both the indictment and the jury panel, Gus faced Wayne L. Hartman, district attorney for the Twenty-fourth Judicial District of Texas; Cullen B. Vance, county attorney; and William H. Hamblen, independent prosecutor for the family and a native of Edna. Gus would refer to them later as "such able lawyers." He recalled, "I was sandwiched in between the arguments of the handsome young district attorney, a dynamic and eloquent speaker, Mr. Wm H. Hamblen, an orator of the old school, and the very capable county attorney, Mr. Cullen B. Vance. Needless to say, we were buffeted about pretty badly."[65] Gus, however, was feigning humility after achieving victory. The fact is, opposition like this simply energized him, and so did the possibility of a major victory.

Gus called as his first witness Gena Lee Lawrence, a district clerk who had held her position for fifteen years. After establishing her credentials and experience by asking her about her job, he quickly turned to the point at hand. "Have you known of a person of so-called Mexican or Latin American descent to be appointed a member of a jury commission in this County?" As expected, Lawrence answered no. She was then asked whether she had "heard" of anyone of the aforementioned being a member of the grand jury in the county. The answer: "I don't recall having heard of it." Gus then went to "ever seen or heard" of a person of Mexican or Latin American descent being drawn on a venire for a petit jury. The answer: "I don't think so."[66]

The line of questioning then shifted to one of proving the status of Mexican-origin people in the county. Gus asked Lawrence whether Mexicans were considered a "different race." The district clerk did not take the bait and answered with an "I don't think so." Gus persisted and asked whether people in the county differentiated between "Mexicans" and "white people." The clerk again refused to be drawn into a battle of racial definitions. "I think we all understand that the Latin Americans are considered white people," said Lawrence. Gus then shifted to the treatment of public establishments of Mexicans, but Lawrence again refused to acknowledge any differential treatment. The questioning again shifted, this time to the eligibility of Mexican Americans to serve on jury duty. The clerk responded that only the tax collector would know who paid their poll tax, and refused to speculate whether any Mexican American actually paid their poll tax. Gus continued pressing, and after considerable prompting, Lawrence admitted that "generally speaking" Mexicans were "of rather low economic status."[67]

This early exchange must have convinced Gus that the Anglo residents of Jackson County were not going to provide him any ammunition by engaging in prejudicial charges or making inappropriate comments. These Texans did not believe—or allow themselves to believe—that their relations with Mexicans and Mexican Americans in their vicinity were out of the ordinary. In the 1950s, people in central Texas did not filter their racial views through civil rights or constitutional lenses. They were more concerned with the way things worked, and for them things worked well. Lawrence's unwillingness to engage in racial talk was on par with the way Anglo officials in Texas thought then. They never spoke about Mexicans in public terms but rather in private ones. That is, Mexicans were racially different in private conversations, in backroom politics, and labor disputes, but in the public discussions, when propriety was a rule and others besides Texans were listening, Mexican Americans were white with all the rights and privileges of citizenship. This was particularly true when pressed by Mexican Americans themselves. Texas officials simply did not accept that they were anything but fair.

When the prosecution took a turn cross-examining the witness, Gus must have cringed at the hairsplitting that Texans would go through to point out the fallacy of Mexican American charges of discrimination. The prosecution lawyer Hartman asked the clerk whether she was willing to testify that no one with "Mexican blood" had ever served on a jury. "It is highly possible some or many of them [jurors] might have had Latin American blood to a certain degree and not have had a Latin American name, is that right?" "Yes, sir," came the answer.[68] Hartman then asked the clerk whether she had ever seen an officer of the court discriminate against Mexican Americans. He followed the negative response with questions on whether Mexican children went to the same schools, played on the same football teams, and whether their parents belonged to the same parent-teacher associations or attended the same theaters. All the questions drew an affirmative response. Then the prosecutor ended by asking Lawrence whether she—in her official duties—had ever discriminated against a Mexican. "I have not" she responded.[69]

Hartman was relying on years of Texan-Mexican interaction to discredit any notion that Anglos and Mexicans did not interact or did not get along. He understood that de facto discrimination had always allowed a certain amount of fluidity among the races in Texas and because of that fluidity there were Mexican Americans who could prove to be the exception in every case. While most Mexican American students had been relegated to segregated schools, an occasional one was allowed into Anglo schools. There was always one elite Mexican American farmer or cattleman who participated in the Chamber of Commerce or the region's politics. There were also a few instances of intermarriage, which undermined any notion of rigid racial segregation. What Hartman was doing was playing the white/black binary of American legal and social thought. If Mexicans did not suffer the rigid and legal Jim Crowism that blacks did, they had no case.

He also wanted to debunk any notion that Texans believed in a "Mexican" race. "Isn't it also true [that] sometimes Bohemians are referred to as 'Bohemians?' . . . and Polish people as 'Polanders?' . . . and Germans as 'Germans?'" he asked.[70] As we will see later, the Texas courts had refused to accept "Mexican" as a racial category. It was a term of nationality and thus its adherents were not subject to protection under the Equal Protection Clause of the Constitution. The Texas courts had decided that there were only two races, black and white. To add another one, especially a Mexican race, would have created major legal and social problems for Anglos in Texas and the rest of the Southwest and West.

On re-examination, Gus quickly countered by getting the clerk to admit that people did mean something different when they spoke about a "Mexican and white man" than when they spoke about a "Bohemian and a white man" or a "German and a white man." He then asked the clerk whether she "knew" of a Mexican with an Anglo name. The clerk said no. Then Gus asked her again whether she recalled any Mexican or Latin American who had served on any jury. "I don't recall any." Then the questioning turned to the schools. "Do you know how long the children of Mexican parents and the children of American parents have been going together here to school?" The clerk responded that it had been "several years," to which Gus responded with, "You would not say it was since the year 1948?" That was the year that a federal court in California had ruled segregation in school unconstitutional as it applied to Mexican Americans.[71] That same year, Gus had prodded the state attorney general to declare that no school could segregate without some scientific reason. Gus, sensing the witness's discomfort, then asked whether apart from the PTA were there other organizations such as the Kiwanis, Lions, and Optimists that allowed Mexican Americans in. The clerk could not answer affirmatively.[72]

At that point, Hartman stood up and told the court that the "State will stipulate that for the last twenty-five years there is no record of any person with a Mexican or Latin American name having served on a jury commission, grand jury or petit jury in Jackson County."[73] Gus had his first victory. Hartman and the prosecution team knew that to hold out on the point that it was impossible to tell if someone with "Mexican blood" had ever served, was to maintain in discussion what everyone in the courtroom knew— that most people were aware of who the "Mexicans" were. These were the people who worked for them, who only recently had sent their children to segregated schools, and who were still barred from some establishments in town. They were the people whom many Anglo parents in Edna pointed to and told their children to "stay away from."

The next witness called by the defense was Claudius Branch, the county tax assessor and collector, who testified that to his knowledge there were Mexican Americans who both owned property and paid taxes, and were thus eligible for jury duty. During his cross-examination, Hartman made sure that the county official admitted that he did not know the exact number of Mexican Americans who owned property and paid taxes and of those how many read and wrote English or how many were women—who under Texas law were ineligible to participate in jury duty. He then asked the tax assessor if he knew of any time when there had been discrimination in his office against a "Mexican or Latin American because of his nationality." "No sir. We carry them on the tax rolls as white," said the county official. "And they are looked upon in your office as 'whites' just the same as a German or Pole or Bohemian?" asked Hartman. "Yes, sir." Gus then asked whether the official was in position to judge whether other people in the county looked upon Mexicans as whites. "No sir," came the answer.[74]

By this time, it was becoming clear to the prosecution that they could win a legal battle in Jackson County, but they were doing it by making everyone in the courtroom uncomfortable. For if there was one thing clear in places like Edna, throughout central Texas, south Texas, and most of the rest of the state, it was that Mexicans were not like whites. Most whites would not accept that they were, and every Mexican knew better. Hartman knew he had to follow the legalistic route by strictly adhering to the letter of the law, while Gus knew he had to take the "common knowledge" approach. Everyone knew that what was on paper had little to do with what really happened on the outside. That was the difference in places like central Texas where blacks were legally subordinate and Mexicans were socially second-class.[75]

Lewis Watson, the county sheriff, was then placed on the witness stand. He claimed he knew of only one restaurant in town that did not serve Mexicans, and that it had only recently removed a "No Mexicans Served" sign that hung on the outside. When asked if there was a distinction in usage of the term "white man" from "Mexican," he responded, "I have heard it, yes sir." When asked if there were three groups in the county "whites, Mexican Americans, and Negroes" he responded, "'Latin Americans' are white and the Negro is a Negro." Under cross-examination, Watson stated that sometimes different groups were referred to by their language: German speakers as "Germans," Bohemian speakers as "Bohemians," and so on. The prosecutor then asked Watson if his son played football at the local high school and if so, were there any Mexicans in the first string. The answer was yes. He was then asked if he treated all prisoners the same. The sheriff added that he put all prisoners together except for "Negroes." "Have you ever seen a sign 'No Bohemians Allowed' or 'No Bohemians Served?'" countered Gus. No, said the sheriff. "But you have seen a sign 'No Mexicans Served'?" "At one place," was the answer.[76]

"No Mexicans Served" was a sign and a phrase with which most Mexicans and Mexican Americans were familiar. It served as a social commentary on their public lives. Mexicans were needed for their labor, and Anglo ranchers and farmers often went to great lengths to recruit and keep them. There were even times when Anglo bosses might befriend some of their workers, but bringing them into their social circle was often a different matter. While Pauline Kibbe of the Good Neighbor Commission of Texas went to great lengths to explain in 1946 that posting blatant restrictions in public places was not a widespread practice, most Mexican Americans understood that the few incidents—in 1943 there were 110 complaints—were indicative of a much larger problem. Few communities in Texas existed where Mexicans were not barred from at least one establishment or more.[77]

Kibbe, in her book *Latin Americans in Texas*, cites one flagrant example in which one Feliciano Mendoza sought to buy his wife a coat in the town's leading dealer of women's apparel. The dealer tried to dissuade him from doing so because he doubted Mendoza could afford it. When told they cost $150 and up, Mendoza put $300 on the counter and asked, "Will that buy two coats?" To which the dealer responded, "Now Feliciano, I don't want to see you waste your money. I tell you what you do. Schwarts next door here, has some second-hand fur coats. You go in there and buy your wife a cheap coat and save your money."[78]

The message did not have to be transmitted to every Mexican American in Texas. Those perpetuating the rejection understood well that word of mouth was enough to let other Mexicans know that they were not wanted. For every one of the 110 individuals who filed formal complaints for not being served, there were hundreds of others who did not protest, or who simply avoided such places. Even when they were served, some were treated so rudely that they did not return, and simply told their friends and neighbors, "They don't like Mexicans there," which in Mexican barrio language meant the same as "No Mexicans Served." Thomas Sutherland, later a director of the Good Neighbor Commission, explained that "in the social context of Texas, Mexican Americans [do] not need a direct no or refusal to interpret . . . a rejection."[79]

Gus's next witness was Oscar Bonds, superintendent of schools. Bonds had been in the position for only one year but had served the district since 1938 as an elementary teacher. Gus quickly put the superintendent on the defensive by asking him when it was that the "Mexican school" in Edna had been closed. Bonds responded that he could not say, since he "did not have anything to do with that." Upon more prompting, he guessed it was three or four years earlier. Gus pressed him on whether it had been before or after the federal courts had ruled that the segregation of Mexican American children in schools was unconstitutional. Bonds responded, "I would not say." Asked if the Mexican school was considered "another"—or segregated—school before it was abandoned, Bond responded that it was not "100 percent for Latin Americans." Asked why it was then called "the Mexican school," Bonds said it was "chiefly" for Spanish-speaking children who did not know the language, but then he quickly added that children were not required to go there if they spoke English. He also told those present that some children left the school or transferred to the other school before the fourth grade.[80]

Bonds admitted he did not know if children took language tests before being placed in the Mexican school, nor did he know how many children were permitted to transfer to the white school. Were there "few or many?" asked Gus. "Few," came the answer. Gus then asked why four years. It was up to the teacher said Bonds. "Were there Latin American children . . . permitted to go to the other [white] school from the very beginning?" "I don't know about that," came the response. "You don't recall of any instance?" pressed

Gus. "I am not positive," said Bonds, "I believe it was after the teacher had them a while." Was the school in the same location? "It was not."[81]

When asked if the theory of separating children on the basis of language was wrong, Bonds responded that he had not made that decision. When queried on how many of the district's 1,555 students were of Mexican descent, the superintendent stated that he did not know, but after further questioning admitted that most were in the first four grades. "The larger percent drop out around the sixth grade." When asked for percentages, he corrected himself—after admitting ignorance of the figure—and said "a large percent. I will not say the larger percent." Gus tried to pin the superintendent down on who could give him the numbers, but he was only able to get Bond to commit to give him a school roll.[82]

Hartman used the cross-examination to reaffirm that students were only separated because of language difficulties. "Not because," he asked Bonds, "the school system and its teachers were discriminating against them because they were of Mexican or Latin American descent?" Bonds admitted he really did not know the "basis" for the creation of the Mexican school. Asked again if he had any evidence of discrimination, he responded that he had none. Hartman then inquired if other "nationalities" dropped out of school too. "Yes sir." "They did not all finish?" came the question. "No sir." And "you don't undertake to say why they dropped out of school?" No, came the answer.[83]

Several times during the interrogation, Hartman used the term "it" to refer to individual Mexican children: "It was kept there just so long as it was necessary for it to overcome the language difficulty?"; and "after that it was transferred to the other school"; and "at any time the teacher that was teaching the child felt—into the regular class it was brought over?"[84] Whether Hartman was that insensitive or simply that indifferent toward Mexican children is difficult to know, but his usage of the term "it" seemed to have caused no reaction from the judge or even from the defense. Yet, given how many insensitive comments Herrera, De Anda, and Gus were used to hearing, it was not surprising to have them simply ignore the terminology.

When asked if anyone was ever denied a transfer after he or she was ready, Bonds said he knew of no case. He added that there were two schools presently, one for white students and one for black students. Once in the white school, he did not expect that the Mexican students faced discrimination. "They attend the same classes?" asked Hartman. "And sit in the same seats and use the same restrooms and play on the football team, there is no discrimination at all?" "No sir."[85] Gus responded by trying to get the superintendent to take a firm stand on whether the segregation of Mexican students was good or bad pedagogy, and whether teachers in the Mexican school were overburdened. The school official, however, refused to make any definitive statements. Hartman then emphasized the teacher's competence in determining which students were ready to transfer. He stressed that "Latin American students were given the same opportunities to graduate from school as those children of any nationality." Gus responded by reaffirming his earlier points.[86]

This particular witness, whether he understood it or not, was in the midst of re-engaging a battle Mexican American civil rights advocates believed they had already won, and in which they had the federal courts on their side. But Hartman was continuing to do what most Anglo educators and policymakers were doing throughout Texas and the West: denying that they had done anything wrong, thus, denying the validity of the rulings themselves. But they treaded on dangerous ground and they knew it. Civil rights litigation and the federal courts' movement toward integration—as slow as it might have seemed to reformers—made it difficult to defend segregation, especially when no legal justification existed. Mexican Americans had been segregated educationally for many of the same reasons as African Americans, but because there was no legal or constitutional framework to legitimize the process, politicians, educators, and community leaders had developed the issue of "language difficulty." They moved toward segregation by exploiting an issue that most people, including Mexican Americans, understood as relevant to the discussion.

Most Mexican children did not know the language well and this was causing them to fall behind. Mexican American reformers understood this, but they saw it was critical that their children not be separated. They knew well that in the American educational system "separate" was indeed "inherently unequal." It did not have to be, but Mexican schools were a prime example of how it was. The schools were usually housed in dilapidated buildings, far away from the main campus, staffed by lesser qualified teachers and nearly forgotten by school administrators. While some state educators bemoaned the horrific dropout rates and sought to counter it, most local school officials ignored or even exacerbated the problem.

With the consensus on segregation crumbling, school officials and politicians had clung even more tenaciously to the "scientific" and "educational" reasons for separation. What had been an excuse to keep them away from white children became a "concern" for the linguistic challenges of Mexican American children. Failure to shift to this "concern" meant that school officials were in fact discriminating and doing so without the cover of law, as was the case with the legal segregation of black children. There is no doubt that there were educators in Texas and the rest of the Southwest who empathized with the plight of the Mexican school children, but unfortunately, there was no education theory or methodology that comprehensively dealt with the issue of Mexican American educational progress.[87]

Gus understood that legal precedence was on his side, but he wanted to make sure the historical record also supported his contention. While white officials wanted a "presentist" approach to the discussion of segregation and discrimination that emphasized that things were different now, Gus sought to prove that the larger Anglo community moved only when coerced by the courts. While not able to accomplish it with the reluctant witness, he also wanted to establish a record of proof that Mexican Americans were seen as different, which in this community, given the practice of jury discrimination, meant "unqualified." More important, for years Gus had heard numerous rationalizations in litigation against school districts that segregated.

The state called as its first witness L. S. Horton, one of the jury commissioners charged with selecting the grand jury and a petit jury panel. A resident of nearby Ganado, he was now retired but still worked for the Mauritz Rice Storage Company. Hartman asked him if he or any of the other commissioners discriminated against persons of Mexican or Latin American descent in forming the grand jury panel. But Gus quickly protested the word "discrimination," and called on the prosecution to provide a definition.[88] Gus knew that in the minds of most white residents in Jackson County, "discrimination" was a word more appropriate to their relationship with "coloreds." Rarely did they see their interactions with Mexican Americans as "discrimination." They simply followed community norms in the way they treated, paid, educated, and associated with Mexican Americans.

Insisting that the term be defined, Gus sought to destroy the nuances associated with the treatment of Mexican Americans, and force the commissioner to be more explicit in explaining the actions taken by the jury commission. Hartman ignored the request and shifted his line of questioning and led his witness through a discussion on the process of jury selection. The witness testified that only the "best qualified" were selected and that neither the instructions nor the discussions among commissioners was designed to exclude those of "Mexican or Latin American" descent.[89] Gus then asked Horton if the commissioners considered the value of jury members who could understand Spanish since a number of those charged with crimes in the county were illiterate in English. Horton replied that it had not been discussed. Hartman then asked if in fact the ability to read and write English was a legal requirement. Gus responded by asking whether commissioners even considered the notion that a Mexican American could serve. "No, sir," came the reply. Hartman asked again if the "matter"—meaning discrimination—had been discussed. Said Horton, "There was no racial discrimination discussed. We selected them irrespective of nationality. We did not turn this man down because he was Bohemian, or this man because he was a Pole, or this one because he was a Negro, or this one because he was Spanish. We selected good levelheaded men that are outstanding for good common sense for our Grand Jury."[90]

Later Horton reiterated that "we selected the men, not the nationality." To which Gus responded, "and in carrying out that policy, you just did not have to select any people of Mexican descent on your jury panel?" "That is right . . . we had a tax roll and that was what we used." Hartman quickly asked if anyone had been left off because of nationality. "No, sir." "It is just not customary for people of Mexican descent to serve on Grand Juries?" asked Gus. Horton simply said he did not know.[91]

The next state witness was Shirley Schroeder, secretary of the Jackson County Chamber of Commerce. She testified that one Mexican American had current membership in the county chamber, which had 170 members, and that two different pairs of Mexican Americans had served on the board of directors in 1949–1950 and 1950–1951. When Hartman asked if they were welcomed into the chamber, Schroeder responded, "They are invited," and that no law restricted them from participation.[92] The reality of two pairs of "Latin Americans" serving on the board of directors pointed out one of the major differences between the Mexican and black experience in Texas and the Southwest. Mexican Americans had always participated in one form or another in the political, social, cultural, and business life of Texas. The problem was that their participation was extremely selective, and that it did not in any way mean participation as a whole. In the end, it was class and racially based. The whiter and richer Mexican Americans could participate. Yet, they did so only as long as they maintained the notion that all was well in Texas.

The prosecution called the other four jury commissioners who repeated the earlier assertions that nationality had played no part in their selections. Gus, seeing the futility of poking holes in their story, asked no questions, realizing that every time they denied discrimination, they strengthened the prosecution's assertion, and weakened his own. The prosecution went on to call a tax collector for the school district who testified that he remembered some "students of Latin American descent who had played on the [high school] football team." Gus questioned him on segregation and graduation rates among Mexican Americans, but got mostly "I don't know."[93]

Gus called his two assistants, Herrera and De Anda, to rebut the claims of nondiscrimination in the community. Herrera had been handed the graduation rolls from 1951 in which he found two "Spanish surnames" in a list of sixty-three names. But during a recess, he had also stumbled into a gigantic symbol of differentiation between Anglos and Mexicans in Jackson County. Asked if he had gone to the "privy" during the recess, Herrera responded that he had and found that there were two, one which said "Colored Men" and under it were the words *Hombres Aqui*, which he translated for the courtroom audience upon Gus's request as "men here."[94] Herrera's testimony dramatically drove home two points. One was that in a community where 14 percent of the population was of Mexican American descent, only two had graduated the year before. And the restroom signs indicated the preference of whites not to have Mexican Americans in their washrooms. It was a "preference" because legally they could not bar Mexican Americans from the main toilet. Still, the signs served to make clear the place of those whose whiteness was questioned. After all, there was no Spanish lettering on the one for whites. Hartman pointed out that there were "Latin Americans" with Anglo surnames, and there was no way to tell from the list whether in reality only two had graduated. In response to the words written on the door of the restroom, he asked whether the restroom without the sign was locked. "No sir," responded Herrera. Asked whether he had used either one, he responded that he had lost the desire after he saw the sign. "But you are not telling the court you could not have used the unmarked simply because your name is Herrera," asked Hartman. "No sir."[95] Ironically, this "accident" would follow the case all the way to the Supreme Court and highlight the fact that in the social binary of black and white, Mexican Americans were perceived to be closer to blacks than most Texas officials were willing to admit.

De Anda, to whom Herrera had given the school rolls, court records, and other documents before taking the stand, testified that he had examined the "consolidated census roll" for the Jackson County School District. In it, he found 211 Spanish surnames out of a list of 1,184. He also found numerous names mostly "Hispanic" struck from the list, but could not account for the reason. Hartman quickly asked if the list differentiated between nationalities. They did not. He also asked De Anda whether the list was designated as the "list of white students?" It was. The transcript then ends for this motion.[96] Here the prosecution had scored a point. The reality was that when African Americans were brought into the equation, Mexican Americans became "whiter." After all, African Americans were "black" by law—that is their color prompted their segregation. It was impossible to regard Mexican Americans as black with the same laws that made African Americans black. Given that situation, Mexican Americans became or could become whiter in the administrative functions of the school regardless of their treatment on the outside. Since there were no laws mandating segregation for Mexican American children, nor any laws that legally supported the segregation of their parents, numerous ways arose for dealing with them administratively. This unofficial discrimination always hampered Mexican American reformers who sought to prove intentional or rigid segregation.

Four days later, another hearing was held to rule on the defense's motions to quash the indictment, to quash the jury panel, and to quash the talesman after the special venire was exhausted. The court had overruled the first motion dealing with the grand jury indictment of Hernández.[97] On October 8 and 9 both counsels examined the potential jurors but were able to select only eleven jurors from the list of veniremen. The court then, under strenuous protest from the defense, instructed Sheriff Lewis Watson and his deputy to summon twelve talesman to report the next day. Gus argued that the jurors had to be selected from the regular panel appointed by the jury commissioners. The judge overruled the protest, saying the process was necessary to complete the jury. Gus then made the motion to quash the array of talesman because no "persons of Mexican descent" had been summoned to serve. He further argued that this new call for jurors was additional evidence of the "custom, usage and practice in Jackson County, Texas, of discriminating against persons of Mexican descent, and of classing them as a group separate and apart."[98] The jurors had been selected from an original list of 130 veniremen. People who observed the process of selection noted that the state prosecution brought up the issue of the death penalty. The prosecution was actively looking for jurors who would be willing to use that form of punishment. It is possible that the prosecutors did not believe that Mexican American jurors would send one of their own to death.

Gus called his first witness, Mrs. Chris Rosas, an Edna resident of twenty years and a native of nearby Victoria. She was a property owner and she and her husband ran a café. A mother of four, Mrs. Rosas was also a member of LULAC, the League of United Latin American Citizens. Her value as a witness revolved around her son being a graduate of the high school that June. More important, her child had gone to the Mexican school years earlier even though she had taught her children English "since they were babies." Asked if she tried to enroll them in the regular school, Rosas responded, "They would not accept him."[99] "Did you tell the superintendent your son spoke English?" queried Gus. "I did." "And what did he tell you?"[100] "He told me that they did not accept any Latin Americans in that school." Rosas then added that she sent her son to the Mexican school for one year and then to a private academy. "I did not want my son to go to school in one room for those four years." Two years later she tried to enroll her daughter in the white school and again school officials had refused.[101]

She described the Mexican school as lacking any "conveniences" common to other schools in the county. There was a woodstove to keep the children warm during the winter, but when it rained, the school became uninhabitable and the pupils were usually sent home. Rosas did not say so, but if the school followed the pattern of others in Texas, it had little to no pavement, no grass, and no recreational areas. Rosas also testified that her son was not allowed to ride to school with the Anglo children, but had to be picked up on a separate trip. The court judge then asked Rosas how long ago these incidents had occurred. She responded that they occurred twelve and thirteen years earlier. Hartman quickly objected to the testimony because "it is too remote in . . . time to the present case." For one of the few times in the case, the judge overruled the objection and said he would allow the testimony, "for whatever it is worth."[102] The last comment seemed to reflect the court's feelings about the jury challenge. The judge continually sided with the prosecution in overruling most of the defense's objections and in sustaining most of the prosecution's motions.

Rosas was cross-examined by Vance. He concentrated on whether the teacher was qualified or certified to teach. Rosas simply responded that she did not know since her son did not go to school there. Hartman then asked if she was charging that discrimination had occurred "in the case we are trying?" Rosas quickly responded, "I think there was discrimination." "Who?" asked Hartman. "The town," said Rosas. "Who?" "The town," she repeated. "The whole town?" "Yes, sir, they discriminated, the town."[103]

Rosas's testimony may have astounded some in attendance, but probably not many. Her testimony proved crucial to the case but not for the immediate trial. Her experience called into question the Anglo excuse that segregation in the public schools had been only for the benefit of those who could not speak the language. The refusal to allow a Mexican American boy or girl to enter a school for which they were linguistically prepared smacked of discrimination, and so did the bus ride. More important, as a business member of the community, her voice could not be "disqualified" in the usual manner used against poor, linguistically-handicapped *mexicanos*. Rosas's charge that the "town" had discriminated may have amused or angered the prosecution—it is hard to say which—but it reflected a view that many Mexican and Mexican Americans had in Texas. They rarely engaged in hairsplitting about which Anglos "discriminated" and which did not. They simply knew that the relationship between the two groups was asymmetric, and few Anglos ever showed a propensity to challenge the status quo. Those who did, were so few that they could not be seen as "the town" as the others who were in the majority could. Mexicans had experienced discrimination and racism for so long and so often that exceptions to the rule did not contradict their reality.

The judge took very little time to overrule the defense's objections to the jury. "I am taking into consideration the testimony that has been heretofore offered by the state in making my ruling," said the judge. As if realizing what he had said, he added, "I'm taking into consideration all the testimony offered by both sides in this matter." This ended the challenge to the jury selection.[104]

"The Mexican People Are of the Same Race"

A life sentence should have been the end of the *Hernández* saga. There was no doubt in the minds of his lawyers that Pete Hernández had no real defense, at least not one that would get him released on appeal. Hernández and his family, however, adamantly insisted that he was innocent and that the lawyers needed to appeal to the Texas Court of Criminal Appeals.[1] Gus García and John Herrera must have thought deeply about the appeal. They knew that their only chance at acquittal or at least a new trial was to pursue the approach used during the pretrial. They had to convince the court that jury discrimination had occurred and had impaired the defense, but experience had shown that this was—or had been—an almost impossible task. By his own admission, Gus had tried "every trick in the book . . . to goad [the prosecution] into some ruling, word, or action" that might make the appeal much easier.[2] Yet no smoking gun had come out of the trial or even the judge's ruling.

Texas judges, prosecutors, and politicians had begun to employ a quasi-scientific response to any accusations of discrimination. When they could, they would use the notion of "helping" the Mexican American. At other times, it was about "efficiency," "appropriateness" or the "civil way." All the approaches were intended to change the discussion of the negative impact on Mexican Americans of the decisions made; it was the "circumstances and actions" of the victims that made both the policy and its results the responsibility of the victim. By never admitting that they had intended to discriminate (or might have done so by their actions) they did not allow the discussion to go any further. They were also quick to take credit for any changes that they had been forced to make. When educational segregation was struck down by the federal courts, they quickly pointed to the fact that Mexican American and white children went to the same schools and participated in the same activities as proof that there was no discrimination. When the courts ruled that there were no legal grounds for discrimination, Texans quickly argued that they did not discriminate because they "could not," given the court mandates.[3]

For Herrera, it must have been rather taxing to even consider the appeal despite his earlier expressions of his willingness to take this case all the way to the Supreme Court. Although quite committed to challenging laws that discriminated, his law firm had tried such an approach a year earlier. They had even prepared a sizeable brief that the appeals court had noted represented a very extensive record.[4] Still, their claims of jury discrimination had eventually been shot down. By this time, Herrera had begun to play politics as much as litigate.[5] In the late 1940s and early 1950s, Mexican American lawyers had become organizers and politicians. They understood that the court rulings could change things only so much. The numerous positive rulings during the late 1930s and most of the decade of the 1940s had done little to change educational discrimination in Texas and much of the West. Politicians, educators, and local officials found ways to circumvent the rulings, mostly because few of them had coercive clauses and those that did were rarely enforced. Putting pressure on politicians by rallying Mexican Americans to the polls and pressuring educators by having parents complain and their children boycott schools had become a way of making officials obey the law. Making sure that Mexican Americans knew their rights and having them exercise them had become the major emphasis of the 1950s. As an officer of LULAC and as a member of numerous other local organizations, Herrera was a veteran of the struggle for civil rights.[6] For that reason, he was quite conscious of which cases could be won and which could not.

Gus saw it as his ethical duty to make the Hernández family think long and hard about an appeal. He later wrote, "I pointed it out to them that even if the case were reversed, it would have to be tried all over again with all the attendant risks." Those risks meant that a new jury could decide on the death penalty. Pete, however, insisted that what he had done was justifiable and his family adamantly agreed.[7] They did not want their son locked up and forgotten, something that happened often to Mexican Americans who were sent to prison. By this time, however, the original fee charged by the lawyers had been exhausted on expenses, and Gus and Herrera began spending their own money. One reason for the heavy expenses had been the hundred-mile roundtrip to Edna from Houston that both lawyers made daily during the trial. Gus blamed "obvious reasons" for the lengthy trip.[8] These reasons were the hostility of the local townspeople and some veiled threats. While much had changed by the 1950s, it was still dangerous for any Mexican American reformer to push his luck in the small rural towns of Texas where Anglos were accustomed to dealing with "meskins" the old-fashioned way.

Because of the limited funds available, the appeal was filed on the last day permissible, giving the lawyers the time to raise the money from friends and supporters as well as from the few functioning Mexican American civil rights groups in the state. On the day that the "Statement of Facts and the Transcript" were submitted to the State Court of Criminal Appeals, William Maldonado, a San Antonio labor leader and fellow reformer, drove a very sick Gus to Austin for the filing and to begin the second phase of the *Hernández* saga.[9] Both the lack of funds and the illness were symptomatic of the situation that Herrera and Gus faced. Their experience at this level was limited though they did have the *Delgado v. Bastrop* case under their belts and a number of other educational cases that had not reached the appellate court. Still, their success rate and that of most Mexican American lawyers at the appeals level was poor. Both were trial lawyers who could dazzle a jury with their courtroom performance, but who understood their limitations in writing briefs for appeal, particularly for cases outside the arena of public school segregation.

Herrera was a journeyman lawyer who worked hard and cared deeply about his clients, but who lacked legal expertise. His young associate at the time, De Anda, would later remember that Herrera avoided the law books, and instead relied on his courtroom savvy to win cases.[10] Herrera grew up as a migrant worker and the constant moving around delayed his high school education and he graduated at twenty-one years of age. He worked for several years and eventually got into the South Texas College of Law. At the time he worked for the city of Houston as a "ditch digger" but later became a cab driver in order to have time to study. After graduation, he took the bar exam three times before he finally passed it.[11] Herrera was street smart and he understood civil rights litigation, but his late start in school and his extremely difficult time in getting through law school had left some gaps in his legal scholarship. Just as important, Herrera neither had the staff nor the colleagues necessary to help him further his legal skills beyond those he needed on a day-to-day basis. Interestingly, one incident that inspired Herrera to become a lawyer occurred when he got a chance to see an aging Clarence Darrow try a case in Michigan. Years later, Herrera adopted Darrow's opening remarks: "You know, every person stands equal before the law . . . it can be the king in his mansion or the pauper in his shack. We're all equal before the law."[12]

Before *Hernández*, Herrera's major claim to fame had been the *Delgado* case, on which he served as second chair to Gus, and his leadership in LULAC, where he sought to challenge segregation and discrimination through the filing of complaints, by boycotts and protests, and if those failed, through litigation. In 1945, in the little rural Texas community of Pearland, near Houston, several families complained to Herrera that their children were being forced to attend a typical Mexican one-room, one-teacher school two miles from the regular elementary. In this shabby building, fifty-one children in grades one to five were segregated because of "linguistic limitations" even though several understood and even spoke English. Herrera rallied the families for an eight-month boycott until the school district moved the Mexican school next to the regular school but kept the students segregated. It was only a partial victory, but the most they could expect given their limited political and economic power. Eventually, however, the Anglo parents complained about the dilapidated building and it was removed and the Mexican children were "invited" into the regular building.[13] This was the type of action that Herrera mostly did in his work as a civil libertarian. It should be pointed out that Herrera had been a lawyer for only eight years when he took Pete's case, though he had already been engaged in a major jury discrimination case before *Hernández*.[14]

Gus, on the other hand, could not have been more different from Herrera. He was smooth, cocky, flamboyant, and extremely articulate in both Spanish and English and a genius in school. Born on July 27, 1915, to well-educated parents, he graduated from Thomas Jefferson High School in San Antonio at sixteen and was its first valedictorian. He attended the University of Texas on a scholarship and graduated at twenty in 1936, and two years later there he received his law degree. After passing the bar that same year, he served as an assistant county district attorney in San Antonio for three years, and was then drafted into the U.S. Army where he served as an infantry officer and then as a judge advocate in Japan. Gus was adept at making important friends, speaking at the right places, and being at the center of important events, both inside and outside the Mexican American community.[15]

When the United Nations was founded, Gus participated in the inaugural activities in San Francisco, and when the Mexican Consulate expanded its offices in the late 1940s, he served as a legal advisor, representing their interests and those of the Mexican community in Texas. Then in 1948, he was elected to the San Antonio Independent School District Board, where he served for four years as an advocate for the exploding Mexican student population and actively sought to end segregation, with only partial success.[16] Among his friends and admirers and even among his opponents, he was known as an incredibly tenacious and successful lawyer who could win any case that was winnable. Within the circle of Mexican American reformers of the 1950s, there were few who had his presence and few lawyers who seemed to promise so much in terms of personal achievement. Still, Gus shared Herrera's dilemma: tremendous interest in civil rights advocacy but little interest in law books.[17] Despite this limitation, Gus had been involved in numerous public school segregation issues, and by the 1940s was the chief legal adviser for LULAC and the American GI Forum in this area.

In defense of both Herrera and Gus, the times called for litigators, advocates, organizational leaders, and motivators, and seldom for legal scholars. There simply were few opportunities to address issues that went beyond the need to keep people out of jail or get them their paychecks or protest community prejudices. Even in cases dealing with school segregation, it was rare that a case went beyond the local level, notwithstanding the number of cases that were heard and decided favorably in the late 1930s and early 1940s. Most cases also did not go to appeal because of a lack of money and because most defendants had little hope of getting a reversal and feared getting a worse sentence during retrial.

Most discrimination against Mexican Americans was de facto and difficult to litigate without engaging in advocacy and establishing "treatment," rather than the law, as evidence of discrimination. Without a legal structure of Jim Crow, Mexican Americans were always trying to prove "intent" and prejudices without the benefit of a legal statute that offered that proof. Ironically, jury discrimination—even against African Americans—was of a de facto nature and so arguably the type of case that Herrera and Gus excelled in. Still, given the failures of the past in winning these types of cases, both lawyers knew they had to bring an expertise to the table that neither of them had. To this end, they brought on board Carlos Cadena, a law professor at St. Mary's University in San Antonio, and according to Gus, "the best brain of my generation."[18] Unfortunately, at the writing of this book, there are no biographies on Cadena or even an encyclopedia article detailing much of his life. There are also no collections of his personal papers and what is known of him comes from obituaries and a few newspaper articles.

We do know, however, that Cadena had won a major federal case in 1948, but one which was outside the area of public school segregation, where Gus and Herrera had the most experience. In *Clifton v. Puente*, Cadena argued successfully that racially restrictive covenants used against Mexican Americans in real estate transactions constituted state action, and the Supreme Court had ruled in *E. Shelley v. Kraemer* that the state could not deny an individual's right to due process under the Fourteenth Amendment.[19] This was a major victory for Mexican American civil rights as it struck a blow against residential segregation that made public school segregation an even greater problem. It was also the first major case not involving school segregation, and which pointed out that this insidious separation of the races was not limited to the educational arena. At the time, Cadena was a thirty-year-old lawyer with less than four years of legal experience. In 1952, he became part of the law faculty at St. Mary's University in San Antonio, an accomplishment none of his peers would equal.[20]

By the time of the *Hernández* appeal, De Anda, who had written the impressive brief for Herrera's prior case on appeal, had begun his move to south Texas to pursue his own legal practice, and where he would eventually become a renowned civil rights lawyer and later a federal judge.[21] Chris Aldrete, a young lawyer already known for his reform activities against public school segregation, replaced him on the legal team.[22] Maury Maverick, a longtime liberal politician and lawyer and friend to Mexican American reformers, rounded out the team, although in his case (as in Aldrete's), it was mostly in an advisory capacity.[23] The legal team would remain basically a three-person team with no staff, little money, and uneven rank-and-file support.

With the appeal, Pete and his lawyers reached the apex of an important phase in the more traditional civil rights movement of the Mexican American community. In the first seven years of the decade at least fifteen educational legal challenges were filed in Texas.[24] While most would not go very far, there were some that did have an impact on the continuing segregated environment in the Southwest. By 1949, Mexican American lawyers and their allies had convinced the federal courts to rule that segregation of Mexican children was a violation of the Equal Protection Clause of the Fourteenth Amendment. For all practical purposes, the notion of "separate but equal" had been discarded as applying to Mexican Americans. But more important than the flurry of lawsuits was the changing nature of civil rights activity. Mexican American reformers were, by this time, aware that litigation had to be accompanied by grassroots organizing and, when possible, by hardball politics.[25]

This approach underscored what most civil rights advocates understood—their victories in the courtroom had remained legal victories and not political or social resolutions. Simply put, no groundswell for change existed in Texas or in much of the West. Mexican Americans found themselves constructing a civil rights paradigm piece by piece. In 1949, educator and civil rights advocate George I. Sánchez had written Hector P. García, president of the American GI Forum and invited him to be part of a "larger discussion" on the issue of segregation in Texas. Describing the current efforts as "pulling teeth," he called for a grand strategy to deal with educational and, indirectly, all segregation. He argued that Mexican Americans had to stop "begging and cajoling" as it led nowhere. Pointing to the important court victories of the last few years that had all but declared "separate but equal" as unconstitutional in the case of Mexican Americans, he called for taking off the "kid gloves" and attacking segregation and all forms of discrimination. To fail to do so would be to "admit stupidity."[26]

Yet, how to "take off the gloves" was a complicated question given the strategy that Mexican American reformers had been following for at least three decades. Their approach had been to seek recognition as good citizens and to maintain an agenda that emphasized "civic duty," education, and the learning of English. In many ways, the three decades before the *Hernández* case had been dedicated—in the minds of middle-class reformers—to proving themselves "good" Americans.[27] This meant that Mexican American reformers had unconsciously (or perhaps consciously) hardened the political borders within their own community. Composed of native-born, naturalized, resident, recently-arrived, and longtime undocumented workers, the Mexican-origin community had found a way to survive socially and culturally intact. But the rise of a Barrio Americanism had given rise to political and ideological boundaries.[28] These boundaries were not particularly clear but they did engender an implicit difference between those who claimed citizenship and loyalty to the United States and those who still looked toward Mexico or who simply found it hard to integrate into what continued to be a hostile environment.[29]

In the early years of World War II, however, a new political philosophy began taking hold in the Mexican barrios, particularly among those who were native-born and longtime residents. This philosophy centered on what can be described as a "politics of similarity." Mexican American elites sought to cast themselves and their experiences as being very much like those of "mainstream" Americans. The war made this approach more sensible and much more likely to succeed, at least in the minds of Mexican American reformers. There were two reasons for this: first, most of them had served honorably in the armed forces; and second, the war had been the one great "generational experience" that brought "all groups" of Americans together—with the exception of African Americans. That Mexican

Figure 3. Two of the *Hernández* case's strongest supporters pose with Gustavo "Gus" García in an earlier period. From left to right are Hector P. García, George I. Sánchez, and Gustavo "Gus" García.

Americans had served in integrated combat units and that they had been decorated for their performance in combat negated any arbitrary differences that some wanted to construct after the war.[30]

For this reason, the challenge to exclusion from jury duty became imperative. It was certainly not a new issue for the community—there are records that trace this struggle to the 1920s—but what was important now was that challenging jury discrimination fit very well an emerging "notion" held by many Mexican American middle-class reformers that there was a "new," more open attitude in the American people. While their predecessors had often doubted American compassion, these new reformers believed in the "fairness" of American society. They were not necessarily naive, but they were trapped into an ideological phase that depended on American compassion and a sense of fair play. If they could not believe in the fairness of American society—and some were not too convinced of it—their approach would be completely undermined.[31]

Seen in this context, it is clear why Gus, Herrera, and Cadena jumped at the case after their initial hesitation. Early on, the often-hyperbolic Gus had assured anyone who would listen that this case was "headed to the Supreme Court."[32] It is not likely that he really felt that way once the case began, but after some time he again became convinced that it was possible, if only because Gus could not litigate unless he was slaying legal dragons. Jury discrimination was one such legal dragon. No educational legal case could compare in representing a clearer debate on the Mexican-origin population's place in American society. Jury duty represented an even greater expression of one's civic duty than voting. In the jury box, the citizen stood to act upon the law, to interpret it, and to provide judgment on its usage. Being chosen meant that the people—through the actions of the state and the defense—had found them worthy to stand in judgment of one of their peers.

Here, if chosen, they stood as assessors of someone's fulfillment of the obligations of the law. While the *Hernández* case involved a Mexican American charged with murder, a precedent could be set for future cases in which a Mexican American would be judging a white person's guilt or innocence. The consequences were not lost on anyone. The opportunity to pass judgment on the white community was something that no other civic duty at the time could provide. Mexican Americans knew that this was a necessity in order for them to be seen as equal. Anglos also understood that to have a Mexican judge them was to breach the social and cultural barriers that kept the communities apart. Bestowing jury responsibility on Mexican Americans meant bestowing them all the rights of citizenship.

It is likely that for many whites there was a feeling that Mexican "clannishness" was not good for this civic duty. Were they capable of acting as good citizens? Or were they going to use this right to free their own kind? Anglos were not convinced that Mexican Americans understood the responsibility of citizenship. One superintendent in central Texas believed that Mexican Americans lacked an understanding of the principles of democracy. "Participate, mix, think, society will accept you when you are ready, not just because you are entitled to those rights," he declared to reformers seeking changes within the school district. "They [Mexicans] will never attain our white level until such time they prepare themselves and accept responsibility in our community."[33]

Mexican Americans were seen as not ready because they had not "accepted responsibility," but reformers argued that it was impossible to "prepare themselves" and to act responsibly when the opportunities for doing so were not available. Jury duty provided that opportunity and it also provided another forum in which to prove Mexican American "civic adequacy." In some ways, this was a "safe" forum. The rules for participation in jury duty were such that only Mexican Americans who understood the language and could read and write would be able to participate. In the case of the Mexican American community, this meant that only the middle class could hope to participate. For reformers, quite conscious of their image and rather sensitive to Anglo criticism of their behavior, this was a good situation. Educated, civic-minded individuals from the barrio would be able to participate and to show that they were capable of upholding the civic role.

Anglos were not so certain. To them, most Mexican Americans were uneducated, uncultured, and untrained in the intricacies of democratic citizenship. Since women and most working-class whites were already excluded through law (in the case of women) and practice (in the case of poor whites), they felt a certain standard had been achieved and allowing Mexican American participation would lower that standard. During the 1940s and 1950s, Texas jury commissions were under federal mandate to allow more African Americans to participate in jury duty. But while blacks had won that right years before, in Texas they continued to be excluded when possible.[34] White middle-class males were the only acceptable people to participate in this civic function. It is important to note that in the year that Hernández killed Espinoza, the Jackson County White Man's Primary Association had voted to disband, believing that they had accomplished the task of bringing order and discipline to local government. White males felt they had achieved their stated goal of securing all the political and civic space for themselves.[35]

Before reviewing how Mexican Americans had challenged their exclusion from jury duty, it would be well to examine how jury duty had become "democratized" for most groups. The story is one of constant struggle and judicial innovation in the obtaining of the right to sit in judgment of one's fellow citizens. The barrier to inclusion in the juror selection process was based on two important legal foundations. One was that the potential juror had to be a citizen and that he (not a "she" until the late twentieth century) had to be white. Jurors were required by law to be white until the three amendments to the Constitution following the Civil War. But in reality these amendments only changed the situation for African Americans; most other people of color still had to prove that they were white.

Black participation in the jury system was first based on the rights they received from legislation following the Civil War. The Civil Rights Act of 1866 to some extent provided African Americans the right to participate more fully in the society at large. In terms of jury duty, it meant that they could participate in both petit and grand juries and they did so in most of the South, including Texas.[36] The Civil Rights Act of 1875 more fully integrated African Americans by making it a misdemeanor to discriminate against prospective jurors "on account of race, color or previous condition of servitude."[37] But only two years later, most states had begun excluding blacks from juries. The Compromise of 1877 created the climate for unrepentant whites to strike back, and they soon received support from the federal judiciary when the U.S. Supreme Court ruled in 1883 that sections one and two of the Civil Rights Act of 1875 were unconstitutional.[38] These dealt with "full and equal enjoyment" of public facilities regardless of race. This occurred in spite of the fact that in *Neal v. Delaware* (1880) the court had ruled to slightly enhance black legal integration. But for the next seventy years, the courts vacillated between expanding and contracting jury participation of African Americans.

In 1880, the Supreme Court found a West Virginia law discriminatory because it barred "coloreds" from participating in both grand and petit juries. This ban, reasoned the court, branded African Americans as inferior and thus stimulated race prejudices, a violation of the Fourteenth Amendment to the Constitution.[39] In 1935 the court followed the protection of black rights to jury duty with a ruling in *Norris v. Alabama*. Here the court again reaffirmed that exclusion of African Americans "solely because of their race, or color, from serving as grand [or petit] jurors" was a violation of the Equal Protection Clause of the Fourteenth Amendment. This ruling, however, attempted to prevent all forms of discrimination and to place the responsibility more squarely on the shoulders of the state.[40]

Without doubt these and subsequent rulings were positive indications that African Americans had rights to jury service that were protected under the Equal Protection Clause. Furthermore, they sought to entrust government with the responsibility of maintaining those rights. Unfortunately, from the first ruling to the last one of the pre-*Hernández* period, the courts quickly moved back toward the concept of "proof of purpose," a position that weakened a potential black juror's claim of discrimination. According to the *Norris* ruling, "if discriminatory purpose is found, discriminatory acts, whether they be in the selection of venire or the exercise of a peremptory challenge, will be eliminated. If discriminatory purpose is not found, discriminatory acts are absent and the system is operating within the proper parameters of the Equal Protection Clause."[41]

This construction of when discrimination was present provided the courts tremendous leeway in ascertaining whether charges of discrimination were in fact applicable. That is, the courts would decide whether something was discrimination and thus either allow or disallow a challenge on that premise. Making things worse, in *Strauder v. West Virginia* (1880) the

Court had emphasized that no defendant had a "right to a 'petit' [or grand] jury composed in whole or in part of persons of [the party's] own race."[42]

Because the Court assumed that the American legal system was free of "racism" and unaffected by the social context of the time or the region, it could provide an unbiased assessment of whether discrimination existed or not. Worse for black defendants and potential black jurors, the courts had no obligation to be inclusive but only the responsibility to make sure that they were not exclusive. The failure to put inclusion outside the realm of the courts made it less difficult for state prosecutors and state courts to avoid putting blacks on juries. Simply put, whites were in charge of deciding whether blacks were discriminated against and whether exclusion was detrimental to a case. Thus, state courts, where most violations occurred and where few people of color had any recourse, would be the ones making the determinations on jury discrimination.

A further vacillation from the *Norris* ruling can be seen in several other Supreme Court cases dealing with jury discrimination. In *Smith v. Texas* (1940), *Akins v. Texas* (1945), and *Cassel v. Texas* (1950), the Court promoted two views detrimental to African American participation in juries.[43] First, they argued that if the jury commissioners and the state courts had been instructed to "not discriminate" then things were proceeding in accordance with the law and no discrimination could be alleged. Second, the Court ruled that race played no part in the fairness of a court proceeding or ruling.[44] In the *Cassell v. Texas* case, Justice Reed declared, "an accused is entitled to . . . a jury in the selection of which there has been neither inclusion or exclusion because of race." And Justice Frankfurter added, "The basis of selection cannot consciously take color into account. Such is the command of the Constitution."[45] This, of course, weakened the arguments that could be made for black participation in juries. After all, if black jurors did not bring anything to the equation, why was it important to forbid their exclusion? Yet, it was on this point that all black protest was predicated. Black jurors were seen as a potential counter to the white supremacist views that condemned all black defendants to harsh sentences. It was by having a different view on the jury panel that defendants could hope to find a more open and proper discussion of their guilt or innocence.

The history of jury discrimination, then, was littered with small steps forward, large steps back, and a freezing of the social context of discrimination. Black jury struggles reflected two important and contradictory notions. One was that African Americans did have a constitutional basis for full participation in jury duty, but that they also had to repeatedly return to the courts in order to practice that right. When they won, the ruling was subject to strict guidelines so as not to "guarantee" proportional jury representation. Also, most states were willing to try their luck at challenging federal judicial interpretation, and so, almost every year at least one new case of jury discrimination made its trek toward the federal courts. Still, the black experience with regard to jury duty was not one of total loss.

Unfortunately, the situation with Mexican Americans represented a complete opposite. Their status within the American legal system was virtually nonexistent. Unlike in the case of African Americans, there existed almost no legal framework for dealing with issues affecting Mexican Americans. The earliest legal foundation arose after the U.S.–Mexican War. The document ending the war and ceding much of Southwest to the United States did provide legal status for those Mexican citizens who stayed in *el norte* after the war. They could choose to stay and claim American citizenship or they could simply stay and be given citizenship status. The treaty, however, did not envision Mexicans wanting to become American citizens and so it failed to consider a process to deal with this eventuality. But this became an issue in the 1880s, when Ricardo Rodriguez, a citizen of Mexico, applied for naturalization and sparked a philosophical and legal firestorm.[46] Briefs rebuffing the idea that Mexican Americans could naturalize came from scholars and others, claiming that Mexicans were Indian or Mongolian—not "white"—and thus not eligible for naturalization. One even argued that the Texas Revolution's declaration of independence had declared them to be "unfit to be free"—a detriment to citizenship—and "incapable of self-government."[47]

Still, there were others who believed that, at least in theory, groups of colored people were eligible for naturalization based on the treaty after the U.S.–Mexican War. Eventually, a perplexed district judge, T. S. Maxey, ruled in the *Rodriguez* case that "when all the foregoing laws, treaties, and constitutional provisions are considered . . . citizens of Mexico are eligible to [acquire] American citizenship." But he did so only after affirming that "if the strict scientific classification of the anthropologist should be adopted, he would probably not be classified as white."[48] Absent the treaties between Mexico and the United States, Rodriguez would surely have been denied the right of naturalization, at least in Texas. In California, the issue had been resolved in 1870 through the case *People v. de la Garza*, but Texas had been seen as excluded from the treaty because at the time the state was already part of the Union.[49] Still, the immigration court came to believe that the treaty provided de facto naturalization to those already in the territory and rights of naturalization to those who applied later. Yet, years later, the courts still seemed unsure of whether "Mexicans could be naturalized."[50]

What re *Rodriguez* meant was that Mexicans and Mexican Americans had become part of a complex contradiction. They were white because they could naturalize—something most "dark" people could not do—but they were people of color because "scientific classification" deemed it so.[51] This meant that their "whiteness" was subject to legal application and thus had no place in the social construction of status or in the qualification for full rights of citizenship. It becomes logical to argue that this legal decision created the opening for a two-tiered citizenship that provided the minimum of legal protection but also encouraged the adoption of means to deny the rights to full protection and full participation. Without fully being accepted as white and without specific constitutional protections such as those that the Fourteenth Amendment afforded African Americans, Mexican Americans were simply left out of the legal framework. Legal scholar Clare Sheridan argues that "by depriving (Mexican Americans) of the opportunity to exercise their right to participation on the same terms as others, the state denied that they were peers or equal members of the polity." This, she continued, allowed them to "maintain and reinforce social distance and erect legal distinctions by not treating Mexican Americans as peers."[52]

Reformers and civil rights activists understood that this exclusion cre ated a severe burden on Mexican American search for equality. For this reason they energetically sought "discussion" of their status. They understood that unless they pushed the issue, they would be left out of the discussion. As early as the 1920s, jury participation became an important issue and one that brought some local success as when the Order of Sons of America were able to force the courts in Corpus Christi to allow Mexican Americans to serve in juries.[53] But this victory was made possible by the large Mexican American population in the city and the fact that segregation was only just beginning to solidify in south Texas. According to social historian David Montejano, segregation would reach its zenith in the late 1930s and the early 1940s and then begin to slowly unravel.[54] The victory was also limited and had little impact in Edna just a hundred miles or so from Corpus Christi.

The more usual outcome of challenges to jury discrimination were those that came from several cases beginning in the late 1920s and ending only a year before Hernández killed Espinoza. The first such case was *Ramirez v. State*, which the Texas Court of Criminal Appeals actually heard twice.[55] The case dealt with Geronimo Ramírez, also known as Herman, who was charged and convicted of castrating nineteen-year-old Lucio Arevalo in Mernard County, Texas. According to court records, Arevalo had "gone off" with the defendant's stepdaughter, a formerly married woman with two children. After being gone for "eight or nine" days, the couple was found by Ramírez and his wife, and were on their way home when the incident occurred. Ramírez testified that he was taking the couple home so that the injured party "could get his divorce fixed" and thus allow the runaway couple to marry. On the way home, however, Ramírez stopped at a windmill to get some tools he had purportedly left there during a job. After failing to locate the tools, he started back to his car when his wife confronted him. "What do you want to do with this man down there?" she asked. "What are you going to do with that dog?" Ramírez replied that he was taking them home, to which the wife responded that she did not want "that dog around the house." She then added, "he [Lucio] has been making love to me and having intercourse with me and double-crossed me and then ran off with my daughter and did the same thing."[56]

Infuriated, Ramírez ordered Lucio to get out of the car. Taking a rope from the car, he then tied the young man, cut off both his testicles, and threw them on the ground. He then untied the young man and left him there to fend for himself, about a mile and half from the nearest house. Ramírez testified that he did "not believe in killing" and that his religion taught against such actions. Once at home, he told no one about the incident, but after several hours he decided to take a "white man" and go for the young man. When they found him they took him to some friends and the injured man "got out [of the car] and walked off."[57] While the records from the appeal do not specify the wife's actions, they do refer to the fact that she was also charged and convicted for the act, but that she received a suspended sentence of five years. Ramírez himself received the minimum sentence of five years in the penitentiary.[58]

The criminal act happened sometime in the fall of 1928 and the case went to court in October of that year. Ramírez was sent to jail for his conviction on the charge of castration. But his lawyers were able to appeal successfully for a reversal in the Texas Court of Criminal Appeals on a technicality.[59] Even before the grand jury had been sworn and impaneled, the attorney for Mrs. Ramírez challenged the composition of the jury on her and her husband's behalf.[60] It is obvious from this challenge that lawyers for Mexican American defendants had already begun to use these challenges as a strategy. The fact that Ramírez—and probably his wife—were represented by white lawyers and that they used the legal strategy adopted by Mexican American lawyers who followed, indicates that racial discrimination in jury composition was seen as relevant in the cases of most Mexican American defendants. No record is available on the discussions of the legal strategy in the case or whether there was a concerted effort on the part of defense lawyers to use that as a strategy. But it is likely that some defense lawyers believed that "justice" in Texas was rarely on the side of Mexican Americans. It is important to remember that this was a case that got to the appeals level, something many others did not, and this could very well indicate that many other trial cases were challenged on the issue of jury discrimination.

The strategy, it should be noted, did not imply that lawyers were necessarily looking to get their clients acquitted. Rather they were attempting to minimize as much as they could the length or severity of sentences handed down. This was because all the cases of jury discrimination that did reach the appeals level were rather simple open-and-shut cases and the evidence was strongly against the defendants, or at least it seemed to be according to the court records. Ramírez never denied the charge against him, but only wanted extenuating circumstances to be considered, such as that the passion he experienced was able "to render his mind incapable of cool reflection." Maybe he also believed that one or two Mexican American jurors might be more sympathetic to the "dishonor" that had been brought on him by Arevalo's relationship with his wife and his stepdaughter.

In challenging the jury selection, the defense questioned three witnesses, all of them officers of the court. The first witness was the county attorney, Joe Flack, a fourteen-year resident of Menard County, who was serving his fourth year as the county's chief prosecutor. Flack testified that he knew of no Mexican having been selected as a juror in his time in residence or his tenure as county attorney. But he added that he did not believe that any of them were "qualified" to sit on a jury, as those in the county did not know English well enough and "were otherwise ignorant." Yet, the county attorney argued that he knew of "no special discrimination against Mexicans as a race in the matter of their being selected on the jury." He also added that he knew of no instance of the court discriminating against Mexicans because of their race.[61]

The sheriff, who also doubled as the tax collector, followed with a similar testimony. In office for two years, he knew of about "thirty-five or forty" Mexican families in the county and about 150 total residents of Mexican ancestry. He knew of only twelve who had voted in the last primary election in the county. He also confirmed that no Mexican American citizen had ever been called to jury duty while he lived in the county. And he firmly added that he had never called "a Mexican on the jury when it became his duty upon direction of the court to go out and summon jurors." The sheriff doubted that the Mexicans of Menard were "intelligent enough or spoke English well enough or knew enough about the law to make good jurors." Besides, he added, their "customs and ways were different from ours."[62] In his mind that disqualified them to serve as jurors. He admitted that there were probably "one or more" Mexicans who could qualify to serve at least as well as some whites who had served before, but added that he did not consider those white jurors well qualified anyway. He ended his testimony by stating that the court had never "at any time by act or otherwise said or done anything that would indicate that he was discriminating with reference to races."[63]

Finally, Albert Nauwald, a jury commissioner, was called to testify. He started out by declaring that he would not select a Negro to sit on the grand jury or petit jury even though the black man was as qualified as any white man. He also opposed Mexicans on the jury. He did not consider them in making up the jury list because he did not believe them intelligent enough to make good jurors, but he added his name to the other two witnesses who testified that the court had "never said or done anything to discriminate against any race of people because of their race or color, and none of the agents or officers of said court had ever done so in so far as he knew."[64]

In three quick strokes, the witnesses stated what most white Texans felt about "their Mexicans" and revealed the complex circumstances of Mexican Americans in the Lone Star State. By the late 1920s the subordination of the Mexican worker population had reached a point where it did not garner much discussion within Anglo circles. The Mexicans were a necessary part of the economy; in fact Texas could not survive without them—but they were not a part of the social or intellectual structure of the white community. Their presence was distinctly noticeable and they were not far from the public's scrutiny, but they simply did not matter as an issue of discussion. More important, most white Texans believed, or chose to believe, that Mexicans understood their place in the region's social structure. They were not to share the same benefits and privileges as whites, and once that was understood, it was fair to have an exclusionary system.[65] Exclusion from participation in the larger society was not discrimination. That is why at least two of the witness could, in their minds, honestly declare that they knew of no "special discrimination" against Mexicans. What exactly they meant by "special discrimination" is unclear, but enough can be surmised from their testimony to underscore that treatment had to be much more severely discriminating before the white community could be made to confront its prejudices.

The court agreed with the witnesses and rejected the appeal. The Commission of Appeals declared, "the proof did not show that there had been discrimination against the Mexican race; and other than the proof that about a dozen Mexicans voted in the County at last primary election, there was no evidence that there was any Mexican in the County who possessed the statutory qualifications of a juror."[66]

In a motion for rehearing, Judge Lattimore reiterated, "we think the evidence wholly fails to show any discrimination against the *Mexican race* in the formation of the grand jury that returned this indictment" (my italics).[67]

The next case to be heard by the Texas Court of Criminal Appeals involved the murder of an Anglo couple by their ranch hand Antonio Carrasco in 1934.[68] It was a gruesome murder that surely must have infuriated the predominantly white community of Culberson County in Texas. Carrasco's written confession—which he later denied making but that was still submitted into evidence—went as follows: "Mrs. Smith and I took the body of Mr. Smith up to the house after I had killed Mr. Smith. I picked up a stick of wood and hit her on the head with it. It was about 7:30 last night that I killed Mrs. Smith."[69]

No more details are available from the court records, but it is likely that Carrasco and his lawyers understood that this was a capital murder case that could bring the death penalty. They were right. It is also probable that as in the Ramirez case the first strategy was to immediately challenge the composition of the jury. In this case there were 585 qualified voters in the county; sixty of those were Mexican American, but only six made it to the jurors' pool. Carrasco's lawyers argued that no Mexican American had been called to serve on a grand jury since 1932. The court disagreed with Carrasco that jury discrimination had played a part in the selection of jurors. "There is nothing in the record to indicate that Mexicans were excluded or discriminated against solely because of race. There is nothing to show that the sixty Mexicans residing in said county were male voters. That Mexicans had not theretofore been rejected is shown by the fact that they had served on grand juries as late as 1932. The indictment herein was returned in October, 1934."[70]

When the court ruled that "nothing in the record" indicated discrimination, it disingenuously avoided the heart of the challenge. Rather than apply the principle of *Norris v. Alabama*, or seek to fully understand the problem of exclusion, it simply accepted the lower court's decision without much discussion. The court did note that a reversal and a new trial with the same facts would not bring about a different conclusion.[71]

This was not a simple acquiescence to the process of the lower court, but a reaffirmation of the social status in Texas. Justices must have been aware of the discrimination that Mexican Americans faced in Texas, and they were also aware of how they were treated as a class apart. To not even acknowledge that a problem existed was to ignore—or confirm—the reality of Texas justice, thus providing judicial cover to discrimination against Mexicans and Mexican Americans. Had the justices expressed biased racial judgments, then grounds would have existed for further appeal. But by simply ignoring the possibility of discrimination, they were able to effectively end the appeal process.

The Carrasco case would be one of the weakest of the jury discrimination cases to reach the appellate level because of the small number of available qualified Mexican Americans jurors, and because little was offered as evidence of prior exclusion. But its importance lies in the way it reveals the complex situation of Mexican Americans in the rural counties in Texas. There their situation was often impacted by class, complexion, time-in-country, education, and ability to mingle with the larger Anglo society. Elite Mexican American families had always found crevices within Anglo society to find their niche. If they understood the limitations, made particular alliances, and maintained a certain degree of propriety, they were able to function, and to some extent prosper, in predominantly Anglo counties. So it was not surprising that Mexican Americans had served on juries in Culberson County, although it is likely that they had not served often or over a long period. For in sparsely populated counties like Culberson, there were few Mexican Americans—only seventeen were qualified voters—and the more acceptable ones were recycled in and out of county functions when needed.[72] They could also be called upon to be just as harsh on Mexican Americans as were whites. They did so because they could only maintain their "distinction" by showing no signs of favoritism to their ethnic brothers and sisters. For whites, Mexican American class divisions, amplified by social perceptions, made it possible to discriminate against most of them while promoting the "equality" of a chosen few.

On February 15, 1938, Genaro Lugo confronted an off-duty "peace officer" at midnight in the town of Odem, Texas. Still angry from having been pistol-whipped by Officer Dick Chisholm two weeks earlier, Lugo took out his gun and cried out to him, "We are going to kill each other." He then fired the first two shots, and after the officer was dying on the ground, came up to him and fired a third shot at his head. Lugo then took the deceased man's pistol, eight dollars, and a pocketknife. Several days later, Lugo was arrested in Corpus Christi and charged with murder with malice. The prosecution would argue in court that Lugo had made an oral confession, which was later transcribed, and had signed it. He told the officers of having stalked Chisholm, shooting him, and then stealing from him. He also told the officers where to find the pistol and the pocketknife. Lugo was convicted and sentenced to death for the crime.[73]

The importance of this case comes from the fact that this was the first case handled by a Mexican American lawyer, and a well known one at that. M. C. González was one of the founders of what was probably the most important and well-known Mexican American advocacy organization of the twentieth century.[74] The League of United Latin American Citizens (LULAC), founded in 1929, became a consistent advocate for Mexican American civil rights.[75] González's involvement brought into the jury discrimination debate new "twists" that reflected the changing nature of advocacy among Mexican American reformers. He introduced his first witness as a "native American and a World War I veteran," providing him a status not usually rendered Mexican Americans, and which sought to dispel the notion that Mexican Americans were foreigners and not loyal citizens.[76] By the late 1930s Mexican American advocates were emphasizing their citizenship to distinguish them from the immigrant, who was seen as taking away jobs from Americans during the Great Depression. Claiming veteran status was also a strategy that began slowly after World War I and would become the major "exhibit" for Mexican American legitimacy during and after World War II. Recognizing Mexican Americans as loyal warriors became another, mostly middle-class, strategy to rebuff accusations that Mexican Americans were neither loyal nor had they earned their rights of citizenship.[77]

González understood that in Texas and most of the Southwest, Mexican-origin people had to be found "acceptable" before they could socially be granted the rights of citizens. This, however, did not mean that González shied away from pointing out the injustices. He reaffirmed in his appeal that while San Patricio County had a large Mexican-origin population not one of them had served on a jury. He pointed out that Mexican American children were segregated in the public schools until the sixth grade, "thus showing in an uncontroverted manner that racial prejudice exists against the Mexican race, to which appellant belongs."[78] He was willing to go further than the previous Anglo lawyers in suggesting the extremes of racial attitudes. He reminded the appeals court that Lugo had been assessed the death penalty "by Anglo-Americans for killing another Anglo-American" in a county where "the belief is prevalent that Mexicans are aliens and illiterate and incapable of taking an active part in the administration of justice."[79]

González chose not to expand on his accusation, but it could hardly be misunderstood that he was indicting the whole system of Anglo justice. In several cases before and after the Lugo case, Mexican American defendants would deny making confessions but their denials were never affirmed by the courts. It may have struck González as strange how simple these cases were to prosecute. While the records are too sketchy to make an informed assessment, it would have been easy for him and other civil rights advocates to infer that in criminal prosecution Mexican Americans were just as much victims as they were on other social matters.

In his ten-page motion for rehearing, González began to set the groundwork for future civil rights lawyers who spoke to the "legitimacy" of Mexican Americans as potential jurors and to the unfairness of the whole social and legal system in Texas. He also extensively connected the African American legal victories to the plight of the Mexican American. He also tied the Ramirez case to this one, thus seeking to develop a body of Mexican American legal arguments against jury discrimination.[80] Eloquently, he raised the issue of the "Mexican race," arguing that Mexicans were "intentionally excluded" on account of their race and their color, and in doing so had been differentiated from being a "so called American." This was a direct violation of Lugo's constitutional rights, and simply reflected that "there [was] so much prejudice in [the] county against his [Mexican] race."[81]

González clearly attacked discrimination, rather than just pointing it out, as earlier lawyers had done. His origins in south Texas and practice in San Antonio provided him a deeper understanding of discrimination against Mexican Americans. Unlike places where earlier jury compositions had been challenged, San Antonio and south Texas were areas where a great number of Mexican Americans confronted discrimination in spite of being citizens, owning property, voting, and serving in the military. San Patricio County was also such a place. In that county were Mexican Americans who were professionals, business people, and even government officials, yet they still confronted discrimination, and were treated as second-class citizens.[82]

This historical presence and visibility in the county added an important element to the case. González called witnesses who argued that more than 300 Mexican Americans there owned property and were American citizens. The deputy tax collector also testified that there were anywhere between 300 and 400 "Mexicans . . . who were qualified voters," though he did not know how many actually could read, write, or understand English.[83] San Patricio was located in the northern part of south Texas, a region Mexican Americans had long occupied. Near the city of Corpus Christi, this county had a long history of Mexican American participation in the civic life of the community. Mexican American elites had managed to retain property, establish businesses, and even dabble in politics. Ethnic tensions were often high, but at least among the elites, relationships remained stable. But as revealed in the court testimony, there were limits to Mexican American participation in the legal arena.

The sheriff recalled that in his fifteen years in office, he had called a number of Mexicans to jury duty but remembered only two actually serving. Four jury commissioners also testified, arguing that they had selected the men best qualified to perform jury duty. Had they known, they argued, that there was "any citizen of the *Mexican race* qualified for service" (my italics), they would not have hesitated to place his name on the list of jurors for the term.[84] This was a blatant attempt to excuse the exclusion through a "sincere" ignorance of Mexican American qualifications or availability. Here they could imply that there were no Mexican Americans for the jury box and still maintain a notion of fairness in their deliberations. Clearly, they were playing to an Anglo audience of justices who understood that denial was the first and usually most important line of defense against accusations of discrimination.

The court ruled that the burden of proof rested on the appellant to show an intentional exclusion by the jury commissioners. Since the commissioners had testified that they would have placed Mexicans on the jury if they had found qualified ones "on the tax rolls," the court did not find any proof of discrimination. On the motion for rehearing, the court took further aim at the defense's contentions, arguing that most of the Mexican Americans referred to as qualified to be jurors were in fact ineligible. "Looking to the testimony . . . it is observed that . . . not all of the men . . . referred to as being able to read and write the English language were property owners." Justice Christian quoted one defense witness who said, "the majority of the persons that I have named would require an interpreter if it were necessary for them to come to court here and testify in a case." The witness added that even those who knew English well would probably need an interpreter.[85]

The witness, a man cited only by his last name of Peña, revealed a major roadblock for Mexican Americans in their efforts to participate in their civic duties.[86] Many of them struggled with the English language, and even when they could read, write, and speak it they were simply not socialized enough into American civic society to feel comfortable in a courtroom. The courtroom, like most other white institutions in the community, had been off-limits for so long that few Mexican Americans had any familiarity with it. Although they might know the words and understand the questions at face value, they were unfamiliar with the implications of the law or with the social meanings of the inquiries. That they would be intimidated because of their accents and their social standing was an accepted fact among whites and even some Mexican American advocates conceded the fact.

Yet Mexican American reformers knew that unless they were allowed into the jury boxes, they would never become socialized into this particular civic duty. Only by having them there would others feel more comfortable coming forward, and only then could some changes be made for accommodating Mexican American citizens. None of the jury discrimination cases dealt with the issue of interpretation except this one, but implicit in the discussion of the interpreter was a sense that the courts had to make accommodations to the circumstances of Mexican Americans. Yet, this accommodation would not then or now include interpreters in the jury room. Mexican Americans were thus constricted by both the racial discrimination of the jury commissioners as well as by the small numbers within their community who could actually participate within the socially restricted interpretation of the law.

Mexican Americans were capable of participating, seeing the evidence, discussing it, and making a rational judgment. They also could bring a particular sensitivity to the situations confronting the accused, but what they could not do was articulate their contributions to their Anglo colleagues in the jury room. In addition to the language barriers, social obstacles prevented them from being seen as contributors in the courtroom. The courts were not willing to entertain the notion that as citizens Mexican Americans should be accommodated in one form or another. Instead, the court simply ruled that the "appellant has failed to discharge the burden of showing that there was purposeful discrimination against Mexicans because of their race." Implicit in the ruling was the notion that whites had nothing to do with the circumstances in which Mexican Americans found themselves.

By the 1940s, the courts began to consider another way to rebuff the jury discrimination challenges that now seemed routine for those defending Mexican Americans on trial. In the 1944 case of Serapio Sánchez, accused of killing a white man who had attacked his father, the appeals court first rejected the argument of jury discrimination by pointing out that few of the Mexican Americans in Hudspeth County paid their poll tax. Though some officials claimed "forty or fifty percent" of the county's population was of Mexican origin, only fifty-eight had paid their poll tax and "some . . . were women." Others were in the Army. While state law allowed the courts to go beyond the poll tax lists if the numbers of potential jurors were limited, few courts considered there to be a need to look for more Mexican American citizens to serve.[87]

The court also refused to reconsider the trial court's overruling of a motion for change of venue. Sánchez's attorney argued that Hudspeth was hostile to members of the Mexican race and he could not receive a fair and impartial trial.[88] The court, however, ruled that the witnesses did not provide a solid case for discrimination. It pointed out that the witnesses had revealed differences in opinion among the citizenry about the case. Some were favorable to the defendant while others were hostile. The state's two witnesses were unanimous in their declaration that Sánchez could get a fair hearing. The court thus ruled "it is the rule in this state that if conflicting theories as to prejudice arise from the evidence, the trial court has the discretion of adopting either theory, it being his [sic] duty to weight the evidence. A judgment denying the application will not be disturbed unless it be made to appear the trial court abused his discretion with respect thereto."[89]

Left to the discretion of local judges—or possibly almost any judge in Texas at the time—it was highly unlikely that the defendant could win out. The court, however, went further than simply rejecting the defense's argument; it set a precedent that would hamper other cases that came after.

Sánchez's lawyer cited *Norris v. Alabama* to argue that his client had been denied equal protection under the Fourteenth Amendment. The court responded (in the first such response recorded up to that time) that the case applied only to the Negro race. "We have discovered no case wherein the [Supreme Court] has applied the same rule to members of different nationalities," wrote Judge Davidson on the motion for rehearing. He further added, "in the absence of a holding by the Supreme Court of the United States that nationality and race bear the same relation, within the meaning of the constitutional provision mentioned, we shall continue to hold that the statute law of this State furnishes the guide for the selection of juries in this state, and that, in the absence of proof showing express discrimination by administrators of the law, a jury so selected in accordance therewith is valid."[90]

The appeals court was willing to accept that discrimination was grounds for a reversal but it was unwilling to accept that *Norris v. Alabama* applied to Mexican Americans. That is, it was unwilling to shift the burden to the state to prove that it was not engaging in discriminatory practices. More important, and of crucial importance to Mexican American defendants, it was not willing to provide constitutional support to charges of jury discrimination as it pertained to non-black groups. In essence, the court was reaffirming a white/black binary in American jurisprudence. To accept any kind of constitutional standing for Mexican Americans would be to open a political and social can of worms in Texas, because by the 1940s Mexican Americans were beginning to catch up to African Americans in their demands for civil rights.

Two years later, M. C. González was back in court representing Victoriano Salazar, a prowler convicted of killing a policeman in a shootout.[91] This time, he argued that jury commissioners had discriminated against

Salazar's "Mexican nationality" in "intentionally and deliberately" refusing to call a Mexican American to serve on the jury even though Cameron County had sufficient Mexican Americans qualified to serve.[92] The use of "nationality" was likely to circumvent the earlier ruling that refused to acknowledge that the "Mexican race" had the same constitutional recognition of either white or black. It is also possible that by the 1940s, there were more middle-class Mexican American advocates who were pressing to have their people recognized as white. After coming back from the war, many Mexican Americans were uncomfortable being classified as "different" by their Anglo counterparts, especially when different meant inferior.[93]

Whiteness as an issue had been in the Mexican American community for several decades, but only now was it coming into play in the courtroom. The strategy, however, proved troublesome. It was one that would create future problems for Mexican Americans even though it brought them a temporary victory in both the courts and in politics. The difficulty revolved around the fact that whiteness both presented them as people who merited inclusion and full rights, but it also allowed them to be lost within the larger white population. Mexican American advocates of whiteness wanted it both ways. They wanted to be seen as "similar" but they also wanted attention to their educational, social, and political problems. While in the earlier decades of the twentieth century inclusion had been the major demand, by the time of the *Hernández* trial Mexican American reformers were demanding governmental action to resolve their plight.[94]

The court refused to take the bait or to reflect on nuances. In its ruling it pointed out that the complaint had explicitly made an issue of discrimination against nationality, not race. "The Mexican people," ruled the court, "are of the same race as the grand jurors. We see no question presented for our discussion under the Fourteenth Amendment to the Constitution . . . and the decisions relied upon by appellant, dealing with discrimination against race." In other words, there really were no "questions" because race was not an issue—Mexican Americans were white—and nationality was not recognizable in constitutional law, according to their interpretation.[95]

The *Salazar* and *Sánchez* cases signaled a strong shift by the Court of Criminal Appeals to put an end to the continuous challenges of Mexican American defendants to the jury system of Texas. Questioning qualifications or merit had been useful tactics in blocking Mexican American jury participation in the prewar years. By the end of World War II, however, using these tactics was becoming more difficult given the number of Mexican American veterans who were becoming much more likely to register to vote and participate in the political process. In fact, the postwar years brought a revival and expansion of Mexican American civic participation and many more Mexican Americans were arguing for full rights of citizenship. Ironically, that so many of them were arguing their "whiteness" made it easier for the courts to throw a new roadblock in their way in the cases of jury discrimination.

It would be quite logical to argue that Mexican Americans had done it to themselves. They wanted to be "white" but they wanted to argue for "equal protection" because they were of the "Mexican race." But the situation was much more complicated than that. Mexican Americans were still debating identity, both racial and national, in the mid-1940s. It would, however, be more accurate to say that middle-class Mexican Americans were unsure where they fit in the mosaic of American society. They were often American by birth or naturalization but they usually lived in the barrios, restrained from entering the American mainstream by economics and by discrimination. They saw themselves as white but felt that they were treated as a separate "Mexican race." Proud to be American, they were rarely ashamed of who they were and so they maintained a bilingual and bicultural existence.[96]

Yet, because of this ambivalence, they were often attracted to contradictory positions in regards to their identity, their politics and their social space. If being white was what it took to be accepted and allowed to participate fully in society, then they were white. If being Mexican provided group solidarity and a chance to distinguish their needs from those of others, then it was also usually acceptable, although most preferred to be seen as "Americans of Mexican descent." Among them were many who also had a strong dislike for their Anglo counterparts, whom they saw as "less American" because they did not live up the American ideals that they themselves so fiercely clung to.[97]

Given this situation, there did not develop among middle-class advocates any particular group racial or national identity. This should not mean they were confused about who they were or that they did not fully value their heritage, only that no ideology developed beyond a Barrio Americanism that saw them as Americans with particular constraints in the mainstream.[98] Thus no one wrote about any underlying principles in their advocacy and not one political intellectual or philosopher, with the possible exception of scholar George I. Sánchez, stood out from among them.[99] In fact, with a few exceptions, this was a paperless generation that left little in terms of thoughts and ideas about their racial or national identity.

They debated among themselves and even at times engaged in a rhetorical debate with whites in public, but they did little writing on the matter. They simply could not resolve the internal contradictions within their middle-class civic views. Unlike earlier and later generations of reformers who seemed able to step back and assess American society and their place within it, these reformers were too constricted by their patriotism, the Cold War, and Anglo resistance to develop a notion of themselves outside of the American mainstream. The openings they saw in American society were simply too small and tenuous to not be taken advantage of when they appeared. Civic duty and inclusion were thus the determining factors in their civil rights litigation, even when it seemed militant or radical.[100]

In 1948, the appeals court heard the case of Robert Bustillos, charged with the murder of Julio Herrera, a policeman. Filing a motion to quash the indictment, Bustillos's lawyers argued that "there were many Mexican people in Lubbock County who possessed all the required qualifications of grand jurors, but that the jury commission . . . intentionally and designedly failed and refused to select any person of the Mexican race as a grand juror." The court, however, found that the appellant had not shown that these Mexican Americans actually qualified as potential jurors. "It is not shown that they were free-holders in the state, householders in the county, nor that they could read and write the English language. . . . We do not think that any discrimination is shown under the proof presented here." In making the decision, the court cited *Sánchez v. Texas* and *Lugo v. Texas*, in which they believed that they had set a standard of proof.[101]

These cases had two things in common. First, the defense attorneys were white, and second, the evidence presented in the challenges was simple and limited. Beyond trying to show that there were "eligible" Mexican Americans available for jury duty, not much else entered into their discussions. No perspective was accorded the courts and no scholars or witnesses took the stand on behalf of the defendants. It seems that these objections to the composition of the juries were just some of numerous "bills of exception" presented to get the defendant a lesser sentence. The strategy was simply one of finding the best defense for the particular accused. It would be the Mexican American lawyers who took the strategy further and who sought to make "law," and not just to win the cases at hand. And this effort would coincide with the larger civil rights reform movement occurring in Texas and the rest of the West and Southwest.[102] It would also represent an attempt to replicate the legal victories in the educational arena.

Caucasian Cloak

Mexicans "White" for Judicial Conveniences

One more important case dealing with jury discrimination predated the effort at ending Mexican American exclusion through *Hernández*. Like several other cases before it, it did not make it past the appeal process but if compared with M. C. González's last case, it provides an interesting contrast on what was happening outside the courtroom and within Mexican American civil rights reform just before Hernández's conviction was first appealed. These two cases revealed how the Mexican American community's fight for the rights of citizenship was changing. M. C. González would litigate his last important jury discrimination case in 1946, and in 1951, newcomers De Anda and Herrera would argue their first.[1] The *Hernández* brief, as we will see, benefited much from those two efforts.

By the mid to late 1940s, returning World War II veterans began taking over the helm of the fight for Mexican American civil rights. These veterans were to form new organizations and take the battle to the national level and into politics. They were a new breed of men—allied with a number of non-veteran women—who saw the fight for inclusion in a different light. They no longer saw inclusion as the major goal. For them, participation in the democratic process, economic prosperity, legal equality and social acceptance were all part of the rewards for their participation in World War II. Theirs was a politics of "similarity"; they saw no reason to be treated differently at home when in the trenches and battlefields they had been simply "American soldiers," fighting and dying like everyone else. Unlike the case of African Americans, the military had not segregated them and a number of them had been able to advance within its ranks. Most came back from the war experience feeling either that they had been accepted or that they were going to be accepted because they had earned that right.[2]

No one really knows how many actually served in the military or in the defense industries or sold war bonds and participated in defense of the homeland. What is certain is that returning veterans who became involved in the civil rights struggle in Texas, New Mexico, Arizona and California soon began to interpret the recent history of Mexican Americans as a "war experience." This was made possible by the fact that most were born during or shortly after World War I and had grown into men during the second conflict.[3] That the Mexican Revolution had endured from 1910 to 1928 probably impacted those who were more recent arrivals. Whether it was the "war to end all wars," "the fight against fascism and Aryan supremacy," or the "fight for land and peasant rights," Mexican immigrants and Mexican Americans between their twenties and forties had seen their emotional and intellectual lives framed by war.

It is likely that many were not as conscious as their leaders would be, but it was easy to remind them or convince them that they were part of this "war experience," simply because these events had happened during their lifetime. For individuals such as Hector P. García, founder of the American GI Forum, a Mexican American veteran's organization, it soon became possible to see all people of Mexican-origin as "veterans" even if only by proxy. That is, collectively, the Mexican American community had paid the price of freedom because its young and old had gone to war and conducted themselves with bravery and gallantry.[4] For them, American rights had been paid for in blood and they were not going to go back to the way things were, though they would find that many Anglo Americans thought differently.

Most Anglos in Texas and much of the Southwest saw nothing particular in the participation of Mexican Americans in the war effort, after all, they had served too. And they had fought to "defend their way of life," and for the longest time, this "way of life" had differentiated them from the Mexicans who did the undesirable, but much needed labor. What they fought for was the maintenance of their "white world" where their skin color, their culture, and their unaccented English distinguished them in a superior fashion. It was then quite discomforting for them to see Mexican Americans use the war experience and their veteran status as a passport out of the social order that they themselves found so comforting. The new reform approach also made them uncomfortable because it used their own high-sounding rhetoric, so common during the war, against them.

With the rhetoric came a new, more aggressive militancy that not only sought inclusion but that implied or even demanded that Anglos see them as "similar" not only equal. That is, they were citizens, veterans, Americans, and they had contributed to the building of the nation and to its defense. They were also more and more taking to calling themselves "white."[5] This, of course, was becoming extremely problematic for Anglo Texans. It created a real dilemma for racial segregation in that the only way to keep the segregation intact was to both allow and deny Mexican Americans their whiteness. But the contradictory approach only worked if it was played out in different arenas.

As discussed before, Mexican Americans were seen as anything but white in the way they were treated in the labor markets, in the political arena, in the schools, and in the social arena. But as seen in the jury discrimination cases, the courts understood that segregation and discrimination could be maintained only if Mexican Americans were seen as white. Being white undermined any charge that Mexican Americans had about "racial discrimination." Without an "official color" Mexican Americans stood on a slippery slope. For whites in Texas, constantly being challenged by African Americans in terms of jury discrimination, having another racial minority demanding their rights was an unwelcome event. So officially, they had to do what they refused to do in reality, and that is to proclaim Mexican Americans white.

Mexican American reformers, however, also faced a dilemma. To accept that they were white was to accept that there was no discrimination. To accept that they were colored, was to add an extra burden to their plight. So they chose to deal within the concept of not who they were but how they were "treated." In this way, they could be both white in the way they wanted to be treated and brown in order to fit into the law. It is important, at this juncture, to remember that not everybody wanted to be white and there were also many who did not want to be brown. More crucial was that the debate over identity was far from being resolved within the confines of the barrio, and that complicated much of what the reformers wanted to do. It also forced the "best and the brightest" of the barrio to deal with that dilemma in their politics and their litigation.

M. C. González was probably the finest lawyer of the pre-*Hernández* era and one of the first ones to deal with this issue. A reformer, organizational leader, and a decorated war veteran of World War I, González epitomized the best of the early twentieth century Mexican American reformer. Like many of his cohorts, he promoted inclusion of his community into American society. He—and many others yet to be fully recognized—engaged in profound discussions on what it meant to be a Mexican living in the United States. His generation was the first to begin calling itself Mexican American, and to collectively call for civic responsibility on the part of barrio residents. Yet, they saw this civic responsibility as part of their "honored" racial origins.[6] While most would see themselves as white in a country where the only choices were black or white, among themselves and their people, they were Mexican. They were proud of their American citizenship, and did not look south for their political and philosophical foundations. But they understood in a way that only Mexicans could understand, that they were of mixed origins. For at least a century and a half, most Mexican writers, politicians and philosophers saw their *mestizaje* as a formation of a new race.[7] While American and European anthropologists resisted the notion of another race beyond those scientifically accepted, Latin American ones had long accepted a different reality.

Limited to calling itself white by American society's black/white binary, this generation "knew" it was really a different race.[8] Subsequent middle-class reformers would either forget or downplay this notion, but most people in the barrio knew otherwise, and that "knowledge" remains intact today. More important, that notion became popular again in the 1960s and came to be the fundamental operating notion in the ideology of many Chicano activist organizations. Even today it has strong supporters among writers, politicians, and community activists.[9]

González's generation knew that being racially different was not enough to develop a group identity that would serve their purpose in driving for full civil rights. They needed to be situated politically and civically within American society, so they became the first Mexican American generation to strongly emphasize citizenship status and the English language. More than any generation of reformers before or since, they advocated, promoted and maintained a commitment to a dual reality: they were Mexican by descent and they were American citizens by choice—either their choice or their parents' choice. They had to be proud of both and their actions were to bring honor to both heritages. They maintained—and some excelled in—their Spanish fluency and they spoke excellent English. They promoted education, but not only the one received in school. They were well read, conducted themselves with dignity, and demanded only opportunity without affirmative action, believing that their community could overcome most of its problems by simply having the doors of opportunity opened to them. They asked for nothing that was not part of the lot of all Americans.[10]

It was through this lens that they understood their reality and through which they approached their fight against jury discrimination. In his extensive and extremely well-written brief to the Texas Court of Criminal Appeals in 1946, González emphasized the exclusion from jury duty of the "Mexican race, precisely because of their race." In support, he introduced the testimony of several Mexican American witnesses, each representative of at least "300 to 500" Mexican Americans who met all the legal requirements and who "would like to serve on the jury." He also quoted Anglo officials who made it clear that Mexican Americans would have a hard time getting on juries because "none of the jury commissioners personally knew any of them that were qualified as jurors." One even added that it would be "embarrassing for me to have selected a Latin American."[11]

The point was that Mexican Americans were qualified, that they were willing to serve, and that only Anglo intransigence kept them from fulfilling their civic duty. He quoted the Supreme Court ruling in *Glasser v. U.S.*, decided only four years earlier, which declared that a jury had to be a "body truly representative of the community, and not the organ of any special group or class."[12] But like most in his generation, he did not want to simply make Mexican Americans another racial group. He probably also understood that most Americans did not want the expansion of the "racial problem" and so he emphasized that "racial groups [need not] be recognized." After all, what González wanted to do was prove racial discrimination against Mexican Americans, not create a racial ternary of white/black/brown. It served no purpose, before *Brown v. Board of Education*, to be colored in the United States. It offered very few protections and added many additional burdens. If Mexican Americans wanted "color," whites were more than willing to give them the burdens that came with it.

González also argued that unlike the three major previous cases dealing with jury discrimination against African Americans, his defense of Victoriano Salazar had more convincing evidence that there actually was a significant pool of eligible citizens who could serve on juries. He sought to emphasize the white middle-class aspect of Mexican Americans in Bee County, but he also sought to do what lawyers had failed to do in the aforementioned cases, and that was to establish a statistical case for the recognition of a Mexican American "pool" of eligible jury participants.[13] González quoted the dissenting opinion in *Akins v. Texas:*

> The equal protection clause of the Fourteenth Amendment entitles every person, whose life, liberty or property is in issue, to the benefits of grand and petit juries chosen without regard to race, color

or creed. This constitutional principle is a fundamental tenet of the American faith in the jury system. The absence of such a principle would give free rein to those who wittingly or otherwise act to undermine the very foundations of this system and would make juries ready weapons for officials to oppress those accused individuals who by chance are numbered among unpopular or inarticulate minorities . . . Racial limitation no less than racial exclusion in the formation of juries is an evil condemned by the equal protection clause.[14]

Three important points came out of this selective quote: (1) the Constitution applied to all groups, races or classes; (2) that juries were often used as "weapons . . . to oppress"; and (3) selective racial inclusion was a trick to disguise racial exclusion.[15] A fourth one, more implied by González than explicit in the ruling, was that Mexican Americans were not allowed to "judge" whites. Keeping Mexican Americans from juries in cases involving other Mexican Americans was simply a way to guarantee that they would also not serve on juries that would hear and decide on Anglo–Anglo litigation.

In the end, González's meticulous articulation of the appeal did not yield the desired outcome. The conviction was sustained and we have no record of what happened to Victoriano Salazar. But what is clear is that Mexican American lawyers and jury integrationists had found neither the strategy nor the conditions that would provide them a judicial victory. The courts saw no reason to accept the arguments by González or others, as neither the times nor the current interpretation of constitutional protections prompted them to do otherwise. González and his allies continued to face a social wall that, while cracking because of economic and Cold War pressures, still remained formidable nonetheless.

When Aniceto Sánchez walked up to Hilario Semersky in the spring of 1950, and fired his twelve-gauge shotgun almost point blank into Semersky's cheek, little did he care about potential jurors; he was acting on fear, quiet rage, and humiliation. The blast, which entered through Semersky's left cheek, "carried a large part of the head" and thrust Sánchez into the last jury discrimination case considered by the Texas Court of Criminal Appeals predating *Hernández*.[16] And like previous jury discrimination cases, it was a rather simple case to prosecute. There were numerous witnesses, a murder weapon on hand, and a confession.[17] It was a brutal murder that initially seemed to have no motive. According to eyewitnesses, Sánchez was talking to some friends outside his house when Semersky came over.

He lived in the adjacent house in the Sugar Land Plantation, where scores of agricultural workers lived side-by-side during the sowing and harvesting season.

Upon arrival, or two hours later, depending on the eyewitness, Semersky began singing a popular Mexican song, *Tu, solo tu.* Sánchez simply walked inside and then came out with the shotgun and fired. Then he waited around until the plantation guard came and took the gun and called the sheriff. The defendant's version would not differ much regarding the actual events but varied greatly regarding the motivation for the killing. While the witnesses testified that the men did not exchange words, Sánchez testified that he told Hilario to leave; he didn't want him around his house. After all, he had discovered him in his house several weeks earlier, under the bed of one of his sons. Semersky had brandished a gun at him and threatened to kill him if he came near him. Sánchez's wife had been in bed, scarcely dressed, in another room. Frightened, the plaintiff had gone on to work. The episode, however, had confirmed in his mind what Semersky had been jokingly saying out in the fields. "I'm going to take your wife away," said Sánchez, repeating Hilario's words. Believing that Semersky was trying to seduce his wife and flaunting the fact that Sánchez knew what was going on among friends and acquaintances, he decided to act to retain his pride and to keep his wife.[18] The court proceedings did not reveal much about the alleged illicit affair or whether it was simply a figment of Sánchez's imagination, though in Texas it might well have served the defense's cause.

There is no record as to how Sánchez came to select John Herrera as his lawyer, but De Anda—fresh out of law school that year—remembers that on his first day at work with the Herrera firm, he was assigned to do the research on the *Sánchez* case. On their way to the town of Richmond in Fort Bend County, where the defendant was incarcerated, Herrera thought out loud why he had never seen a "Hispanic on the jury in any case" he had tried in the area. He then turned to De Anda and said, "I want you to look into the records over there and see why I've never seen a Chicano on the jury while he's all over town."[19] De Anda undertook the task of looking at county venire lists for the last several years and found that no Mexicans had ever served on "actual juries to try the lawsuits, on the grand jury panels, nor the grand jury commissioners." Excited over the findings, he told Herrera, "Johnny, I think we got . . . grounds for filing a motion here and see if we can't get this indictment knocked out . . . and do some good work for the folks."[20] Herrera then assigned De Anda to prepare a challenge to the jury selection. The evidence was faulty given that some Mexican

Americans had Anglo surnames, but Herrera must have figured that those who did were a very small minority.

It would be appropriate to pause here and to discuss in brief the disconnection between lawyers of Herrera's generation and those of González's. What was discussed then and what De Anda would say fifty years later in remembering the *Hernández* case indicates that neither the younger nor the older lawyer knew much about what had happened in the past, and how much work had been done before. De Anda would discover the cases only after "doing an awful lot of research."[21] It would be appropriate to ask why Herrera did not know about these cases and why he did not contact González even after he found out about the older lawyer's earlier work. The latter is an assumption based on the fact that no letters exist between the two and the fact that the more experienced González never came into the picture.

The question may be answered in two ways. First, Herrera was a trial lawyer as we have seen, much more comfortable in the courtroom than in the law library where he might have discovered González's brief on the Salazar case. De Anda remembers that when he came to work in Herrera's office, the law books were covered with dust and seemed as though they had been unused for a very long time.[22] In the short time that he served with Herrera, he remembered him as someone more able to "orally persuade a jury" and less adept at writing legal memoranda and understanding constitutional law. Herrera would later jokingly remember that he took the bar exam "either six or seven times."[23] As mentioned before, while in law school he supported himself and his family as a cab driver and as a pick-and-shovel man for the Sanitation Department of the City of Houston. His coworkers would rib him for not being able to "get out of law school." But once he did, he became an expert on reading people, understanding their body language, and working a jury. He would eventually have a rather healthy practice, but at the time, he was still finding his own place in civil rights litigation.[24]

A second reason for the disconnect was the growing separation between reformers of the prewar and early postwar eras, and the returning veterans who launched a new phase of the Mexican American civil rights movement. Some of that difference has been mentioned earlier, but it is important to emphasize some other important differences between the two groups. One is the perception each group had of itself and what they might have thought of each other. Mexican Americans of González's generation had been concerned with and had focused on developing a group identity that situated them somewhere within the American mosaic. They were the ones who developed the notion of the "Mexican American," a term used mostly among elites and reformers during Herrera's time. Still, this notion of an ethnic American was important and correlated well with the notion of America as a land of immigrants, where people came to share the same values and politics but did not have to fully lose who they were. In González's time, there were still many ethnic clubs, associations and private schools that retained their ties of identity with their nation of origin and their particular culture. An effort at full assimilation—mostly for European ethnics—did not come until the end of the Second World War, although World War I had exerted pressure on some groups more than others.

González's generation also saw acceptance as being won by performing civic duty, becoming educated, and participating in society. They were particularly meticulous in presenting themselves to the larger society, which they believed would accept them if they only knew them better. Still, while angered by rejection, they had created their own "internal communities" that allowed them to prosper and rise in stature even if they were rejected by the larger Anglo community. Elites by education and profession or by familial connections, they protested the harsh lack of accessibility as much or more than harsh treatment. And accessibility to them came with no strings attached, that is, they wanted no special favors, seeing themselves more than capable of competing on their own.[25]

Herrera's generation had come of age in World War II, as can be seen from the fact that Gus, Cadena, De Anda, and Herrera himself had served in the military during the war. Through the prism of this experience, they saw themselves as future congressman Henry B. González liked to say, "Americans who happen to be of Mexican descent."[26] Thus, they were not very interested in discussing identity or their particular place in American society. In fact, many of their internal battles often resulted from discussions regarding the use of a hyphenated label. Were they Latin Americans, Spanish Americans, Americans of Spanish descent, or Spanish-Speaking Americans? They were much happier and felt more secure when seeing themselves as Americans, similar to the Anglos they knew or associated with. This, of course, had come through their experience in the war, where all were the same "in the foxhole." The fact that they did not serve in segregated units, and that they were allowed immediately into combat units, gave them a sense of being the same.

But to retain the similarity required them to distinguish themselves from those who were more recent arrivals and who carried all the characteristics of being "foreign." They allowed the political boundaries of the border to become cultural and social borders that were added to class borders.[27] While the two generations overlapped, by Herrera's time the veteran generation was already in ascendance. They came aggressively seeking equality, ready to challenge any notion that they were different from other Americans. It was clear to them that difference meant inequality. Unlike the earlier members of LULAC, they were less concerned about being proud of their racial past or their indigenous glories, and more concerned with what their citizenship meant for them. Like so many Americans of that era, they saw themselves as citizens of the most powerful nation in the world, and they marveled at what that could mean for them and their community. One thing it meant was differentiating themselves from those who still clung to the old world, or those who sought to "merit" the rights of citizenship through their behavior and their education. These new reformers, most of them combat veterans, did not want to hear that they "still had to prove" something to white Americans.

One can see the divergence of the two groups on the issue of immigration, legal and illegal. Particularly offensive to Herrera's generation was the Bracero Program, a bilateral agreement between the United States and Mexico, to provide Mexican workers to the agricultural and other related industries during the war years. Rather than ending at the conclusion of the worldwide conflict, the program was periodically extended until its demise in 1964. Led by Hector P. García and the American GI Forum, post-World War II reformers attacked the program as being catastrophic for Mexican American farm workers who could not compete with their counterparts from the south. Though prohibited from doing so by the agreements between the two countries, farmers and executives of the agribusinesses in the Southwest lowered their wages, forcing Mexican American workers to migrate to the Midwest, Northwest, and California to find better paying agricultural work.

Using language that later generations would find offensive, these reformers ended up blaming the victim for the labor problems caused by both governments and agribusiness. Over time, the contracted worker became synonymous with the "wetback," and both became synonymous with crime and deviant behavior. Two studies supported by the American GI Forum were so offensive in their use of stereotyping and unfounded accusations that their attacks on unscrupulous farm bosses, government officials, and labor contractors got lost in a backlash by immigrant groups and old elites. Old-time reformers blasted the American GI Forum and other anti-immigrant Mexican Americans for legitimizing stereotypes, and for taking food from "children's mouths."[28] They were also appalled by the characterization of border patrolmen as heroes who were protecting the nation from barbarians. Old-timers quickly understood that these new reformers did not see Mexican Americans as a part of a traditional community with a long history, but rather as a constituency group that needed to lobby for its rights and to be lobbied for its votes.

The new Mexican American reformers were not particularly insensitive so much as they were ambivalent about some of the concerns that the Mexican community had about living in the United States. Herrera's family at times followed the Texas migrant stream and De Anda came from immigrant parents who migrated to Michigan seeking work.[29] Yet, they were not burdened with conflicting loyalties between the United States and Mexico, nor were they debating internally whether to assimilate or not. Their view was that Mexicans born in the United States or who had basically given up going back to Mexico had the obligation to become civic-minded and participate in the political process as Americans, not as an ethnic group seeking only to shield itself from discrimination. They were seeking a commitment to integration and, to an extent, assimilation by the Mexican community into the larger American society. Part of this effort stemmed from their belief in the American way, but part of it was intended to diminish the hostility that some directed at them because of the growing influx of undocumented workers. Sandwiched in by their desire to be seen as full Americans and their desire to reduce hostilities, they found a scapegoat who could not fight back. But they lived to regret it because they fundamentally misunderstood that immigration, legal and illegal, would be a defining issue for every succeeding generation in their efforts to integrate into American society.

The old-timers understood it better because they were much more connected to their people, even if only because they were the elites within those internal communities. Possibly even more so, because as enlightened elites, they saw it as their responsibility to represent and advocate for those less fortunate in their communities. They were not beyond stereotypes themselves, or alliances with Anglo political machines that did not serve the interests of their community, but they more fully understood that their own status depended on the collective effort of all Mexican Americans. The new reformers tended to be more individualistic and imbued with Horatio Alger concepts of success rather than with notions of collective actions. It would not be until the late 1950s and early 1960s that they came to realize more fully that their own success was dependent on bringing the community along with them. So, in the 1950s, even as they advocated for civil rights reform, they saw Mexican Americans as a confederation of individuals rather than a true community.

One more point to emphasize is that this new generation of reformers was, with a few exceptions, totally devoid of historical knowledge. Unlike the older generation who extolled their Mexican and Spanish heroes, and to a lesser extent the great Indian civilizations of Mexico, as well as some of the original Mexican Americans elites, the new reformers could go back no further than World War II. For them, the great conflict had given birth to the "new" Mexican American. And for several decades after the war, they would distinguish themselves as veterans who had earned their rights in the foxhole. Hector García would remember the old reformers coming to his town and expounding on culture and history in the town square. Few, except for some academicians of his generation, would do the same during their organizing efforts.[30]

This should not imply that the post–World War II reformers were indifferent to their community's concerns or hostile to the immigrant. Rather they thought—or sought to think—like Americans, and their relationship to immigrants, to Mexico, and to their past was contextualized within this search for America. Some had relatives in Mexico, others were proud of their indigenous heritage, and still others were resentful of Anglo racism and rejection, but they had little alternative to clinging to their citizenship and veteran status. They could neither go back to Mexico as some immigrants did, or simply play the role of "elites" within their community. They wanted what America offered and they saw no other way of getting it other than through integration, loyalty (combined with a healthy advocacy for their rights), and by differentiating themselves from those who were foreign in their birth, their loyalty, or their actions.

When De Anda had done the research, he concluded that to have any chance of winning on the grounds of jury discrimination, they had to "establish a theory of identifiable minority" that would allow them to get past the Texas Court of Criminal Appeals' prior rulings that Mexicans were simply "Caucasians and there were [already] Caucasians on the jury."[31] This was, of course, only partly new for both Anglo and Mexican American lawyers who had tried these types of cases before. The new part was the establishment of a "theory." That is, lawyers in the past had simply tried to take common knowledge that Mexicans were different and present that as a point of contention in the composition of the jury. What was needed was a framework that could be discussed and debated—or litigated—in a constitutional sense.

Herrera and De Anda set out to prove that the county had engaged "over a period of thirty-five years, [in] a systematic, continual and uninterrupted practice of discrimination against Mexican Americans as a race, and . . .

as a class separate from other white Americans."[32] While the lawyers used the term "race," they would actually de-emphasize it, except when using it to distinguish class, as in "racial class."[33] This reveals this generations' discomfort with the notion of being racially apart. While most understood the notion of "race" within their community's context they also realized that most outsiders considered the term to deal exclusively—at least in a legal sense—with African Americans. Whites might see Mexicans as another race, but when they talked about race and the law, the term always referred to black Americans. The desired theory required that Mexican Americans stand on their own as a distinguishable minority group. It is also important to distinguish their use of race from its more classical definition. They were not arguing for a racial classification as much as they were describing a group identity constructed by segregation, discrimination, and lack of governmental and judicial protection.

De Anda pointed out in the appellate brief that one of the Grand Jury Commissioners, a W. L. Ansel, had testified that people of Mexican descent could be "distinguished from other people merely by looking at them."[34] Another witness, Joe Hernández, claimed that the Chamber of Commerce of Fort Bend County divided the county population into three groups. one-fifth colored, one-fifth Latin American, and the other three-fifths in a third group. In essence, the chamber saw the population divided into three racial groups. De Anda emphasized that while Mexicans were "members of the white race," they were not so considered in Fort Bend County. This argument had its drawbacks, as we will see later, but it would nonetheless set the groundwork for the *Hernández* case.

Herrera and De Anda also emphasized the qualification of numerous Mexican American citizens to participate in the jury system, and here they believed they had a stronger case than did previous defense lawyers. This was probably because they had not really looked at all the documents related to the Victoriano Salazar case. Fort Bend County had over 6,500 citizens of Mexican descent, and that population had remained steady for several decades.[35] Of those, the lawyers argued, there had been many "qualified voters . . . able . . . to read and write the English language and . . . of good reputation."[36] Their exclusion, thus, could not be seen as anything but discrimination based on "said class," and this exclusion sought to "avoid and evade the equal protection clause of the Fourteenth Amendment of the United States and of the statutes of the State of Texas enacted pursuant thereto."[37]

De Anda introduced a point not originally promoted in the previous challenges to jury composition. He argued that the jury commissioners not only failed to choose any Mexican Americans for juries, but that they made no "affirmative" effort to look for those who might be qualified to serve. After all, if jury commissioners only went to those they knew or knew of, it was rather clear that most Mexican Americans were not going to be considered. This was supported by the fact that no one could show that there had been at least one Mexican American juror "during the last thirty five years, or within recollection of the memory of any of the witnesses."[38] De Anda based his argument on the ruling in *Patton v. State of Mississippi*, which clearly delineated that a defense showing that no members of any particular group had ever served on a grand jury was prima facie proof of discrimination toward that group.[39]

In the actual litigation, the counsel for the state was so confident in its position that the prosecutor, R. A. Bassett, even asked the court, "Do you care to hear from me?" When told it was his choice, Bassett simply countered with the point that the defense had not "proven" that a "Latin American" had not served or been summoned for service on the grand jury. He pointed out that one had been called but had been excused because he did not speak or write English. He then followed that argument up by stating that a Latin American "is a white person, the same as you and I, or anyone else." To argue for Latin American representation, said Bassett, was to demand representation by nationality for all those indicted.[40] He acknowledged that the Supreme Court had distinguished "darkies" from whites when it came to jury representation, but no such interpretation existed for Mexican Americans.[41]

Herrera quickly responded that the burden of proof rested on the prosecution, and it had not countered the proof that Mexican Americans had not served on juries in the last thirty-five years. "Our argument," said Herrera, "is that the people were here. They are available and qualified . . . and the burden of proof is on them, because they have not be able to show that a grand jury commissioner or grand juror of Mexican descent has ever served."[42]

"Just a second," Bassett responded, "counsel is trying to mislead the court. The burden of proof is his [Sánchez's] to show that he has been discriminated against. It is not to the state." On that final note, Judge T. M. Gupton declared, "Well, I am going to overrule the Motion to Quash the Indictment,"[43] and, so ended the case at the district level. It is interesting to note that in approving the bill of exception to be filed for appeal, the judge put two qualifiers in the document: first, he pointed out that some of the defense's own witnesses had testified that no deliberate discrimination had been involved in the choosing of jurors; and second, that the "defendant did not place anyone on the stand who swore that there had not [ever] been Latin-Americans on the Grand Juries in Fort Bend County."[44]

It seems rather amazing that the judge stipulated that point in the bill of exception. After all, the defense had brought witnesses to testify that they knew of no one serving as juror, and they also asked to put into the court records all the county documents that named every one of the jurors who had served in the last three decades. The fact that no one had "sworn" with complete knowledge that no Mexican Americans had served in a Fort Bend County jury was beside the point. Herrera and De Anda conceded the point that some might have been considered, and even called but not selected, but what was really important was a pattern of exclusion that kept most if not all Mexican Americans from serving. The judge sought to rigidly interpret "legalities," and, in doing so, defuse the impact of the myriad of witnesses who presented a clear testament that Mexican Americans were excluded. A severely strict interpretation of the testimony sought to counter the fact that the prosecution had no counter to the charges of jury exclusion beyond a play on words about proportional representation of nationalities.

De Anda immediately took issue with the judge's interpretation in his brief to the Court of Criminal Appeals of Texas, submitted on November 14, 1951. This followed the conviction on March 20, which sentenced Sánchez to ten years in prison. It should be noted here that Sánchez was initially unwilling to appeal his case. He considered the ten-year sentence a rather light sentence and he wanted to serve and get back to his wife and sixteen children.[45] De Anda and Herrera, however, believed that they had successfully established a "theory of identifiable minority" in the case of Mexican Americans, so they immediately appealed the judge's qualification, arguing that they in fact had presented, "uncontroverted" testimony that no Mexican American had served on a grand jury based on the "memory of witnesses" who had "lived in said county for periods ranging from twenty-six to fifty-one years." Furthermore, they wrote that Sánchez was part of a "class or race also known as Latin-Americans," who were between 15 and 20 percent of the population, many of whom were qualified and willing to serve as jurors but had never been called to do so.[46]

Citing *Patton v. Mississippi*, the defense lawyers pointed out that in the case involving a black defendant, the United States Supreme Court had ruled that the fact that no "Negro" had served as a member of any jury created a strong "showing" of systematic exclusion based on race. Given the situation, "It became the duty of the state to try to justify such . . . exclusion as having been brought about for some reason other than racial discrimination."[47] The brief then cited the case of *Pierre v. Louisiana*, in which the court similarly ruled that the fact that no "Negro" had been selected for grand jury service within "the memory of any witness" created a "prima facie case of systematic exclusion of Negroes . . . because of race and . . . established a denial of 'equal protection.'"[48]

De Anda, who wrote most (if not all) the brief, then took on another of the judge's qualifications that argued that the grand jury commissioners had all testified that they did not deliberately discriminate against Latin Americans. "One," wrote De Anda, "stated that he was unaware as to which Mexicans were citizens . . . that he did not know of any that were qualified . . . and that no affirmative effort was made to obtain any Mexicans to serve on the grand jury. Another," continued De Anda, "stated that he did not know of any Mexican qualified to serve and that the topic never entered the discussion."[49] A third commissioner admitted that he knew there were a "qualified" number of Mexican Americans but that their names never came up. De Anda cited *Cassell v. Texas*, in which the court ruled that "When the [jury] commissioners were appointed . . . it was their duty to familiarize themselves fairly with the qualifications of the eligible jurors of the county without regard to race and color."[50] He also quoted Justice Reed in *Hill v. Texas*, who wrote, "The statement of the jury commissioners that they choose only whom they know, and that they knew no eligible Negroes in an area where Negroes made up so large a proportion of the population prove the intentional exclusion that is discrimination in violation of petitioner's constitutional right."[51] Finally, the defense brief cited *Smith v. Texas*, where the court ruled that "where jury commissioners limit those from who grand juries are selected to their own personal acquaintance, discrimination can arise from commissioners who know no Negroes as well as from commissioners who know but eliminate them."[52]

The defense understood that their presentation was the most elaborate ever presented on behalf of any Mexican American appellant seeking a reversal on jury discrimination grounds. But they also understood that the major stumbling block had been the appeals court itself. It had already expressed a reluctance to extend the rules of jury discrimination against blacks to jury discrimination against Mexican Americans.[53] De Anda then went on to quote Judge Davidson of the appellate court, who argued that "we have discovered no case in which the [United States] Supreme Court meant to apply the ruling to anyone other than members of the Negro race."[54]

Declaring that all the subsequent rulings had been meant to apply to all racial groups not just African Americans, the brief quoted the court in *Patton v. Mississippi*, which stated that jury discrimination against "a large group of Negroes, or *any other racial group*" (my italics) would invalidate any indictments or verdicts against them.[55] Then, in an ingenious move to distinguish the court's former decisions, the brief referred to several of the jury discrimination cases filed on behalf of Mexican Americans, and pointed out that while they had been rejected, the appellate court had done so because it found no discrimination against the "Mexican race" and not because the court had rejected the possibility of a Mexican race.[56]

On November 21, 1951, the appellate court issued its decision on the appeal, rejecting the appellant's arguments. While seemingly impressed by the "exhaustive brief on the subject," the court had by now adopted the political strategy of Texas's white elites who had found a way to impede Mexican American progress by allowing them to see themselves as white but treating them as different or brown. "They are not a separate race," ruled the court, "but are white people of Spanish descent, as has often been said by this court. We find no ground for discussing the question further and the complaint raised by this bill will not be sustained."[57] That one sentence ended the Sánchez saga. With the defendant reluctant to push his luck and with no funds available, Herrera and De Anda decided not to appeal, though De Anda would say years later that the case was winnable, and possibly an even better test case than *Hernández*.[58] It is quite possible that he was right since Fort Bend County had more Mexican Americans who qualified to be jurors than Jackson County, and the jury commissioners had been more forthcoming, thus, showing more clearly the discrimination. It would, however, take a flashier courtroom lawyer, a constitutional scholar, more funding, and a more aggressive Mexican American civil rights community to take the challenge to the next level. Of course, a more amenable court was also extremely helpful.

The two cases revealed the evolution that Mexican American exclusion from juries had gone through since the first *Ramirez* case in 1929. During this time, the exclusion of Mexican Americans from the jury panel had evolved from individual exclusion because of discrimination to a systematic exclusion because of "race" or "class." While racial prejudices had existed for nearly a century, it was not until the early part of the twentieth century when labor, housing, and public school segregation became more rigid because of their numbers that Mexicans and Mexican Americans became an excludable class. In trying to combat this form of discrimination, M. C. González provided a beginning framework for challenging jury exclusion by highlighting legal precedence that prohibited such action. No Anglo lawyer had done so before as they had instead relied on convincing the courts that this practice was "logically" unconstitutional.[59] For their part,

De Anda and Herrera contributed the "theory" of an identifiable Mexican "class," whereby they could make the claim that Mexican Americans merited, by the nature of their racial or class grouping, protection under the Fourteenth Amendment. These steps were an important foundation, but it would take someone of Cadena's brilliance to take the next step, which would define Mexican Americans as a "class apart," both white and racially different, thus "equal" both because of their whiteness and because of their status as a protected group under the Fourteenth Amendment.

No one could change the dynamics of the *Hernández* case and jury discrimination litigation for Mexican Americans more than the brilliant Cadena, who was not only a friend to Gus but also a law partner. At the time, he was also on the faculty of St. Mary's University Law School in San Antonio, Texas. Not as flashy or well-known as Gus, Cadena, nonetheless, had a solid reputation as a meticulous litigator who knew the law well. He brought to the case the two ingredients missing in both Gus and Herrera, and which were still slightly raw in De Anda: constitutional knowledge and experience in legal writing.[60] Ed Idar Jr., a leader in the American GI Forum and an eventual litigator before the Supreme Court, remembers that few in the civil rights circles knew Cadena well, but they knew his reputation and trusted him. More important for civil rights leaders like Idar, Cadena came at a crucial time in the case, when there was some grumbling, especially by those organizations that were being asked to raise funds, of the way Gus was conducting it.

Gus, seemingly always in debt and confronting a growing problem with alcoholism had become "distracted" from the case. What exactly that meant is uncertain, but Idar threatened to stop supporting the case unless Gus withdrew or allowed Cadena to become the lead attorney for the case. Cadena became key to keeping the case alive. There is no paper trail to allow us to fully understand who played which part in the defense team, but it is clear that by the time of the appeal to the Texas Court of Criminal Appeals, Cadena had become the most important figure in the case.[61]

In his legal expertise, Cadena gave no ground to González or De Anda when it came to understanding and writing about the law. In his briefs on behalf of Pete Hernández, he continued to refine the notion of Mexican Americans as a definable racial and ethnic group who merited protection under the Fourteenth Amendment. He combined the legal articulation of González with the innovation of De Anda. He also brought a much more forceful voice to the litigation, reflecting the more aggressive approach of his generation of war veterans. While it is hard to know what part the De Anda and González briefs played in his initial construction of his own, there is no doubt that he built on them even as he used a much more extensive body of rulings from past cases than did his predecessors.

In the brief to the appellate court, Cadena outlined the pertinent issues: no Mexican Americans had served on juries in the last twenty-five years; there were qualified members of that group; and, they were considered and treated as a separate race. Citing *Hill v. Texas*, the defense also argued against having to show burden of proof that Hernández would be found innocent with Mexican American representation in the jury. In that case, the Supreme Court ruled that the courts were not "free to grant or withhold a constitutional privilege merely as they deem a defendant innocent or guilty."[62] This was seen as critical because the Texas appellate court had made such a ruling in *Ross v. Texas*, placing the proof of innocence before that of a violation of constitutional rights.[63] The court reasoned that without proof of innocence, the defendant could not show he was technically harmed by the constitutional flaw, and to remedy the flaw would not necessarily change anything. The Supreme Court ruling, then, was critical as having to prove Pete's innocence would completely demolish their case as none of them really saw him as innocent.

By now, Mexican American lawyers understood that any justice would have to come from a higher court, or by a radical change of view of the Texas-based court. So Pete's lawyers directly took on the views of the appellate court throughout the brief. The second challenge to the court's view was its previous rulings that exclusion of persons of Mexican descent from jury duty was not a violation of the Fourteenth Amendment. The lawyers took a two-pronged approach to the challenge. First, they set out to show the court had "not correctly interpreted the Fourteenth Amendment," and second, to show that the present case "presents a fact situation not heretofore considered."[64]

The brief first referred to the *Ramirez v. Texas* case, the first to bring up the issue of jury discrimination, and alluded to the fact that the court had simply ruled that the allegation had not been "established by the evidence." This, the lawyers sought to point out, meant that if the evidence was "established," the court needed to deal with the issue of jury discrimination. They pointed out that in *Patton v. Mississippi*, the Supreme Court had found that only twelve "Negroes" in the county met all the requirements for jury service, and still it had ruled in favor of the defendants. In contrast, Jackson County had at least 6 percent of the Mexican American population qualified for jury duty. To assume that all of them were "utterly disqualified by want of intelligence, experience . . . moral integrity or because of inability to read and write," was a "violent presumption."[65]

The fact that the jury commissioners had denied any discrimination against Mexican Americans was not sufficient to ignore the charge. After all, in *Norris v. Alabama*, and *Smith v. Texas*, the Supreme Court had rejected jury commissioner testimony as "not sufficient to overcome the conclusion which was compelled by evidence of long continued exclusion."[66] The testimony could also not explain the long continued exclusion by prior jury commissioners. Even more important, the *Smith* ruling and the one in *Cassell v. Texas* castigated the state for allowing commissioners to only select those jurors that "they knew." In *Cassell* particularly, the court had ruled that jury commissioners had the obligation to "familiarize themselves fairly with the qualifications of the eligible jurors of the county."[67] In not doing so, according to *Hill v. Texas*, "discrimination necessarily results where there are qualified Negroes available for jury service."[68]

Given those rulings, Cadena, Herrera, and Gus argued, the testimony of the Jackson County jury commissioners actually "showed a course of conduct" from which "discrimination necessarily results."[69] They added that if Hernández had been Negro, the court would have had to rule in his favor and agree that discrimination had in fact occurred. More important, the appellate court had in fact accepted that notion in their ruling in *Sánchez v. Texas*. But the court had found a way out by ruling that *Norris v. Alabama* applied only to members of the Negro race.[70] "We have discovered no case," wrote the court in 1944, "wherein that [Supreme] Court has applied the same rule to members of different nationalities." The court went on to state that until the Supreme Court declared that nationality and race "bear the same relation within the meaning of the Fourteenth Amendment," they would continue to limit those protections to members of the Negro race.[71]

In a line of argument that could come only from a constitutional scholar like Cadena, the brief then takes the court to task for inserting the issue of "race" into the interpretation of the Fourteenth Amendment. Citing *Hirabayashi v. United States*, decided in 1943, which declared questions of race in regards to the Fourteenth Amendment as "irrelevant and therefore prohibited," Cadena described the appellate court's earlier rulings on Mexican American jury discrimination as "mere hornbook law of the most elementary kind."[72] After all, in *Gibson v. Mississippi* the Supreme Court had declared in 1896, "In the administration of criminal justice, no rule can be applied to one class which is not applicable to other classes."[73] The Texas Court of Criminal Appeals, argued Cadena and his colleagues, could not apply a rule against Mexican Americans that it did not also apply to Negroes, and which created a heavier burden of proof. Worse, the court should not have the right to defend its action on "purely racial grounds."[74]

It is important to note here that Cadena was in fact setting up the argument that Mexican Americans were white, but that to rule against them on that point was in itself a violation of the Fourteenth Amendment. He cited *Yick Wo v. Hopkins, American Sugar Refining Co. v. Louisiana, Juarez v. State,* and *Truax v. Raich,* which broadly agreed that oppression or discrimination based on color, race, nativity, religious opinion, political affiliations, etc. was a "denial of the equal protection of the law to the less favored class."[75] More important, in the last case the court had provided protection to an Austrian national, stipulating that the Constitution protected foreign nationalities. If this was the case, asked Cadena, "will this Court hold that discrimination based on national origin is valid?" Failure to do so, he continued, meant that the Fourteenth Amendment protected the alien more "zealously" than it did so a citizen of the United States.[76]

Here, Cadena was placing Mexican Americans within the framework of being "white" and being citizens. They were not to be perceived as being different or foreign, unlike those who enjoyed the full protection of the law. In presenting the case this way, he was trying to use the court's own interpretation of Mexican Americans as white against it. By claiming color blindness, Cadena was forcing the court to be on the side of racial prefer-ences, something the Texas court was not going to be comfortable with. It was a strategy that had no logical conclusion given the prior rulings by the Supreme Court, but it was one that strived to disarm the court and make it less confident in simply dismissing the case as having no merit because Mexican Americans were not Negro and thus under no protection from the Constitution. In fact, Cadena was trying to argue that Mexican Americans should not have needed special protection because due process was a given right for white Americans.

The reason it had no logical conclusion was that to bolster his own argument of jury discrimination, he had to continue to go back to Mexican Americans being seen as "another racial class." Following this path, the brief then began to cite cases in which the federal courts had ruled that Mexican Americans were indeed protected by the Fourteenth Amendment. *Mendez v. Westminster School District* had declared that segregation of Mexican-origin children violated the Fourteenth Amendment's Equal Protection Clause. *Lopez v. Seccombe* held that exclusion of Mexicans from the city's swimming pools violated the individuals' constitutional rights; and *Gonzales v. Sheely* held that segregation in separate school buildings because of national ori-gin was a denial of equal protection of the law.[77] Finally, the brief referred to *Clifton v. Puente,* the last Mexican-focused case decided by the Texas Court of Civil Appeals and one litigated by Cadena, which ruled that a Texas court could not enforce a restrictive covenant prohibiting sale of land to persons of Mexican descent without denying equal protection of the law.[78]

The lawyers then cited a case of jury discrimination that involved a Spanish-surnamed individual, but which was not about racial discrimination but about bias based on religion. In *Juarez v. State*, the appellate court ruled that "the State cannot do indirectly through its officers or agents that which it could not do directly by legislative act. If the legislature of this state should pass a law saying that hereafter no man holding to the . . . Roman Catholic faith should ever be permitted to serve on a grand jury . . . the validity of such a law could never be sustained."[79] In the same vein, argued the brief, legislative action barring Mexicans from jury duty "could not be sustained," so why should it be so through the courts?[80]

Returning to the argument of "whiteness" Cadena argued that to forbid exclusion of Negroes but to allow the exclusion of Mexican Americans because they were members of the white race, amounted to discrimination based "on purely racial grounds." He reminded the court that the Fourteenth Amendment not only precluded the expulsion of Negroes from juries, but also forbade the "exclusion from juries of the white race."[81] He reiterated what Gus had argued in the trial, and that was that the Texas statutes governing juries were fair on their face, but to use them to exclude Mexican Americans by "administrative fiat or caprice" amounted to depriving them of their liberty without due process of law. This would then make the statutes themselves unconstitutional.

The effort to establish the fact that the appellate court had previously been wrong in its rulings against Mexican Americans took most of the brief. The argument to "distinguish" this case from the rest took less than two pages, and then it really did not focus on proving the point but rather on presenting a strong public policy language that Cadena hoped the court would adopt in its ultimate opinion. The brief chastised the "sovereign state of Texas" for using the "Caucasian cloak" to protect its political interests. "It is only when the issue of discrimination and denial of constitutional rights is raised that some signs saying 'No Mexicans Allowed' disappear, and the county officials insist on the witness stand that 'Mexicans' are white—for purposes of judicial conveniences," wrote Cadena.[82]

He added it was not sufficient to say that "Mexicans" were "white people of Spanish descent." The fact was, wrote Cadena, most Mexican Americans were actually classified as *mestizos*, persons of mixed Spanish and Indian blood, with the Indian heritage "generally predominating." While anthropologists debated racial categories, the "sovereign state of Texas" had simply used racial terms to "shamelessly deny to this large segment of the Texas population the fundamental right to serve as jury commissioners, grand jurors, or petit jurors.[83] This was a line of argument that he would continue up to the Supreme Court, and one that underscored the tensions over identity that Mexican Americans were confronting during the 1950s.

More important, rather than simply seeking to be fully on one side of the racial equation of black or white, Cadena was trying to provide a new space for Mexican Americans to occupy. At the appellate hearing, Cadena was not yet using much of the sociological and educational scholarship on Mexican Americans in American society. That would come at the next level. For now, Cadena was simply articulating in a brief some of the notions circulating within the barrio and among Mexican American reformers. He would come to define even more clearly his interpretation of these ideas in his brief before the Supreme Court, and thus provide one of the few documents of that generation that sought to understand the racial and cultural notion of being a Mexican in American society. In doing so, he also developed a case against Texas by playing the politics of the Mexican American generation that sought to nationalize the issues that impacted their community, and find a sympathetic ear to counter the prejudices common among the politicians, educators, and community leaders in the Lone Star State.

4

"May God Permit You Triumph in This Most Grand of Campaigns"

If Cadena and Gus had any hopes of reframing the argument on jury discrimination against Mexican Americans, they were dashed on June 18, 1952, when the Texas appellate court affirmed the lower court's decision and then refused a rehearing on October 22 of the same year. The appeals court described the defense's claim as being based on the "so-called rule of exclusion" by the Supreme Court, which indicated that a sustained exclusion of "Negroes" from juries when they were available and qualified "constitute[d] a violation of the due process and equal protection against members of that race."[1] The ruling's rather dismissive tone seems oblivious to the fact that the "rule of exclusion" had been sustained in four cases that involved the state of Texas. But that dismissive tone continued throughout the ruling. It recognized that "much testimony" had been introduced to show the systematic exclusion of Mexican Americans from juries in Jackson County, but then disregarded the evidence as "of no greater probative force than those stipulated by the state and the appellant." The state had admitted that no Mexican American had served in a jury commission, grand jury, or petit jury in Jackson County. Thus, in the view of the court, no new evidence had been presented nor had any testimony been given that suggested "express or factual discrimination against appellant or other Mexicans." To them, the defense had incorrectly relied upon the rule of exclusion in their case.[2]

The court saw this theory as unacceptable given that it had already stated in *Sánchez v. State* that the Supreme Court had never ruled that nationality and race bore the same relations within the Fourteenth Amendment.[3] They also pointed to the ruling in *Smith v. Texas* that declared that the statute providing for the selection of juries in the state was "not in itself unfair" and could be "carried out with no racial discrimination whatsoever."[4] Given the validity of the statute and no proof of expressed or factual discrimination, the court was unwilling to see any validity in the challenge to the jury. The court also rejected Cadena's argument that the ruling in Sánchez was in fact extending "special benefits to members of the Negro race," arguing that such interpretation called for a reconstruction of the Equal Protection Clause beyond its intent. After all, the Fourteenth Amendment was "adopted to secure to members of the Negro race . . . the full enjoyment of their freedom."[5]

The court continued, "To our minds, it is conclusive . . . the Fourteenth Amendment . . . recognized only two classes as coming with that guarantee: the white race . . . and the Negro race."[6] The court then repeated its *Sánchez v. Texas* declaration that "Mexican people . . . are not a separate race but are white people of Spanish descent." To argue that they merited special consideration, the justices continued, would classify them as a special class within the white race, and this would violate the Equal Protection Clause because it would extent to them "special privileges" not given to other members of the white race.[7] They "reminded" the plaintiffs that no defendant had the right to demand that a member of his class serve on the juries that tried him. To do so would "destroy our jury system" because it would be impossible to meet such demands.[8] It ended with the following assertion: "Mexicans are white people and are entitled at the hands of the state to all rights, privileges, and immunities guaranteed under the Fourteenth Amendment. So long as they are so treated, the guarantee of equal protection has been accorded to them."[9]

The court's ruling was a stinging rebuke to Pete's lawyers made worse by the court's reminder that neither in the original case nor in the appeal briefs did anyone challenge the statement that Mexican-origin individuals were white.[10] To accept being white, in the mind of the justices, was to give away the ace in the hand, but to insist that they were another race was of little value as the court was unwilling to do what it claimed the Supreme Court had not done, and that was to include Mexican Americans as a protected group under the Fourteenth Amendment. The justices simply refused to read into the Constitution any of the implied inclusions of groups other than African Americans, and this did not leave much room for maneuvering. After a number of reversals in jury discrimination cases, the appeals court of Texas was willing to use a narrow interpretation of the higher court's decisions to block any expansion of the Equal Protection Clause.

The defense lawyers were disappointed but must have realized that they were honing their strategy and that in fact the appeals court had provided them some ammunition by using their whiteness against them and by narrowing the Equal Protection Clause beyond what the higher court had done in the past. By "recognizing through denial" that Mexican Americans were a special class, they were handing Cadena, Gus, and Herrera their final strategy. It would not be race or whiteness alone but a combination of the two. Cadena had already introduced this concept in his appeals brief but he needed the court to provide a clear decision that could be challenged and the court did so by specifically rejecting the notion through questionable reasoning. By being so restrictive in its ruling, the court was trying to stem a movement toward greater expansion of civil rights that had begun with the Vinson Court and was to continue under the Warren Court. While most of the cases dealt with African Americans, there were, as Cadena had pointed out, cases already decided that expanded the interpretation of equal protection.

The lawyers for *Hernández* were conscious of what was going on in the arena of school segregation litigation. There, Mexican Americans had made major inroads and all but illegitimated the doctrine of separate but equal as it pertained to Mexican Americans.[11] In spite of the appeals court ruling they were not discouraged. The lawyers left no personal records (at least none found yet) about their feelings after the appeals ruling, but it is possible that they were beginning to feel as Gus did when he first took on the case. Back then he told friends and reporters that this case was heading to the Supreme Court, and he spoke as if he was sure of a victory.[12] It was more than just personal arrogance, because despite numerous setbacks in their civil rights activities, Mexican Americans were starting to crack through segregation's wall. Frustration was evident given the slow nature of the forward movement, but there was also optimism because the number of middle-class Mexican Americans was growing, more groups agitating for reform were joining the fight, and the changing economy of Texas and much of the Southwest created a more fluid landscape.

There was, however, another element to the reformers' hope for greater acceptance into American society. By the late 1940s and early 1950s, the issue of illegal immigration from Mexico had once again flared up. Unlike the past, when most Mexican and American activists had sought to mediate the effects of border patrol raids on their communities and the often ruthless deportation campaigns that impacted both legal and illegal Mexicans, this new generation of reformers saw an opportunity to enhance their community's civil rights and their status as "good Americans" but on the backs of those who were in the country illegally. This situation was not planned but rather arose out of circumstance.

For decades thousands of Mexican American farm workers had picked the fruit, vegetables, and cotton on American farms, and done so for low wages and under extreme conditions. Most middle-class Mexican American reformers had rarely become involved in seeking to alleviate the conditions of those farm worker families. Mostly, they had been involved in issues of job or housing discrimination and political representation. Even in small towns where many of the residents were farm workers or migrant workers, reformers had concentrated on eliminating the worst forms of racial discrimination and in getting Mexican Americans to vote, and not on changing the labor conditions or protesting American agribusiness.

This would change, however, with the rise of the American GI Forum founded by Hector P. García, a physician and former Army surgeon who became involved in labor issues through his work with the Veterans Administration.[13] While not the originator of this concern, his work among farm workers forced the issue of "wetbacks" to be front and center in Mexican American reform. He began visiting farm worker colonies throughout south Texas and taking pictures and interviewing the workers. What he found and presented to the public were horrendous, unsanitary, and abusive conditions: malnourished children who did not attend schools, chicken coops passing for housing, long hours under the sun, and starvation wages that kept families and their offspring in a cycle of poverty.[14]

García was appalled by the conditions and the lack of concern by both local and state officials who turned the other way to appease the strong agricultural interests in the state of Texas. In this, he was joined by other reformers who saw the plight of their farm laboring countrymen as "Exhibit A" regarding the way the nation's leaders ignored the Mexican American community. Unfortunately, Mexican American reformers, including Hector García and Gus, who was the American GI Forum's legal advisor, did not articulate (nor did they have) an alternative plan of action beyond "paying farm workers better" and eliminating the "wetback" problem. Rather than critique an agricultural system that relied on cheap labor and that offered no benefits or mobility to its workers, Mexican American reformers sought to concentrate on blaming illegal immigration as well as contract labor from Mexico for most of the problems of Mexican American poverty.

Illegal immigration was actually not the major source of competition for American farm workers. Instead, it was the labor contracted from

Mexico through the Bracero Program, a guest worker program established during World War II to deal with labor shortages but that continued almost seventeen years after the war.[15] While these workers were supposed only to be imported to areas that had labor shortages, and were to be paid the prevailing wages and given housing as well as protection by a whole slew of safety regulations, they in fact were an army of abused workers with little recourse. Texas farmers often paid less than the contracted wage, provided horrendous housing, and usually requested more workers than they needed, thus depressing the wages even more.[16]

Mexican American farm workers saw themselves competing with workers in worse conditions than theirs and with fewer options. Native farm workers could always go north and west and they started doing so in the 1940s, following a pattern set much earlier by migrant farm workers who went to areas outside the Southwest to find better wages. The constant moving to *el norte* made the native population a shifting one and created difficulties for children who wanted to go to school and for adults who wanted to take part in the social and political life of their communities.

For Mexican American reformers who came back from World War II anxious to participate more widely in American society, and much more concerned with their communities' ability to sustain them in their economic and political efforts, the Bracero program and the illegal migration it encouraged was unacceptable. But their concerns about the issue went further than economics, and extended to the political and social realms. It presented them with not only an opportunity to demand governmental action on their community's poverty, but a forum through which they could prove their Americanism.

As early as 1947 Mexican American reformers were demanding that the Truman Administration do something about discrimination against Mexican Americans in employment and they tied this demand with an urgent plea to do something about "illegal aliens" and also the foreign workers being contracted in the Southwest through the Bracero Program. In a letter to Robert K. Carr, who headed the President's Committee on Civil Rights, professor and civil rights reformer Carlos E. Castañeda argued that at the "base of the various forms of discrimination suffered by [Mexican Americans] in the political, social, economic, and educational fields, lies the economic."[17] Wages paid to Mexican Americans, he wrote, "are, in the final analysis, plain and simple exploitation, based on an assumption that the Mexican is inferior in ability and in physical endurance."[18] Growers in Texas were able to maintain a salary of as little as twenty-five cents an hour because they had a surplus of workers.

When Mexican and American negotiators signed the guest worker agreements, they stipulated that the "prevailing wage" would be paid to the workers. This meant sixty cents an hour in California but only twenty-five cents in Texas. Texas reformers like Hector García wanted seventy-five cents an hour to keep the Mexican American worker home instead of in the fields of California or the Midwest. They saw the thousands, even hundreds of thousands, of Texas migrant workers traveling north and west during the picking season as a disruption of the social, educational, and civic life of the Mexican American communities in the state. They particularly worried about the effects such traveling had on the children's education. Every year thousands of children would leave their schools in mid semester and go to work in the fields with their parents. This constant movement and educational disruption diminished any hope that the migrant children could break the cycle of poverty and transience that they inherited from their parents.[19]

These children, were, of course American citizens or at least resident aliens, and they were being forced from their homes mostly by men from Mexico who were willing to work for any wage to feed themselves and send money to their families back home. "Mexican alien labor," wrote Castañeda, "is . . . being used to force Mexican American citizens, *who pay taxes and are citizens of this country*, to lower their standard of living . . . or remain unemployed" (my italics).[20] The result was that Mexican Americans were "taking to the road" and taking their problems with them as they arrived in communities with a need for housing, labor, food, and schooling. "When winter comes," continued Castañeda, "and seasonal employment is over, many will return . . . with little or nothing." Others, he added, remained to become public charges to those communities that had lured them with low wages that were at least higher than those in Texas.[21]

The biggest problem from all of this, concluded Castañeda, was that Mexican Americans would remain illiterate. Being "ignorant, miserable [and] discontented" they became vulnerable to the "enemies of democracy" who would turn them against the "American way of life." The solution was the end of labor discrimination, better wages, and (although not mentioned by the author) a greater restriction of the illegal alien and the end of guest worker agreements with Mexico. The end result would be a higher standard of living among Mexican Americans, which would lead them to "become . . . better American citizen[s] and . . . staunch defender[s] of a democracy that is a reality."[22]

Less than two years after Castañeda wrote these words, Gus García joined two other prominent reformers in denouncing the "wetback problem of the Southwest." They wrote a report that began with an emphasis on the fact that of the 3 million Spanish-speakers in the Southwest, 80 percent were citizens and many of them had been here "since Spanish Colonial days." "These people," continued the document, "have repeatedly demonstrated their loyalty to this country, in war and in peace . . . they have a record second to none among the minority groups of this nation."[23] But after one paragraph of reaffirming their loyalty, the document quickly went into the deplorable conditions in which Mexican Americans found themselves. "Since the Southwest was annexed and occupied by the United States, most of these people have been 'pushed around,' 'jim crowed,' and otherwise mistreated—by individuals, by organizations, and even both state and federal government agencies—to such an extent that today, after 100 years of U.S. rule, they are still largely unassimilated."[24]

While Gus and R. A. Cortez, president of the League of United Latin American Citizens (LULAC), were co-authors, it was George I. Sánchez whose imprint was firmly on the document. A University of Texas professor of education, Sánchez represented the most militant of the middle-class reformers of the 1940s and 1950s. Unlike most other reformers, he constantly described the Southwest as an area "invaded and occupied" and continually described the Mexican American situation as comparable to, or worse, than that of "the Negro." The other point of emphasis was the unassimilated circumstances of most Mexican Americans. While Sánchez was often critical of Mexican Americans who did not try harder to assimilate into American society, he laid most of the blame on American society. In his view, it was hard for Mexican Americans to integrate into the larger society when their children went to poor schools, their families lived in substandard housing and their labor wages barely kept them above water. Rampant discrimination also served to push them away. For the university professor, assimilation did not mean losing one's culture or sense of identity, it simply meant being a good citizen and adopting those characteristics that would allow one to succeed in American society.[25]

The document expressed alarm that notwithstanding all the ills that Mexican Americans currently faced, a "new development" threatened to "sink them deeper in the mire of socio-economic under-privilege."[26] This development was the increasing number of workers from Mexico who were entering the country illegally and working for fifteen to twenty-five cents an hour and displacing native-born farm workers. The influx of undocumented workers was seen as a source of unfair competition that drove most Mexican Americans further into poverty. It was made even more unfair by the fact that government agencies were assisting in this "illegalization" of the fields. The authors pointed out in particular the involvement of the Immigration and Naturalization Service in finding workers for the Texas growers. Rather than deport many of the workers they caught, they simply channeled them to where they were needed, and only deported them at the end of the picking season, or when they formed a large surplus of unneeded labor.[27]

Beyond depressing the wages and forcing Mexican American workers to migrate, they also posed a national security risk. Here again, Mexican American reformers used the Cold War scare to move the Mexican American worker into the American mainstream by finding an "other" whom they could blame for undermining organized labor, maintaining a caste system, manipulating government, "and even for subversive action."[28] The authors warned of irreparable damage to the country and to the Mexican American community if the "emergency of national significance" continued. Their solution: stricter border control, penalizing employers who used illegal labor, and the "immediate" appointment of a presidential commission to investigate the problems of the Spanish-speaking population of the Southwest.[29]

Reformers in Texas would follow up their correspondence with President Truman by commissioning several studies to gauge the impact of the foreign workers on the labor markets in the Southwest. One exhaustive study directed by Sánchez focused on the undocumented worker in south Texas. Unfortunately, that study and another one commissioned by the American GI Forum and the Texas AFL-CIO (American Federation of Labor and Congress of Industrial Organizations) were drowned in controversy as other voices within the Mexican-origin community took issue with the portrayal of Mexican workers and with the call for strengthening the U.S. Border Patrol.[30]

Still, Mexican American reformers persisted in dividing the Mexican-origin community between those who were legal and those who were illegal. In doing so, they followed one current while fighting against another one within the Mexican American community of Texas and the Southwest. There were, without doubt, those who saw illegal immigration as a threat to Mexican Americans not only in jobs but also in the biases they attracted. Those old enough to remember the 1920s and 1930s knew that the increase in workers on the burgeoning agricultural fields in Texas and the rest of the Southwest had brought with it an increase in racial prejudices as Anglo Texans resented the growth of Mexican communities throughout much of the southern and western part of the state. Most workers were poor, illiterate, and spoke no English. The Anglo reaction was to lump all Mexican-origin individuals into the same category of "meskins" and to increase their hostility toward every class of them.[31]

For some, the only way to respond to that reaction was to draw a line of distinction between themselves and those recent arrivals from Mexico. For others, it was to protest the actions against them by law enforcement, growers, policymakers, and other Mexican American reformers. But by the 1950s, however, this group was smaller and less influential because it had always depended on immigrant organizations and labor unions to provide it with strength. But the immigrant community had now gone through several deportation and expatriation campaigns, and while these campaigns had not been fully successful in stemming the tide of Mexican workers coming to find work, they had been successful in stripping that community of much of its leadership. Also, with the end of the conflicts in Mexico, and the growth of agriculture, the kind of Mexican immigrant coming changed from the political and economic exile to the migrant farm worker. These were the people most vulnerable to exploitation and often the least able to defend themselves and also the least likely to organize against such treatment. The labor unions of the early twentieth century had heavily recruited Mexican laborers, but during the postwar era there was much opposition to their joining unions.[32] Civil rights organizations that were strongly pro-immigrant had also mostly declined during the war and postwar years.

Those organizations taking center stage were those most anxious to integrate into American society and were more self-conscious of how they were perceived by the larger public. They were veterans who wanted to prove their Americanism. While not anti-immigrant, this community had begun to see itself within the context of its citizenship or legal residence. They saw small openings in society but were profoundly conscious that entrance into mainstream society depended on their acceptability. As a senator from New Mexico would tell a gathering of Mexican American voters, "When a boy named González goes off to war, he doesn't wear a Mexican uniform. He wears the uniform of the United States of America. There's nothing for him as a Mexican, but there is everything here for him as an American."[33]

This generation was clearly conscious of the political line at the border and the debate on immigration provided them the forum in which to prove their Americanism. They could claim that they had no particular animosity to their Mexican counterparts, but they were Americans and had to look after their own first. To do so and find credibility within their own community, they had to find justification for creating rigid borders where in the past there had been fluid ones. To blame illegal aliens for low wages, disease, bad housing, educational problems, and potential national security risks allowed Mexican American reformers to accomplish two purposes: first, they defined themselves as Americans instead of foreigners; and second, they could demand American government action as citizens under duress because of a foreign population. The fact that most illegal aliens were "Guadalajara Joes" as one reformer called them, made it easier to distinguish the reformers and their community from the "Mexican," and made it easier to claim whiteness for those who chose to.[34] It also made the reformers' efforts to take leadership of the Mexican community much easier because it made them the only logical leadership in a community some reformers believed was spiraling toward integration.

The stand against undocumented immigrants would culminate in what many Mexican Americans would later see as a shameful act of support for the massive deportations of the 1950s known as Operation Wetback.[35] This government response to nativist complaints of an out-of-control invasion of brown hordes from Mexico involved massive neighborhood roundups, illegal house searches, unprovoked roadblocks, and an often ruthless separation of family members. Like deportation campaigns of the past, it also meant that hundreds if not thousands of American citizens of Mexican origin were deported along with those in the country illegally. The deportation campaign, unfolding in every Mexican neighborhood in broad daylight and under the cover of night, created a backlash that would once and for all end reformers' support for deportations and a strengthened border patrol, but not before subjecting the Mexican community to trauma. But clearly, whatever the later reactions, the deportations strengthened the hand of those advocates of Americanism.

The defense's position in *Hernández v. Texas* fit well within this strategy to promote Americanism to the Mexican-origin community while allowing them to demand recognition from the larger society as citizens. Ironically, Hernández's own father was an immigrant from Mexico who came to the United States as many Mexicans did before and after the border patrol was established to control the borders. Luckily for him, he did it before it became illegal to cross the border to look for a job.[36] But the irony was lost on the lawyers, or possibly it simply fit in with the complex and often contradictory view of most middle-class Mexican American reformers, who sought to define themselves by creating borders to the south while demanding open borders to opportunities in American society to the north. Their approach was not racial or even class-based but rather citizenship-based.

Pete, by all accounts, was an American citizen. The only thing that distinguished him from those poor, undocumented, brown-skinned Mexican youth who worked the cotton fields around the Edna area, was his citizenship and the fact that he could speak English well enough to function in American society. But like them, he was poor, basically uneducated, with no real future and quite unacceptable to much of Texas Anglo society. Yet, his citizenship mattered and it was his ticket to momentary fame and a temporary reprieve from a life sentence. More important for reformers, it was his rights of citizenship that were central to the case, because despite his similarities to the other Mexican youths, unlike them, he did have a right to demand justice and protection from the law. That, in the end, was the difference between the Mexican groups, and the one element of national identity that reformers wanted to build on.

Their community would move toward assimilation and political and economic integration only if it saw benefits in leaving behind those customs and habits that limited their involvement in American society. On the other hand, they needed to see a greater commitment by American society to the protection of their civil liberties and a willingness to accept them as citizens with full rights. Mexican American reformers led by George I. Sánchez, Hector P. García, R. A. Cortez, and to some extent Gus García, gambled on this strategy succeeding in getting Mexican Americans focused on integration and the government committed to righting the wrongs in the barrios of the Southwest.[37] The *Hernández* case, more than even the successful educational legal cases of the past, provided a forum in which to argue Mexican Americans' place in American society because it pitted English-speaking, property-owning, and legal Mexican Americans against a state judicial system seeking to limit the Equal Protection Clause of the U.S. Constitution.

It is quite possible that Mexican American civil liberties advocates were, like their African American counterparts, optimistic that the national climate seemed posed to change to their advantage. While Jim Crow remained strong in the South and Mexican Americans continued to be segregated in the Southwest, the previous decade had been good for both groups in terms of court victories reaffirming, if only in a piecemeal fashion, their rights as American citizens.[38] More important, both groups' middle classes were growing, liberalism at the national level was on the rise and concern over the Cold War found diplomats and national politics hedging away from the worse aspects of White Supremacy.[39] In Texas, the expanding economy had begun breaking down segregation by the late 1940s and creating political alliances between progressive Anglos and Mexican Americans. In the rest of the Southwest, especially California and Arizona, Mexican Americans were being elected to office, while New Mexico remained a place where political and social control was contested by Anglos and *Nuevo Mexicanos* as both populations grew.

The changing circumstances for Mexican Americans emboldened the reformers, but it also placed them in what some found to be an uncomfortable situation. The opportunity to prove that they were Americans came with the price of shifting the blame to their countrymen who were either illegals or who were working as contracted labor. Yet, not all were comfortable with this. Having already placed themselves above their community through their education and their activism, these reformers could forcefully speak to a difference—created by legal status and assimilation—in the Mexican communities of the Southwest. The fact that most Mexican American reformers of this generation were second or third generation Americans—with a few exceptions—allowed them the social space to engage in this strategy. Had they remained more within the mainstream of their community, however, they might have appreciated more that in the barrios the enemy was not so much the "wetback" or the "Bracero," but the *gringo* who exploited them. But these men and women spoke from a viewpoint that placed political and social integration above cultural maintenance, not necessarily out of personal choice but out of political expediency.

The issue of illegal immigration, while often uncomfortable for them personally, provided them a forum in which they could publicly debate their rights of citizenship. Publicity was often something they hungered for after so many years as an "invisible minority."[40] Often overlooked, when they did come into the conversation, it was rarely their voice that was heard. Mexican Americans simply did not have a public leadership that could speak at the highest level. They understood this and so they kept speaking to their invisibility.

It was not lost on Mexican American legal advocates that this case was garnering attention in the country's legal journals, though it is hard to know which, if any, of the legal journals they read after the Texas Court of Criminal Appeals rejected their challenge. If they read most or any of them, their hopes no doubt soared because both within and beyond the state, legal scholars agreed with them, one even arguing that if the case went higher, it would gain a reversal.

The *Nebraska Law Review* was the first journal to comment on the case, just one month after the rehearing was denied and four months after the ruling. In a review of recent cases, a law student wrote that the Federal Civil Rights Act already entitled Mexican Americans to claim discrimination based on exclusion, but more important, the "Negro Exclusion rule" aptly applied to Mexican Americans because the main focus of the rule had been to prohibit racial discrimination and Mexican Americans were a discriminated people in Texas.[41] This assumption came after a clumsily written statement arguing that Mexicans might better be placed in the "genus of Red people" instead of white. The author pointed to a scandalous case in Texas where a county attorney refused to prosecute a Mexican American for murder because he felt he might be forced to accept a "Latin American" in the jury box.[42] He also mentioned another county in which officials were prodded into including Mexican Americans in the jury list, but those were soon "systematically" excluded from actually serving. In that case one court official said, "attorneys just would not have Mexicans on the jury." And the author of the story added, "that was the end of Mexican American jury service; there are no Hispanic names on the jury list today."[43] The article concluded that exclusion had been practiced against Mexican Americans throughout the country, and "in some cases even more than [against] Negroes," thus the exclusion rule needed to be "broadened to encompass Mexicans."[44]

Mario Piazzolla, in the *Temple Law Quarterly*, argued that the Equal Protection Clause applied equally to "intra-class discrimination" and pointed to rulings that found a violation of equal protection in cases of jury exclusion of members of a political party, of religious groups, and of women. In those cases, however, "direct proof of discrimination" was necessary for reversal and this placed an unnecessary burden on the defendant. Piazzolla submitted that the holding in the *Hernández* case needed to be reversed. "The Fourteenth Amendment makes no attempt," he wrote, "to enumerate the rights it is designed to protect nor does it attempt to classify the persons whose rights are protected."[45] He added that the court's attempt to differentiate race and nationality was inconsistent with the spirit of the Equal Protection Clause. He concluded, "The Fourteenth Amendment does not contemplate a study of geology, archeology or paleoethnology; and our jurisprudence should not be based on differences in bone structure, nasal profile, lip formation or distinctive colors."[46]

The author in the *Washington University Law Quarterly* found that the Fourteenth Amendment's parameters were "broad enough" to include any race or group.[47] Citing the Supreme Court in *Fay v. New York*, he argued that the Court had "left the door open" for other groups outside the category of race or color, to charge discrimination in jury selection. There, the Court wrote, "we do not mean that no case of discrimination in jury drawing except those involving race or color can carry such unjust consequences as to amount to a denial of equal protection or due process of law."[48] As had the author in the *Nebraska Law Review*, this author questioned whether

Mexican Americans were white. He pointed to federal naturalization statutes that placed Mexicans in a different racial classification than that of the white man. "If such is the case," he wrote, "then the position of the defendant in the principal case and that of the Negro in *Norris v. Alabama* are closely analogous." Given this similarity, the author questioned why the appeals court had not extended the *Norris* case beyond the specific facts and included Mexican Americans in the exclusion rule.[49]

A *Virginia Law Review* author agreed that the burden of proof in claiming jury discrimination for a "class" of people hung heavier on the defendant than did claiming racial discrimination. Nonetheless, the Supreme Court had, according to the journal author, established that a case of discrimination was "proved" when Negroes were systematically and for a sustained period excluded from jury duty. This meant that the *Norris* exclusion rule was "concerned with the manner of *proving* discrimination and not with substantive rights under the Fourteenth Amendment."[50] Hence, continued the author, the rule could be applied to discrimination against Mexicans making such discrimination as illegal as that against "Negroes." By implication the journal article reaffirmed that Mexican Americans were a "class" to be protected just as were African Americans, and this was a victory for the *Hernández* lawyers who wanted whiteness by implication and color only in so far it provided them protection.

If the Texas Court of Criminal Appeals expected some support from Texas journals or scholars, it did not get it. The *Texas Law Review* criticized the Texas court for "drawing a line" between the proof required for discrimination against the "Negro race" and that against Mexican Americans. Calling the line a "fictitious" one, H. Weaver, the author, argued it in effect was requiring separate rules as well as separate proofs for the same constitutional guarantees.[51] He continued, "If the circumstantial evidence of long-continued and systematic exclusion of members of the Negro race from jury duty justifiably serves as proof of discrimination, then the same evidence should be sufficient to prove discrimination against a citizen of Mexican extraction."[52] He added that the ruling was a disappointment for Mexican Americans in areas where they did not ever get into the jury box.

Frank Lady, writing in the *Baylor Law Review*, called the court's decision an "unusually limited" view of the Equal Protection Clause, and added that classifying Mexicans as predominantly white was a "fallacious assumption."[53] He argued that it was settled law that "systematic and arbitrary exclusion" was a denial of equal protection, no matter the group. More important, in his mind, rulings dealing with African Americans and Asian Americans provided a broad umbrella for other groups, countering the black/white binary that the Texas court had adopted.[54] Lady then pointed to a number of lower court rulings that made segregation of Mexican school children a violation of the Equal Protection Clause.[55] While he pointed to cases in California, he could well have included a number of cases in Texas where Mexican Americans had been very successful in winning litigation against segregation.

In countering the notion that Mexicans were part of the white race, he used anthropological studies of the era. In doing so, he clearly showed why Mexican American reformers often were ambivalent about categorizing themselves as a race. Quoting anthropologist A. L. Krober, Lady wrote, "The [Native] American race can hardly have come from anywhere else than Asia . . . their affiliations are generally Mongoloid." He then followed it up by quoting another writer by the name of Stuart Chase, who argued that too few white men ever came to Mexico to provide Mexicans with enough white blood. "There must be far less white blood today relatively and absolutely than in 1790," he wrote, calculating that the Mexican nation was 96 percent Indian and *mestizo*, 3 percent white, and 1 percent foreign.[56] Being their own race made their exclusion from jury duty a violation of the Equal Protection Clause. Given all of his points, Lady declared that if the case were appealed to the Supreme Court, it would likely be reversed, and the Court would declare that there was ample evidence for a prima facie presumption of discrimination.[57]

The published arguments revealed a clear consensus among legal scholars that times were changing and that Mexican Americans were poised for a victory sooner or later in the nation's highest court. They also clearly showed that rampant discrimination was going to be a tough act to defend in legal terms. White supremacy, at least in the law schools and among some legal scholars, had begun to lose support. Many whites might not have been ready to accept minorities as complete equals, but they were becoming more and more uncomfortable trying to defend this separation with racial bigotry. The late 1940s and the early 1950s were a period of transition and were setting the stage for the changes that came with Earl Warren's confirmation to the Supreme Court.

All of the scholarly reviews pointed to a favorable outcome, but the immediate problem for Hernández's lawyers, however, revolved around raising the money to take the challenge to the next step. All of them had experienced life as members of civil rights organizations that tended to survive on nickels and dimes from dances, fundraising raffles, dues, and small donations from the still small Mexican American middle class. There were extremely few wealthy members of the community and no major philanthropies committed to Mexican American civil rights. This would be one clear difference between Mexican American and African American civil rights struggles: the number of wealthy white Americans ready and willing to give money for the long and costly legal campaigns. It reflected, in part, the scarcity of white support for Mexican American civil rights activity. There might have been some sensitivity and sympathy for their struggles but few whites were passionate about working alongside or funding Mexican American reformers' activities.[58]

Another problem facing Cadena, Gus, and Herrera in terms of support, came from a lack of a strong national advocacy group for Mexican Americans. While LULAC could now claim a history of activism for more than a quarter of a century, and the American GI Forum could lay claim to be the fastest growing Latino organization at the time, neither of them had a significant presence outside of Texas. Each state in the Southwest had its own Mexican American organization and most of them had the same financial difficulties, thus any attempt at a national level to raise funds competed with well-entrenched state fundraising efforts. Also, hampering any national fundraising efforts was the limited exposure of the case outside of Texas. Simply put, the national media showed little interest in highlighting one of hundreds of cases that attempted to get to the Supreme Court. Unlike the black newspapers that could be found throughout most areas where African Americans lived and which were written in English, Spanish-language newspapers were more limited in circulation and resources, usually focused on local issues, and were mostly written in Spanish for people much less connected to American society. Even the major Spanish language newspapers, *La Opinion* of Los Angeles and *La Prensa* of San Antonio, did not cover the case initially.[59]

Of course, fundraising hinged on getting the Supreme Court to consider hearing the case, and so on January 21, 1953, almost two years after Hernández shot Espinoza to death, the lawyers filed a petition for a writ of certiorari.[60] Years later they would talk as if it was a given but in reality getting a case heard before the Supreme Court was and continues to be difficult. The petition was filed on the last day allowable as the lawyers harbored misgivings that their petition would be granted. "We had little hope," wrote Gus years later, "because every year hundreds of applications are submitted but only a few are granted."[61] Given that Mexican American civil rights issues were not at the forefront of the debate in the nation's capital, it is accurate to say that the lawyers waited anxiously for a reply. It came on October 12, 1953, and simply stated: "The petition for writ of certiorari is granted and the case is transferred to the appellate docket." It also stated that the chief justice took no part in the consideration "or decision of this application."[62] But it did not matter to the lawyers, who were elated that the petition had not only been granted but that it had occurred on October 12, Columbus Day, or as it was known in the Mexican community, "El Dia de la Raza."[63]

Chief Justice Earl Warren had been appointed to the court only seven days earlier and had not yet settled in when the vote was taken to consider the granting of the writ. A conference list for the week of October 5, indicates that the court had decided by then to grant the writ of certiorari.[64] Of the eight sitting justices, only Justice Stanley F. Reed voted not to grant the writ.[65] Ironically, on the same day that the Court agreed to hear Pete's case, they also agreed to hear *Galvan v. Press*, a case dealing with a Mexican immigrant fighting deportation for "alleged Communist activity after entering [the] country." The case involved the McCarren-Walter Internal Security Act.[66]

Money became an immediate necessity and the first expenditure came within two weeks when the lawyers had to pay $900 for the printing of the record.[67] The money came from the San Antonio chapter of the League of United Latin American Citizens (LULAC), but within days of the case being granted a writ of certiorari, Ed Idar Jr., executive secretary of the American GI Forum, was seeking estimates of the monetary needs to litigate the case. He wrote the president of LULAC on October 27, and asked if the organization was making any further commitments "over and beyond the $900 already given."[68] Ironically, the money given by the San Antonio chapter had been allocated through questionable procedures. The president of the local chapter had called a quick meeting to approve the donation and invited only those he believed would support the request. That action, according to a Cadena letter to Sánchez, had "caught quite a bit of hell" for Pete Tijerina, the local president, and this made LULAC an unlikely donor for more money.[69]

Idar, a very meticulous reformer and organizational leader, wanted to know how much his own organization would need to contribute in order for the case to go forward. He told Albert Armendariz, LULAC president, that he had heard that the Good Neighbor Commission had made commitments to help, but dismissed the idea that an entity that had often been reluctant to help Mexican American reformers in the past would now be interested in helping.[70] The one other large funding entity that they could look toward was the Robert Marshall Civil Liberties Trust Fund, which donated five thousand dollars during October of 1953 for civil rights cases, but only a fraction of that went to the *Hernández* case.[71]

On the same day, Idar wrote Cadena and asked him what kind of commitment LULAC was willing to make to the case to "determine the extent of our aid if we agree to help."[72] The American GI Forum had few personal resources but had in the past been able to raise funds by calling on other Forum participants and on members of the Mexican American community to make small donations. On November 23, the Forum established a three-person committee to consider the merits of the case and consider funding the case.[73] This decision came only a few days after Hector García wrote to the Forum state chairman, Chris Aldrete, to inform him that Herrera, De Anda, and a "fellow Cisneros" wanted to accompany Gus and Cadena. This would add to the costs but García felt that the lawyers needed someone to "crack the whip" over them. Wrote García, "I am afraid of misbehavior or negligence of duty when they go over there in that they may feel too elated and may not study the brief and perhaps even have a little drinking."[74]

García suggested that they send a man of the "caliber" of Dr. George Sánchez to keep an eye on the group of lawyers and make sure "they do the job as we want them to do."[75]

García's letter revealed the anxiety that some Mexican American reformers felt about going to the Supreme Court for the first time. They understood the importance of this act and wondered whether they were up to the challenge. Members of the American GI Forum were particularly concerned with the performance and behavior of Gus. While Hector had not mentioned Gus directly, Idar had done so in his letters to Cadena and Almendariz. To Cadena, he had expressed "much concern with Gus's participation." He accused the flamboyant lawyer of neglecting the case and being cavalier in doing the work to gather the documentation necessary for the appeal, and expressed his disinclination in funding the case as long as Gus was part of it. "I would personally feel much better if Gus were not to participate and Sánchez and I have discussed this at length but fail to find a way to keep him from it since it was originally his case. It seems to me, however, that an attorney who neglects his client's interests in the form that Gus did has no right for continued participation."[76] Idar asked Cadena to assure him that the funds devoted to the case would be kept from Gus's control.

On December 4, Idar again wrote to Cadena, this time asking whether he and Gus had "agreed definitely" to collaborate on the appeal. The letter seems to imply that there had been some discussion as to the makeup of the defense team going to Washington, D.C. In the letter, Idar referenced a letter to Gus that mostly discussed finances and asked for a date when the briefs would be filed.[77] But to Cadena he expressed concern with the composition of the litigation team. Idar requested confidentially in all his letters and he never seems to have challenged Gus openly. There is, however, no doubt that Idar would have discouraged the American GI Forum from contributing funds had Cadena not participated. He made that threat when he told Cadena that "any question as to whether you are to collaborate . . . will have an important bearing on our decision [to fund]."[78]

It is difficult to tell exactly what Gus did specifically to cause Idar's hostility and that of Sánchez, but it is likely to have had something to do with his drinking, his flamboyant "airs," and his lack of attention to detail in his work. He seemed to always be in financial straits and he kept borrowing from friends and from the organizations to which he belonged. Throughout the *Hernández* case there would be a hesitancy to provide Gus any direct funds. In fact, in the final disbursement of funds, Gus's allotted $215 was withheld and applied toward the $315 debt he had with the American GI Forum.[79] Some Mexican American reformers were worried about Gus acting as the face of Mexican American reform in front of the U.S. Supreme Court.

While LULAC had provided the initial $900 for the case, the American GI Forum took an active lead in the attempt to provide the remaining funding. In an undated, open letter to Forum members and other interested individuals, Hector García called for a collective contribution of $1,000. He tried to explain in a concise fashion the meaning of the case, though he did so by leaving out the fact that this was a murder case, and he did not even mention Pete Hernández. This would begin a campaign to promote the case without promoting the reasons for Pete's predicament, which were likely to cause some consternation among both reformers and regular citizens. After all, he was accused of murder and not even his lawyers denied he had been responsible for the killing of a fellow Mexican American. Still, the importance of the case was based on discrimination and not the individuals involved. "If we win this case," wrote García, "then all of the counties and districts as well as the states, will be forced to permit our people to serve on juries."[80] He added that the American GI Forum had already spent $1,500 on the case, and he asked the contributors to be generous because this was a case for "all our people."[81]

Generosity can be described in many ways but for poor Mexican Americans it would be defined by the sacrifice that they had to make to give assistance. The few records available on the donations provided the American GI Forum confirms that no one individual gave more than $25 and only a couple of organizations gave $50 or more.[82] There simply was no middle class big enough to tap and there were almost no philanthropic giants anxious to fund any civil rights effort by Mexican Americans. Whatever white support there was for civil rights in Texas or the Southwest was limited mostly to helping African Americans. Compounding the limitations was the competition by a myriad of local and regional Mexican American civic, cultural, and political organizations vying for the same limited donor base. Still, the efforts to contribute were admirable and revealed the commitment that many rank-and-file Mexican Americans felt to fighting discrimination.

An undated letter from the Midland chapter of the Forum told of an enclosed check for the amount of $50. "We sincerely regret," wrote A. V. Gutiérrez, "that our contribution is small due to the fact that ours is a newly organized group." But he added that if the goal was not reached, they would do their "utmost" to contribute more.[83] On December 14, Hector García received a letter from Simon Moya Sr. in Beeville, Texas. He had heard García on the radio requesting funds for the case, and decided to do some collecting of his own. "We've come to the conclusion that the decision of the Supreme Court . . . will, undoubtedly be favorable for our people in Texas, and end cases such as those in . . . Jackson County." Moya then listed himself at $2 and eight other men at $1 each.[84]

Francisco and Alfredo Martinez, two men barely literate in Spanish and likely illiterate in English, sent $2.50 because they felt it their obligation to be part of the effort against discrimination.[85] Like Gutiérrez they likely heard about the case on the radio. That was the case with Pablo Renaud, a very articulate letter writer who told García that he heard one of the Saturday broadcasts on KWBU radio in which the GI Forum leader asked "for all the possible help to combat" discrimination and segregation. Renaud sent $2 and told García he wished he could send more, but only recently he had lost his vision and was unable to work to provide for his family. But he was sending all that was in his possession, and he hoped that others would make a small sacrifice to fight those "threats that seemed always to hang over" all Mexicans.[86] Juan Montiel, another radio listener, sent $2 and asked that García overlook his bad grammar as he was one of many Mexicans living in the states who had not received much of an education—but he did point out rather proudly that he had a son in Japan who had served in Korea. "May God permit you to triumph in this most grand of campaigns," he wrote.[87]

Manuel García sent $5 in defense of the case "to be heard on . . . the 15th of January before the Supreme Court." Octabiano Canul sent $2, and Jesse F. Castillo sent $5. Castillo wrote from Huntsville, Texas, from the same penitentiary that would house Hernández for nearly six years. "I hope to hear it . . . on the radio next Saturday where [sic] you read all the names," wrote Castillo in badly-worded English, "and I hope to hear my name."[88] A day after Castillo wrote, the Seguin chapter of the American GI Forum also wrote to contribute $25 to the *Hernández* fund. Manuel Castilla Jr. pledged "our present funds and future additions . . . for the benefit of our Latin American people." He added that if the other Forum chapters answered the call, there would be more than enough money. "We must learn to do our part, and you can count on the Seguin Forum for as long as there is anything in the treasury."[89]

The Bay City Forum sent a $15 check for "Mr. Hernández as a small token of our appreciation for his willingness to fight for his civil rights and setting an example for the rest of us." The organization's secretary also promised further cooperation "to the fullest extent" if more was needed for the case.[90] These small donations were very representative of the type of support that the *Hernández* fund received. They revealed the financial situation of most Mexican Americans in Texas, but they also indicated that many were staying abreast of the issue to the extent that they could. What they knew came from Hector P. García's radio broadcasts and from the few organizational newsletters that mentioned the case. Of course, Mexican Americans in Texas were not the only ones in tune with the case.

While knowledge of the case outside of Texas remained limited, some who heard about it also contributed. One such contributor was the Mexican-American Council of Chicago. Martin Ortiz, its director, broke down the contributions as follows: $100 came from the Council, $20 from the Chicago Fiesta guild; $2 from the Hispano-American Company; and $5 from an individual, Sydney B. Wexler. Martinez added that the Council did not really know much about the case but felt nonetheless that it would be important. "We realize," he wrote, "the amount enclosed is small in comparison to the over-all expenses however, we forward this sum to you in the spirit of greater cooperation between the various organizations interested in the welfare of persons of Mexican descent in these United States."[91]

On February, 1954, the American GI Forum announced that it had contributed $1,236.95 to the *Hernández* case, most of it raised by García through his radio program and his letters to Forum members and chapters throughout the state. Of the money, $721.30 were turned over to Cadena for court costs and other expenses involved in the case. Three hundred dollars went for travel expenses for Forum state chairman, Chris Aldrete, an attorney who went as much to see how the money was spent as to assist. The remaining $215 went to Gus García "in the nature of credit to a balance" that he owed the Forum.[92] It is strange that the Forum chose to air

Gus's debt to the organization, but it does seem to reveal that there were some hard feelings against him.

In a letter to Hector García, sent on January 15, Ed Idar informed him that Gus had been given at least $400 for expenses and had not shared any money with Cadena. In fact, Idar noted, Cadena had yet to receive any funds either for expenses or for lawyer's fees.[93] Seven days later Idar wrote Cadena and sent him a check for $296.30 to be used at his discretion to cover court costs. "However, we feel that, in case you have not received any funds to cover your own personal expenses, you would feel free to retain all or whatever part of the contribution which you desire to retain," wrote Idar. He could, the letter added, disburse money to "other attorneys." Idar promised to send any other funds that were late in being reported, and expressed regret that the organization did not have the funds to cover the expenses or provide a "substantial fee" to him and Gus.[94] One month later Idar sent Cadena the last $200 of the *Hernández* fund.[95] This ended the fundraising for the *Hernández* case by the American GI Forum. It is impossible to know exactly how much money was raised for the case. None of the other organizations kept a record as detailed as the Forum's, and there is no way to know how many individuals contributed directly to the lawyers themselves.

We do, however, know what Gus thought of the fundraising efforts and the inability to raise significant funds. He wrote about it in a pamphlet that came out only a month or two after the case was decided. He recalled that "we" had been taken to task by those he called "guard-house lawyers" and "Monday-morning quarterbacks" because "we" chose not to go to the high court on a "pauper's oath." "Look at the Rosenbergs," he remembered being told by the critics. "I would hardly call the ultimate conclusion in the Rosenberg case successful from the standpoint of the defense," wrote Gus. "Secondly," he continued, "we felt . . . the 3 million persons of Mexican descent in the United States, or at least the noisy well-heeled clowns and poseurs who are constantly seeking publicity as 'civic leaders' should be able to provide for court costs and bare expenses in the first case to come before that August tribunal. Have we, because we are in a sense a conquered people, lost all sense of pride?"[96]

Gus had no qualms about criticizing other reformers whom he felt simply talked a good reform game but never actually played one. He was from a generation that in the 1950s was still consolidating its status in a community used to immigrant activists and their nationalist views, and older reformers who always vacillated between being bold and being hesitant about challenging the status quo. He longed for Mexican Americans to be as organized and as "successful" in their civil rights activities as African Americans were in theirs. Gus estimated that the American GI Forum, LULAC, Texas Good Relations Association and several private individuals were able to raise about $3,000 for the cost of the appeal, and he compared that with the "$45,000 to over $100,000 raised for each major case that African Americans took to court."[97] He also believed that black lawyers and civil libertarians were much better compensated for their efforts, and "considerably less" criticized by "bird-brained contemporaries."[98]

Gus seemed to have a running battle with other reformers and it had to do with the difficulty of being a reformer. He understood that life for a reformer was a difficult lot. They were supposed to give and give, and rarely expect anything in return. There is a sense from his writings that Gus was committed to his people and to reform, but it also seems obvious that he wanted to show something for it. The tragedy of Gus García was that he believed he was destined for "greatness," but that status would not be accorded to him except in small towns and obscured courthouses, and each legal or civil rights victory simply led to another fight. Some, like Sánchez and Hector García, lived for the struggle and rarely contemplated any other life. Gus seemed more like the average returning veteran who wanted to fulfill the American dream, and he was often critical of those who saw no other life than reform. But conflicted though he was, he never abandoned the struggle for Mexican American civil rights.

Gus did acknowledge that some individuals and organizations had come through.[99] Despite his apprehensions of the community's ability to rise to the challenge, he understood the difficulties that poor Mexican Americans confronted. Yet, he wanted more from a community that had been left to fend for itself. Given the economic circumstances of most Mexican Americans and the limited exposure of the appeal, $3,000 was actually a good sum, but it did not really provide more than minimal support.

Still, the case had made it to the Supreme Court and Mexican Americans would finally get to litigate on a national stage, and this was something many Mexican Americans lawyers had been waiting and hoping for, for a long time. They saw it as a chance to prove their worth to the Court, to the nation, and to their own community.

"There Must Be a White Man in the Wood Pile"

The stately building of the Supreme Court is unmistakable with its grandeur, and its solemnity reflects the fact that decisions made within it have no appeal. As the head one of the three branches of government, the Court's power is derived from its articulation of what this country stands for, and the fact that its justices—some more than others—are seen as intellectual giants who put aside their own biases to rule for the good of the nation. Of course, it is easy to document where petty biases and profound racism have been the rule rather than the exception, but many Americans still believe in the integrity of the institution if not of the justices themselves. In 1953, still decades away from a time when potential justices are scrutinized for their political leanings and their stand on certain cultural issues, the Court still could strike fear into anyone preparing to stand before the justices for the first time. Gus may well have been too proud to admit it, but his own awe of American institutions made him swell with pride at the opportunity to make history, and to show the American public that Mexican Americans belonged on this stage. Surely he relished the chance to show how good a lawyer he was as well.

Cadena, even more than Gus, must have had sleepless nights knowing he would be litigating before the nation's most important, and at times, most unfriendly, court. A man who felt more comfortable writing briefs, researching the law, and preparing strategy, he seemed uncomfortable as the center of attention. His daughter remembers him as a shy man who seldom spoke about his accomplishments. Years later, his colleagues in the district attorney's office would be amazed that their colleague had actually litigated before the Supreme Court.[1] It is then not surprising that he put such great effort into preparing the brief. At the same time, in a letter to his friend and mentor George I. Sánchez, he told him, "the chances of winning the *Hernández* case are, I think, good." Though he admitted that they had not complied with all the rules, by overlooking the serving of a copy "of anything on the state attorney general," which he described as a "slightly improper procedure" and grounds for dismissal of the petition.[2]

In another letter to Sánchez he expressed his confidence that he and Gus were fully able to argue the case by themselves. This discussion came after he received a letter from Al Wirin, an ACLU lawyer, who offered to assist in the arguments before the Court. Wirin was well known to Mexican American reformers as the lead counsel in the *Mendez v. Westminster* desegregation case in California, which had struck down "separate but equal" in regards to Mexican Americans. At the time of the *Hernández* arguments, he was scheduled to argue a case alongside Dean Acheson, former President Truman's secretary of state. Cadena recognized that it was an incredible offer that Wirin would "forego the pleasure of arguing" with such a distinguished statesman to help with *Hernández*, but he did not feel he needed him nor that he had a place for him on the team. "I am quite familiar with all of the jury cases, and the brief is already written," wrote Cadena. "It may be that I am being a bit capricious concerning Wirin, but my conceit is such that I think that I can handle the chore myself."[3]

No record exists on what Cadena said to the justices in the oral arguments, but we have a magnificent record—in the brief—of how he came to define Mexican Americans before the law. Few pre-1960s documents exist that so well define the thought of a generation of Mexican Americans. The brief served as the best way to illustrate the mind of his generation, a generation that well understood the parameters under which it lived within American society. Unhampered by foreign ideologies or internal philosophies, Cadena wrote for a generation that found its identity within the context of American political and civil thought. Their culture, their national origin, their racial characteristics, and their status as second-class citizens created corollaries within their Americanism, but never substituted as a replacement ideology or identity. Being Mexican American was contingent on their believing in American society, and their yearning for full acceptance.

For the small but growing Mexican American reform community, this opportunity represented the climactic point in their civil rights litigation, and it would be an understatement to say that a number of them wanted to be present. More would have gone if the money had been available, but in the end only seven ended up making the trip. The onlookers who accompanied Cadena, Gus, and Herrera were a diverse bunch who unintentionally represented several sectors of the Mexican American community.

Abel Cisneros of Wharton, Texas, came along because his community had contributed the most, and it is likely that some of the contributors were anxious to ensure that their money went to good use. Of course, it is also possible that they simply wanted a blow-by-blow account of the proceedings in D.C., and in Cisneros they could count on just that. He was a radio commentator, and though no record exists of him or his radio program, it is likely that he was well known in the Mexican community of Wharton and the surrounding towns. What we know of him comes from something Gus wrote shortly after the ruling: "He took copious notes and, after he came home, rendered a lengthy report over the radio to the people of East Texas."[4]

Spanish-language radio was the one medium that most Mexican Americans could count on to keep them abreast of what occurred around them. Disc jockeys were honored guests at people's homes, and they assumed a status rarely obtained by others. They were news givers, critics, counselors, and they lent a sensitive ear to their listeners, all the while taking liberties in their advice. Because most station owners were Anglo and often non–Spanish speakers, they did not know the liberties their DJs took in rallying their listeners to civil rights causes going on in the state. Hector García had used the medium successfully to bolster his American GI Forum and more recently to raise money for the lawyers. Spanish-language radio was also accessible to most Mexican Americans, and it was common for most stations to have call-in shows where listeners requested songs, sold secondhand items, and made commentaries on issues that affected them. Reformers found these radio stations great allies and a way to keep abreast of what was stirring up the community. While most stations promoted civic duty and responsibility, they nonetheless nurtured the community culture and motivated the people in the Texas barrios to take an active interest in what was going on around them.

Accompanying Cisneros was Anthony (Tony) García, director of Municipal Markets of San Antonio, who attended as an observer for the LULACs. He took vacation time and paid his own way to Washington. Gus wrote appreciatively of García's "moral support, encouragement, and his timely suggestions [which were] invaluable to us."[5] It is likely that Tony was a close friend and probably one of the officers of LULAC in San Antonio, which had been the first organization to provide the lawyers money for the appeal.

Chris Aldrete, state chairman of the American GI Forum, also accompanied the lawyers. Aldrete was part of the clique of reformers from the

San Antonio–Austin area who hung together and shared multiple organizational affiliations with the Mexican American community. A graduate of the University of Texas, he had been mentored by Sánchez as had been Cadena, Gus, and Hector García. A recent graduate of law school, he was not certified to litigate before the high court, but for years he would be known as part of the battery of lawyers who represented Hernández.

Rounding out the group was Manuel B. López of San Antonio, who at the time was serving in the Army and was stationed in Virginia. He served as the team's leg man and also became their guide in Washington.[6] While Cisneros represented the community, Tony the LULACs, and Aldrete the GI Forum, López represented the veterans, the military men and the young turks who would one day be expected to take over the reform activities. The entourage also reflected the excitement so many felt about getting a case, their case, before the Supreme Court. Like a car full of family members heading toward *el norte* to pick the crops, this family of reformers were just as anxious and hopeful that the experience would be fruitful. Whether they fully understood the risk is unclear, but in more sober moments, some—at least the lawyers—must have realized that an unfriendly ruling would set them back decades and basically undo what they had done in the lower courts on issues dealing with segregation in the public schools.

There, they had been able to slowly but steadily develop a framework that underscored that among Mexican Americans "separate but equal" was unconstitutional. They had found a niche between white and black. They had done so without having to fully rely on being either white or black— just simply different. They sensed a broader question was involved than simply an issue of who served in the jury box. Even the lawyers who came along primarily as observers understood that jury discrimination reflected broader contours in American society. Deeply conscious of appearance and perceptions—especially those of the larger society—they came to support and encourage the lawyers to victory, and to see if Mexican Americans would finally shed their invisible status. The judicial victory they envisioned included a more inquisitive and curious nation seeking to know more about them. New to the process at the national level, they expected results that were likely beyond the reach of the Court's ruling.

Of course, camaraderie played another part in this venture. These individuals were either friends or admirers of one another and they were anxious to share in both the process and the outcome. Despite their activities and the fact that they seemed to be everywhere, they were part of a rather small sector within the Mexican American community. As discussed earlier, these individuals were often differentiated from other Mexican Americans by their education, profession, by their loyalty to American ideals, and their willingness to see the border as a boundary between their community and Mexico. They did not so much feel disloyalty to their ancestry as they felt the need to find an identity for it. Because of this, they sought comfort and support from others such as themselves who shared these values and outlooks. They were an organizationally-focused group of individuals who were joiners of multiple organizations and who were mobile enough to respond to the call of those whom they admired. While often competitive with each other, nothing brought them together faster than when one of their kind was treated unequally. They collectively celebrated each other's triumphs in Anglo society and just as collectively felt the bitterness of their defeats.

The only records so far found on the activities in D.C. come from Gus's writings and from gossip and personal recollections. It is clear that the budget of over $3,000 went only so far. Gus chose the Mayflower Hotel, a first-class hotel at the time, which charged $10 per person. He (and probably Cadena) arrived first and then came Tony García, Herrera, and Cisneros. Aldrete came later. They later moved into a suite that cost them $36 per day, and in doing so saved themselves $1 per person per day. The suite was big enough to hold all of them even though some slept on the couch and others in a rollaway bed. The room also served as a meeting place to plan strategy and to talk about the historic mission on which the three lawyers and their entourage found themselves. They even managed to hold meetings with members of the press there.[7]

Thrift, however, was a principle followed only after Cadena and the others arrived in Washington. The story goes that Gus got there first and when the others arrived, he greeted them with food and liquor and even servers to be at their beck and call. Another story recounts that when they left D.C. the hotel bill was much more than they anticipated. Gus simply did not know how to suffer even though he would spend much time arguing that Mexican American lawyers were constantly subject to making do with less because of the people's unwillingness to pay more for the services they got. It is, of course, possible that he simply wanted to overcome any anxiety and any feeling among the lawyers and supporters that they might not belong there, which could well have been a prevalent feeling during the initial stages of the trip. He had even hoped to hire a public relations firm in Washington to "get national press coverage and all kinds of publicity."[8] Lack of money finally discouraged the plan.

In letters he wrote to Sánchez before arriving in D.C., Cadena expressed a slight frustration with Gus's antics. He was particularly worried about his friend's drinking, but had been assured that not one drop would be touched until after January 4, which is interesting since the arguments would not come until January 11.[9] Gus had even promised to take his mother and his wife, Nora, possibly as guarantees that he would not "make a jackass out of himself." Still, Cadena was unsure "how long he will continue in his present frame of mind."[10] In a more personal note, he told his former mentor of Gus's intemperance in style. "He is already talking about dressing up in striped trousers, cutaway coat, gray vest, and ascot tie," wrote Cadena. When he told Gus that he was simply wearing a nice dark blue suit, the former threatened not to share the argument before the court. "I told him that I didn't give a damn whether he presented an argument or not." Cadena then added that in actuality Gus could legitimately take the position that Hernández was his client.[11] In the end, Gus pared down his expectations and his clothing did not attract any excessive attention.

Novices to protocol at this level, they found assistance from a few people in Washington who offered to help. Harvey Rosenberg was a young lawyer from Texas who helped them get oriented to arguing before the high court. There was also Dennis Chávez, senior senator from New Mexico who made his staff available to the defense team, and Senator Lyndon Baines Johnson who provided courtesy support and Senator Price Daniels who ended up introducing them to the Supreme Court.[12] There was also Al Wirin. What these individuals attempted to do was provide the lawyers a crash course on the ways of the Supreme Court and, indirectly, a knowledge of how things worked at the nation's capital. As capable and knowledgeable as these lawyers were, they were rather uneducated to the way national politics worked. The Mexican American reformers' experience was ancillary at this stage. Though Gus felt confident about his abilities, he had only recently begun to participate in correspondence and meetings with national politicians and bureaucrats.

It is important to note that at this stage Mexican American reformers were in fact quite removed from the functions of civic government at the national level. Their connections came from knowing a few national politicians and corresponding with federal government bureaucrats about issues such as illegal immigration and the Bracero Program. Time after time, they would be surprised by how little they knew of national politics and how little influence they had upon it. Mexican Americans were simply not seen as a critical constituency in the national political arena. Far removed physically, electorally, and politically, they were often an afterthought when it came to making policy or establishing legal precedence. For these reasons, it was critical to understand the culture and the protocol of the Court and the way things were seen in Washington.

Of course, in the end, the most important aspect of the case began earlier when the court made the decision to accept the case, and when the briefs were filed. It has often been implied that Earl Warren, whose court would be known for its liberal leanings and its landmark civil rights decisions, had been responsible for the case being heard. But as mentioned before, Warren had yet to take his position on the Court when the first consideration of the merits of the appeal were being discussed. It was the leftover members of the Vinson Court who made the decision, and that decision reflected the direction of the Court even before Warren took over as chief justice. Even though several members, like Hugo Black and Tom Clark, had been seen as resistant to integration and African American civil rights, in actuality they had gone along with other more liberal members of the court on enough occasions to change the temperament of the Supreme Court.[13]

Warren would reinforce the move in that direction and contribute greatly to the further expansion of civil rights. What made him do so? Much has been said about the profound regret he experienced after having actively promoted, as California attorney general, the internment of hundreds of thousands of Japanese Americans during World War II.[14] What has been less discussed is the fact that as both attorney general and governor of California he had witnessed the debates and the struggles over Mexican American civil rights in the state. He was governor of the state when *Mendez v. Westminster School District* had been decided in 1947, and was already in politics when the Lemon Grove incident became a major issue in regards to Mexican American children's segregation in the public schools. And he had witnessed the efforts to put on the ballot a measure to include Mexican Americans into the group of legally segregated populations. There is then, no question that Warren was aware of Mexican Americans and their struggles in addition to the knowledge that he had about African American civil rights efforts. He carried with him the memory of the Japanese internment, the struggles of Mexican Americans in California, and the civil rights battles of African Americans, and showed a propensity for moderate Republican politics that tended to be less race-conscious than that of the hardcore conservatives of both parties.[15]

Of course, we know all of this after the fact, but Pete's lawyers were not privy to such knowledge. Unfortunately no record exists of what they expected or how they strategized. There is likely to have been much discussion about the momentous opportunity they had been given and no doubt there were some misgivings about going to argue before the Court with only rudimentary knowledge of what went on there. The only thing

we know of this period is the aforementioned discussion of Gus's preparedness and fitness to be part of the effort. Being appropriate and proper was
of utmost importance to this generation of Mexican American reformers,
and the lingering doubts concerning Gus would surely have worried many
a friend and admirer. Yet, any doubts regarding their preparedness were,
to the lawyers' good fortune, outside of the justices' understanding of the
case. What they knew came from the documents submitted, particularly
the brief.

In that brief, Cadena sought to squarely question the legitimacy of the
Texas Court of Criminal Appeal's reasoning on the notions of due process
and equal protection by arguing that the court misinterpreted the Fourteenth Amendment and misconstrued the petitioner's appeal. The citizens
of Jackson County, wrote Cadena, had taken it upon themselves—through
their jury commissioners—to exclude persons of Mexican descent from
juries. Because the Texas statutory schemes governing juries was fair on its
face and capable of being carried out without discrimination, the citizens
of the county were in fact creating for themselves an authority that had not
been given them by any administrative or executive decree and thus they
had denied the petitioner due process.[16]

The Court of Criminal Appeals, by recognizing only two protected
classes within the Fourteenth Amendment, was in fact denying Hernández the equal protection of said amendment. "Petitioner," wrote Cadena,
"has found no decision by this Court, by the lower federal courts, or by
the courts of any state which supported a two-class interpretation of the
Equal Protection Clause." In its only expression dealing with a group not
of African descent, the Court, in *Strauder v. West Virginia*, had declared: "if
a law be passed excluding all naturalized Celtic Irishmen, would there be
any doubt of its inconsistency with the spirit of the amendment?"[17] In *Yick
Wo v. Hopkins* the Court had declared that the provisions of the Fourteenth
Amendment were universal in their application, to all persons under the
territorial jurisdiction, without regard to any differences of race, of color,
or of nationality.[18]

The Texas court, continued the brief, was reading into the Fourteenth
Amendment a limitation that did not exist, and in fact was contradicting a
ruling it had made twenty-five years earlier. In *Juarez v. State*, the Texas court
had ruled unconstitutional the systematic exclusion of Roman Catholics
from jury duty.[19] "Careful reading of the opinion has uncovered no facts
even tending to show that the defendant in that case was a *Negro* Roman
Catholic," wrote Cadena. Of course, Cadena knew that Juarez was in fact
a Mexican American, but he continued his line of thought by pointing

out that his brief to the Texas court had pointed out the discrepancy of the rulings in *Juarez* and *Hernández* but the court had simply ignored the discrepancy.[20]

"In order to explain the *Juarez* decision," continued the brief, "the two classes theory, through some process of asexual inbreeding, must give birth to a third class."[21] Would the two-classes theory be extended to cases involving discrimination in the field of education? asked Cadena. Lower courts had ruled no in two cases dealing with Mexican American children in both Arizona and California, and even earlier the Texas Court of Civil Appeals had ruled that segregation of Mexican children violated the Fourteenth Amendment.[22] In *Clifton v. Puente*, the Texas court ruled that the Constitution forbade judicial enforcement of a covenant prohibiting sale of land to persons of Mexican descent.[23] It was only the Texas Court of Criminal Appeals, wrote Cadena, that had ever applied the two-classes theory to discrimination or segregation in cases involving Mexican Americans. And there simply was no apparent reason for the application of a unique rule in the jury exclusion cases.

The Fourteenth Amendment did not mention juries, it simply provided that no state shall deny to any person within its jurisdiction the equal protection of the laws. Cadena added that no restrictive adjective followed the word "person."[24] Here, Cadena was embarking on what had become a strategy used by Mexican American reformers to isolate Texas from the rest of the nation, and imply that the state was so backward on race and civil rights issues that its practices should be rejected as standards for the rest of the nation. Without having experienced life in the deep South, they could make claims that Texas was the worst state in the union in terms of racism, though those claims would not be far from the truth. More important, by creating such a view of the state, they could then be seen as victims of a state system so outdated and so backward looking that the rest of the nation could not help but react positively to their appeals. This strategy, of course, was made possible by the fact that many across the nation viewed Texas as a cowboy frontier with racist populists, fundamentalist bible-swearing country folk, and ignorant and corrupt politicians.

Mexican Americans, in essence, presented themselves as an enlightened population that was more American than Texan and that was ready to join the rest of the Union with a little help from the courts. What they did not realize, however, was that part of the backward appearance of Texas—at least in the mind of some—was due to the fact that Texas was full of cows, bibles, and Mexicans. Non-Texans might criticize the Lone Star State for its treatment of Mexicans but the criticism was based on the ridiculous nature of Texans and not on sympathy for the victims. Most Americans in the 1950s were rather oblivious of Mexican Americans beyond the stereotypes they saw in Western movies. Still, the strategy allowed those Anglo judges and politicians willing to move beyond the white supremacy of the 1950s to find a crevice in the legal and social system that they could use to move toward a more liberal notion of race relations by being sensitive to the concerns of Mexican Americans.

Cadena then went from criticizing the Texas Appeals Court to asking what was so sacred about discrimination in the organization of juries that the court would consistently maintain an interpretation not in accordance with the original intent. No federal court provided support for this interpretation and the Texas Court of Civil Appeals had actually discarded the notion of a two-class theory in its rulings on public school segregation. Citing several other cases, he pointed out that the federal courts and the Supreme Court had rejected jury exclusion of members of political parties or factions, of daily wage earners, of women in certain circumstances, of Catholics, and other groups. "Petitioner admits that in those cases the decisions were based on the fact that the exclusions shown amounted to an improper administration of justice," wrote Cadena, "but in these cases this Court was concerned with upholding the tradition that trial by jury contemplates an impartial jury from a cross section of the community."[25] Then Cadena pointed out that the Court had underscored that jury competence was an individual rather than a class matter. To do otherwise meant that a whole class of people would be excluded from the jury system and that would preclude a fair trial for a certain sector of the population.

"Can it be said," wrote Cadena, "that in a county where, over a period of twenty five years, no persons of Mexican descent have been called for jury service, a person of such descent is afforded a trial by a fair and impartial jury?"[26] At this juncture the brief introduced several studies by academicians and social workers that charged that in Texas, Mexican Americans were subject to discrimination in employment, jury service, in access to public swimming pools, parks, and other recreational facilities, and in the public school system. As recently as two years earlier, the State Board of Education had needed to issue an order specifically directing compliance with a 1948 Federal Court ruling that described public school segregation of Mexican American children as a violation of the Fourteenth Amendment.[27]

It was against this background, continued Cadena, that the Supreme Court had to evaluate the notion set forth by the Texas court that Hernández was demanding special privileges as a special class within the white race in the organization of juries. Yet, wrote Cadena, the only special privilege being requested was the right to be free from discrimination in the selection of juries. Besides, he argued, all whites had the right to sit on juries, why could not Mexican Americans? How [would] elimination of discrimination against persons of Mexican descent give to this special class any special privileges that were not enjoyed by other members of the white race in Jackson County? Hernández was not requesting proportional representation in the jury box, and ruling affirmatively in his case would no more make that a reality than past rulings in favor of Negroes and Roman Catholics had created proportional representation in juries for those two groups.[28]

In essence, the Texas court had created and then attempted to demolish a straw man of its own creation. Cadena saw it as wildly ironic that the Texas court attempted to make Mexican Americans part of the dominant class in Texas, but did so by upholding the right of their exclusion. The battle here was in reality not as much about inclusion as it was about battling exclusion. The Texas court was engaging in racial classifications by making Mexican Americans white in privileges but still allowing their exclusion by fact of their membership in the white class. If the Texas legislature, wrote Cadena, passed a statute excluding persons of Mexican descent from jury service, the courts would inevitably rule it unconstitutional; how then could the jury commissioners of Jackson County do what the legislators could not?[29]

This was a critical point in defining the civil rights struggles of Mexican Americans as one of peoples and ways of life. The legal and political system was an accomplice to that struggle but not always the initiator. Mexican Americans confronted a harsh society and its limitations because most Anglo Americans did not care for them, yet could not find a way to define them in a more legally constricted way. Legal treaties were in part responsible for that, but so was the Anglo ambivalence as to where exactly Mexicans fit in a racial context. Even some Mexican-haters were willing to allow them their whiteness and to see them as human. In fact, their humanity was rarely an issue although their evolution was. Whites, unable to easily categorize Mexican Americans, thus promoted a cultural and social standard that most Mexican Americans found difficult to meet.

Challenging the white masses's ability to make the law on their own was the one way to attack de facto discrimination and facilitate the reformers' ability to counter it. In doing so they directly challenged what David Montejano has called the "culture of segregation and inferiority" that had developed over the last half century in Texas and other parts of the Southwest.[30] They wanted the high court to understand this nuance so that a lack of de jure discrimination would not hamper their case.

Jury discrimination cases by the mid-century were now all instances of de facto prejudices even in the case for African Americans. Consequently, *Norris v. Alabama* had become the key case in dealing with jury discrimination, at least in the minds of Cadena and the other defense lawyers. Based on *Norris*, the appellant only had to prove that there were eligible individuals to serve on juries and they were not being considered for jury duty. Cadena then posed the question to the court: "Does the rule of *Norris v. Alabama* apply to a case involving exclusion of persons of Mexican descent from jury service?" Given the declaration by the Texas Court of Criminal Appeals that the Supreme Court did not equate nationality with race, then there really was one rule of evidence for Negroes and a different rule of evidence for Mexican Americans. While African Americans only had to prove exclusion from juries to claim discrimination, Mexican Americans had to show expressed discrimination. No effort, wrote Cadena, "was made to disguise the fact that this denial is based solely and exclusively on the fact that this petitioner is not a Negro." Thus, he continued, the state courts had set a requirement or classification based solely and exclusively on race.[31]

He continued, "By making the outcome of a case depend on the applicability of the rule of evidence and by making the applicability of the rule of evidence depend on the race or color of a litigant, the Texas court has made the outcome of a case depend on the race of the accused."[32] It was clear to Cadena that the conviction in the case would have been reversed if Pete Hernández had been a Negro but it was being affirmed because he was Mexican. Could anyone believe, he asked, that the Fourteenth Amendment not only permitted but actually compelled that incongruous rule of law? Here, Cadena was allowing the polar opposites of black and white to create a space somewhere in between where Mexican Americans could fit. While he sought to keep Mexican Americans within the scope of whiteness because that was the only possible winning strategy, he did not, as some would argue later, simply try to make Mexican Americans white, undistinguishable from the larger white society.

Admittedly, he got very close because he needed to break the black/white binary in the interpretation of the Fourteenth Amendment and to do so he needed to challenge both sides of that duality. He had, in the earlier brief to the Texas Court of Criminal Appeals, challenged the white aspect of the binary by pointing out how Mexican Americans had been marginalized and in fact colorized by their treatment in the larger Texas society and within the state judicial system. In essence they had been found wanting in regards to their whiteness, and had been judged children of a lesser white god. But having been pushed toward blackness—not legally but socially and culturally—they were now being denied the rights that even African Americans were supposed to have. Consequently, Cadena was forced to navigate between the two polar opposites and find a niche somewhere in between.

His challenge was to find an equal footing at the level of Negro rights, and then work toward finding it again at the higher level of white rights. To do so, he needed to get as close to whiteness as he could. African Americans were the beneficiaries of Constitutional protection, and while not the only group to receive such special protection, they were the most identifiable. But those special protections were not supposed to be meted out on the backs of other groups, especially those groups considered white. Citing *Oyama v. California* and *Buchanan v. Warley*, Cadena pointed out that the Constitution also prohibited discrimination against whites.[33]

Even if, wrote Cadena, the Fourteenth Amendment did recognize only two classes—whites and Negroes—it did not, however, sanction discrimination against other white persons by imposing on them a higher burden of proof than that demanded of African Americans. More important, the Texas Court of Criminal Appeals, acting as a judicial tribunal could not escape the reach of the Fourteenth Amendment's prohibition against discrimination. Cadena further argued, "a state court cannot, by adopting a discriminatory rule of evidence, weave a protective cloak behind which local jury commissioners can continue to disregard the plain mandates of the Fourteenth Amendment."[34] In his conclusion, Cadena went back to attacking the validity of the two-classes theory. "While the Texas Court elaborates on its two-classes theory, in Jackson County and in other areas in Texas, persons of Mexican descent are treated as a third class—a notch above the Negroes, perhaps, but several notches below the rest of the population."[35]

This third class condemned them to segregation in schools, denial of services in public places, exclusion from non-Negro restrooms, and to absence from the jury box. This exclusion was upheld by a court that reminded them that they were members of the dominant white class. Continued Cadena, "they are told that they are assured of a fair trial at the hands of persons who do not want to go to school with them, do not want to give them services in public places, do not want to sit on juries with them, and who would prefer not to share rest room facilities with them."[36] Cadena concluded by reminding the high court that Texas was more than proportionally represented in cases in which nondiscriminatory statutes were used to discriminate against certain groups. In order to defend that practice, the Texas court had concocted the two-classes theory and accused the petitioner of seeking special privileges, but in fact the court sought to interpret that theory in a way that excluded Mexican Americans. Cadena ended with a quote from *Hirabayashi v. United States*, which declared that "distinctions between citizens solely because of their ancestry are by their very nature odious to a free people whose institutions are founded upon the doctrine of equality."[37]

As an accompanying document, Cadena summarized in part several of the works submitted as textbooks within the list of authorities. The document emphasized four points: (1) the Spanish-Mexican people had been in the Southwest for over 300 years; (2) Mexican Americans were marginalized after the U.S.–Mexican War; (3) between 1870 and 1920 thousands of Mexicans crossed the border to find a new home in the United States; and finally, (4) that they were treated as, and were in fact, a "class apart." Cadena emphasized that while legally white, the Mexican American was anthropologically Indian and treated more this way by the society in which he lived and by several government agencies that kept tabs on their numbers and their actions. Since 1930 the Census Bureau had been collecting data that distinguished between the two segments of the white population.[38]

Cadena went on to cite other works and government reports that also implied that Mexican Americans were sufficiently different from other whites that it was necessary to categorize them separately and to create specific reports on them. The document went on to note that even the state of Texas had accepted this when a governor in the 1940s had seen fit to issue a proclamation, and the state legislature had adopted a joint resolution, recognizing that Mexican Americans were subjected to discrimination.[39] Those efforts had gone for naught but they nonetheless stood as examples of how Texas society, state agencies, and even federal agencies as well as academicians recognized that Mexican Americans were in fact a "class apart."

Pete's lawyers had set out to marginalize the two-classes theory of the Texas Court of Criminal Appeals, to place Mexican Americans within the polar opposites of black/white, strengthen their rights to jury duty vis-a-vis African Americans, and finally show that academicians, government leaders, and intellectual writers recognized without any qualms that Mexican Americans were in fact a class apart. It is quite likely—since no record exists—that Cadena and Gus were quite happy with their brief and how they structured their arguments. Cadena would later say, speaking of the two-classes theory, "the objective sought by the attorneys for the defendant Hernández was the destruction and eradication of such a dangerous and insupportable legal fallacy. That objective was achieved."[40] There was confidence in the declaration.

Much more confidence it seems than in the opposing brief filed by the Texas attorney general's office, which provided a lackluster defense of the Texas court's ruling. It attempted to dismiss the appeal as much ado about nothing, something many Texans would have understood, as they too believed that much of what Mexican Americans protested was simply unimportant or revealed an exaggerated view of their victimization. But even before this approach it sought to highlight the shortcomings of the *Hernández* legal team by pointing out to the Court that the defense's petition had been submitted one day late and was in typewritten rather than printed copy. Late filing, said the brief in opposition, should have denied petitioner jurisdiction in this matter.[41] "Respondent submits," continued the brief, "that this Court should not be required to take cognizance of this matter because same is of no importance beyond its own particular facts and has been correctly decided on adequate state grounds irrespective of any federal questions discussed."[42] "Of no importance beyond its own particular facts," simply meant that the case was not important except to a few Mexican American reformers who were always advocating or protesting something. "Irrespective of any federal questions," meant to clearly point out that Texas knew better how to deal with its Mexicans.[43] In any case, the state lawyers accused the defense of overestimating the evidence and reaching for conclusions that were unwarranted from the facts.

Nowhere, argued the state lawyers, did the defense show that any plan had been worked out or purpose pursued toward keeping those "white persons characterized by him as Mexican or Latin American" from serving on juries in Jackson County, Texas.[44] They reiterated that Hernández was white, the jury was composed of white men, and no actual exclusion of the white race was shown. To follow the defense argument, they wrote, was to divide the white race into blondes, brunettes, redheads, left handers, right handers, Protestants and Catholics, etc., and that would so encumber the jury system as to utterly ruin it.[45] Furthermore, argued the state lawyers, the only perfect jury would be the one that acquitted the accused and every jury that convicted would be censured by the criminal found guilty.

In conclusion the state lawyers reminded the Supreme Court that Pete Hernández had murdered Joe Espinoza with malice and that both the perpetrator and the victim were of Latin American origin, thus indicating no denial of equal protection of law as might be otherwise vaguely inferred if the victim had been of some other national origin.[46] In plain words, they were saying that if the victim had been Anglo or another nationality, the jury might have had reason to discriminate but in this case it seemed ludicrous to believe that the all-white jury would have had any particular reason for being unfair to Hernández since he killed another Mexican American. Finally, the lawyers declared that using surnames to show that no Mexican Americans had served in the jury system was simply inaccurate because many Mexican Americans had Anglo names. With that, the stage was set for the oral arguments.

The anticipation of appearing before the Supreme Court in early January of 1954 took its toll on the lawyers, particularly Gus, who reverted back to the bottle as he often had before. While there are no records or any public acknowledgement of its authenticity there is a story that has survived for more than fifty years about the early morning of the day of the trial. It seems that Gus went out drinking the night before and came back to the hotel room in the very early hours of the day completely drunk, unable to walk, much less utter a coherent sentence. It was exactly the scenario that Ed Idar and other critics of Gus (both in LULAC and the American GI Forum) feared. Time and time again they had seen Gus either in celebration or depression consume too much alcohol and lose all sense of equilibrium. Whatever emotions Cadena and Herrera and the rest of the party must have had were quickly subsumed to the task of getting Gus ready for the court appearance.[47]

Cadena, Herrera, and others quickly began pouring coffee down Gus's mouth, unclothed him, and got him into the shower. How long they kept him in there or how much coffee they poured into him is not clear, but they did manage to get him dressed and ready to at least walk under his own power to the courthouse. During the time they spent doing this it probably dawned on them that they were confronting the most important case of their—and every other Mexican American reformer's—careers. All the work that had gone before and all their own efforts came down to about an hour's time in front of the most important judicial body in the nation. Even if they gave it their best, and availed themselves of the resources that others had used in the past when approaching the high court, there was no guarantee that they could succeed. But here they were, with few financial resources, no amici briefs, no experience, no Latino legal precedence in their favor, and their top gun at oratory was completely drunk and seemingly unable to undertake the argument of his life.

We don't know what went on in their minds or if they engaged in the infighting that often breaks out among novices before a major event. What we do know is that Cadena and Herrera were probably the right people to have on the team in time of crisis. Herrera was a veteran of numerous political fights, and he rarely seemed intimidated by Anglos or by the structures of power in American society. Because he knew not to take himself too seriously, he could step back and assess a situation as well as anyone. He also knew Gus well and had known him to come through at crucial moments. Cadena seemed to have that quiet resolve that people of great character often do. He was quiet, humble, and methodical. He also knew how to meet his obligations well. It is likely that he assessed the situation and made up his mind to prepare Gus, but at the same time to be prepared to go it alone, if necessary. It could only have been by destiny that these three men had come together. The political genius, the rhetorical giant, and the brilliant legal mind all came to play their part in this historical drama. Herrera's steadiness and Cadena's meticulous preparation were ready to take over if Gus could not rise to the occasion.

In reality, Gus represented an ace in the hole, an uncommon ally to carry the point through its legal and social end. In a courtroom that saw many of the great legal minds of the past century and a half, but which rarely saw them deliver rousing presentations, Gus was an anomaly, because cases here were won by great briefs, not by inspiring presentations. It is safe to say that among the great legal minds of the Mexican American community—and there were few besides Cadena who fit that category—Gus was a strange choice, though no one doubted his courtroom presence. Convincing a jury of everyday folks was quite different than impressing a group of men steeped in law. These men had heard it all and they distrusted those who were more comfortable in show-and-tell presentations than in writing their arguments within the context of written law. They were also men limited by how they understood constitutional law, and while their biases were often apparent, unlike a regular jury, they had to justify their decisions in crafted words that were to be scrutinized and debated by lawyers, journalists, legal scholars, and the civic-minded.

Yet, Cadena and Herrera understood Gus's ability to contextualize the arguments and to give them meaning. They understood that American jurisprudence had no frame of reference when it came to Mexican Americans, as became quite clear from the questions that the judges asked during the legal arguments. They, along with the rest of the nation, did not really have a place for Mexican Americans in their legal structures and in their political culture. Far too often Mexican Americans had been the subject of an occasional story in *Look* or *Life* magazine, or periodically showed up in a government report commenting on their poverty or legal status, but the black/white binary in the legal literature simply discounted them as a case and point in law. Gus had the potential to change that because he had a way of underscoring that Mexican Americans were a people and that they had dreams, and had worked and fought for those dreams. When he spoke about Mexican Americans, it was difficult to continue to see them as a distant minority likely to fade into oblivion as other small minority groups in the country had done in the past. He knew how to give life to a group that had often not enjoyed one in American society.

It was more than friendship then that made Cadena and Herrera much more patient with Gus than their fellow reformers. Though given every opportunity to do so, Cadena rarely engaged in criticism of his law partner and always gave him ample credit for what was accomplished in the case. Herrera would be Gus's friend until the end, using his resources and his moral support to help his friend and colleague stay above water. While sobering him up they surely understood that they could go on without him but would not be able to accomplish their task fully without him. Gus had a way of infusing confidence—when people did not worry about whether he would show up—and getting to the heart of every argument. It was his bravado that had initially made them feel that they could actually come to D.C. and win a case before the Supreme Court.

That confidence was somewhat subdued when the actual litigation began, causing Sarah McClendon, a well-known journalist from Texas, to write that Gus sat through the first part of the arguments like a sad-faced bull fighter.[48] In contrast, Cadena methodically and less flamboyantly argued that the Fourteenth Amendment already prohibited the exclusion of Mexican Americans from jury service, and added that he found it ironic that the Texas courts would deny that right by "reminding us that we are white." He continued, "we are glad to be considered legally white, but we want actually to be so considered legally and socially."[49] Here Cadena underscored the need to put some social context to the law as it applied to Mexican Americans. The fact that the *Hernández* case was in essence dealing with de facto discrimination meant that the justices had to understand the social context. Here he repeated the arguments in the brief about how Mexican Americans were treated and why they had in fact been racialized in the way they were treated.

Following Cadena's arguments, numerous questions were asked, and in McClendon's reporting this is when Gus came alive. Revealing their ignorance of Mexican Americans—in spite of the fact that Tom Clark was from Texas—the justices asked whether Mexican Americans were newcomers in Jackson County and whether they could even speak English well enough to serve on a jury. Gus quickly responded, "Your honor my people were in Texas one hundred years before Sam Houston arrived there." Shortly afterward, he referred to the famous Texas hero as the "wetback" from Tennessee.[50] Gus the politician, however, knew better than to let such a statement stand once back in Texas, and so he clarified that this was said in a jocular vein. He did maintain, however, that all Anglo Americans who settled in Texas were seen as "uncouth foreigners [and] Johnny-come-lately by the rather snobbish Spanish-speaking families (like mine) who had settled Texas in the eighteenth century."[51]

Admitting that he enjoyed deprecating his society-conscious relatives—he came from an old elite border family—he added that he had a soft spot for two Anglos, Sam Houston and Jim Bowie. He liked them because they were unabashed adventurers and they had demonstrated in the most emphatic manner possible that they harbored no notions of racial superiority.[52] This bit of interpretation would be challenged by future historians, but it clearly revealed that Gus admired self-made men who left their mark on history—something he probably saw himself doing. Of course, the way he flung around the statement before the court also revealed his propensity for outrageous statements.

There is no record of any outrageous acts before the high court but the *San Antonio Light* account described an emboldened lawyer ready and willing to answer any and all of the questions put to him with both sarcasm and wit. When Justice Frankfurter inquired whether the brief was accurate in indicating that Latin Americans really lived in Jackson County and not been called to jury duty, Gus emphatically answered in the affirmative. When Texan Justice Clark pointed out that only 6 percent of the Mexican American population in the county were freeholders and thus eligible for jury service, Gus rebutted with "evidently the justice is not aware that in Texas the law does not require a man to hold a poll tax to serve on a petit jury." This was certainly a dig at a man who should have known better.[53]

When Chief Justice Warren inquired as to whether Mexican Americans would assimilate into American society, Gus responded, "we hope so," but then quickly turned the question into a reproach to whites in the Lone Star State: "But two or three places in Texas are giving us plenty of trouble." He then assured the Chief Justice that, given a chance to serve on juries, Mexicans would not dodge jury service as so many white people did.[54] Here Gus reverted back to an old Mexican American reformer strategy of trying to paint Mexican Americans as even more fully committed to their civic duty and their citizenship role than the traditional population.

This was the "Mexican Americans have to be more Americans than others" rationalization so often used by reformers to spur their constituents to be more concerned about their obligations.

The newspaper account described the oral arguments as filled with some dramatic instances interrupted frequently by questions from the justices.[55] There is unfortunately no way to know what these other questions were, but it is likely that they simply sought clarification of some of the points made by Cadena in his brief and by Gus's free-flowing oratory. All of this interaction could not have gone any better than if it had been planned beforehand by Pete's attorneys. The questions, particularly those asked by Warren, allowed Gus extra time to talk, making it one of the few times that the Supreme Court permitted an attorney more than the allotted time.[56] This extra time, of course, became legendary and would be a point cited for years afterward to underscore Gus's abilities.[57]

The attention given the defense's arguments may well have signaled to the State that their side of the argument was not likely to be key to the decision. Whatever decision was given would simply depend on the strength of the defense's position. The newspaper coldly reported that against the array of Latin American talent, the Texas attorney general office sent just one man, Assistant Attorney General Horace Wimberly.[58] All the state lawyer could muster was, "we in Texas regret the situation as we want to live in peace with our neighbors. We deny, however, there was discrimination against the Latin American race."[59] Gus must have felt like screaming with joy at the top of his lungs in response to the state's horrific misspeak. Given a chance to rebut the State's statement, he pointed out that Wimberly had described the Latin Americans as a race. This he added, was another sign of discrimination, or better said an indication that the state wanted it both ways, describing Mexican Americans as either another race or as white, depending on political or legal expediency.

Gus's performance was as virtuosic as only he could have dreamt it. He was serious, aggressive, historical, scholarly, and he even got a chance to make the justices laugh—possibly all except for the Texan Clark—when he declared in his part-humorous, part-indignant tone that "when Mexicans comprise fourteen percent of the population and no Mexican is called for jury duty in over twenty five years there must be a white man in the wood pile somewhere."[60] In the end, he, with the assistance of Cadena and Herrera, had created a picture of Mexican Americans as a community struggling to assume its role as citizens of the United States, and one that had the legal skill, intellect, and oratorical talent to ably present its case before the highest court in the land.

It should be noted that both Cadena and Gus recognized the role that Herrera played in the process even without writing or speaking a word. Gus captured well Herrera's contribution when he wrote, "it was he who kept our heads level when we were bombarded by questions from some of the justices, particularly the Honorable Tom C. Clark." Herrera had simply juggled the notes, the points, and the suggestions, serving as the reservoir of political, cultural, and social knowledge and calming them when the questions had become pointed.[61] Gus made a special effort to point out that neither Cadena or Herrera ever received the full credit due to them. Part of the reason for those two not getting the credit they deserved was that the case was heard one hour earlier than anticipated, and most newspaper reporters were not present when Cadena made his opening arguments. Still, Gus was satisfied with the coverage, as limited as it was.

He felt that the points had been made and that the justices had heard what they needed to hear. He was impressed by Cadena's presentation and fully satisfied with his own effort at knocking down stereotypes and misconceptions and with his ability to quickly rebut misstatements and pointed questions. It must have been particularly satisfying to have diminished any damage that the less-than-friendly justice from Texas, Tom Clark, could inflict with his questions. While Gus and company probably understood that the Vincent Court had been moderating its views toward civil rights, it was not a unanimous decision to move in that direction. Yet, here Pete's lawyers had been able to introduce satisfactorily—in their minds at least—the notion that the law of the land was inclusive of Mexican Americans and its protection was not something that simply rubbed off because of their proximity to African Americans in a number of issues.

It is interesting to note that in the only available taped discussion of the case after the arguments before the Supreme Court, both Gus and Herrera emphasized something other than the merits of the case. Speaking of the case at a San Antonio radio station, Herrera reminisced—only a couple of days after the court appearance—of how proud he felt seeing Cadena and Gus speaking before the nine judges in the nation's premier courtroom. "Two of our own," said Herrera, "showing what we can do." At that moment he remembered all the Mexican American boys who had fought for the country less than a decade before. This case, he said, would show the world that the Mexican American was capable and that he belonged.[62] Gus, in his discussion of the case emphasized the same theme, praising Cadena's brilliance and Herrera's valuable input, crediting him with keeping them in focus. As a team they had made their community proud and shown their abilities and struck a blow against segregation and discrimination.

The show's host offered no questions but simply allowed his guests full access to the microphone. Anyone listening who knew little about the details of the case would have been baffled by what was going on. Of course, loyal listeners would probably have heard about the case numerous times. But for many Mexican Americans, including the lawyers, the case was about more than Pete Hernández or serving on juries. The fact was that few of them would ever be accused of murder or be called to serve on a jury. For those listeners who were not U.S. citizens the latter was not a possibility. What was important then, was the fact that a team of Mexican American reformers had earned the right to advocate for their kind before the nation's highest court. That, in itself, was a major victory and a favorable ruling would be an even greater one.

Herrera sounded optimistic, almost sure of a victory, while Gus seemed more cautious, expressing hope that the Court would see the merits of the case.[63] The caution was characteristic of Gus. While he often boasted of what he could do and what was possible, he tried always to be appropriate, gracious, and humble, and allow his actions to speak for themselves and allow others to heap on the praise. Caution, however, also came from experience, as he had been involved in numerous cases and actions where complete victory rarely came, and where partial victories always brought a backlash by those in power who sought to evade reform. A favorable ruling by the Supreme Court would put reformers in Texas in a powerful position to combat discrimination. It would put the final touch on their judicial struggle to end all forms of sanctioned discrimination. There would be no appeal for the foes of reform.

Why was pride in a job well done so important for Gus, Herrera, and other reformers? The answer can only be understood within the context of how they saw themselves and their community. The fact that the Mexican community had a more fluid relationship with Anglo Americans than did African Americans, meant that the concept of merit remained always a fundamental characteristic in Mexican-Anglo relations. Mexican Americans knew they could accomplish much within American society—there always were examples of those who had, and Anglos seemed always to leave the door open enough to create a few opportunities and many illusions. Also, relationships between the two races were always tempered by class status, money, political connections, geography, and demography.

This fluidity promised much for the individual but rarely provided the same opportunity to the group. Reformers by the nature of how they saw society were always looking for collective openings and opportunities. Lawyers, doctors, businesspeople had all shown that it was possible to slip through some doors, but all these doors were entered only through a merit system developed by Anglo Texans. This merit system was complicated and sometimes insidious and extremely difficult to navigate for the mass of Mexican Americans. Reformers had been trying for decades to find the right formula for a collective group elevation, and had only in the last five years discovered the notion of veteranism. This veteranism sought to make all Mexican Americans worthy of citizenship and full rights through the effort of thousands of their kind who had fought in World War II.

The problem appeared, nonetheless, when Mexican Americans had to prove that they belonged once they were in, and that they could carry the burden of citizenship despite the limitations imposed on them by the larger society. The lawyers themselves proved to be "Exhibit A" to those limitations. They had college degrees, and were certified to litigate, but they continued to attract only poor clients, had no chance of landing an important partnership, and rarely were their losing cases granted an appeal. Gus could speak before the United Nations and correspond with the president's cabinet, but at the end of the day he still returned to his limited practice and his precarious economic situation.[64]

Cadena, the brilliant legal scholar, taught in a small school where he belatedly got the recognition he deserved and continued to struggle to find career stability until late in his life when he was appointed to the Fourth District Court of Appeals after considerable political pressures. It was an important attainment and one he very justly deserved, but one for which he was not groomed in a traditional manner, and for which he had to depend on a number of twists and turns in Texas politics.[65] This never meant that he did not earn his status, only that he could not simply depend on things taking their course to reward him for his merit.

It was thus important that every public legal or social victory be promoted as a group victory and that Mexican Americans take advantage of whatever disruption occurred in the society in which they lived. The reality was, however, that few Mexican Americans were in a position to take advantage of opportunities—and Gus and other reformers understood this. This made it imperative that the victories keep coming, and they be larger and last longer than the ones that had come before.

At the individual and elite level, it meant carrying the burden of the race on their shoulders. Each individual victory then had to be repeated continually because they had such finite legacies. Lawyers in particular understood this; they had achieved numerous legal triumphs over the last decade, and yet segregation and discrimination remained rampant in Texas, California, and much of the West and Midwest. Yet, here seemed the opportunity to strike a major blow for Mexican American civil rights. No longer would their issues be overshadowed by the black/white binary of American legal and civil rights thought. In part their innocence and in part their hope provided them the sense that things would be different this time around. Seeing this opportunity come without the resources and time that African American reformers had invested seemed like a real coup to the three civil rights lawyers, and so they reveled in their triumph.

Lamentation, Deportation, and Integration for "Mexicans"

As soon as the oral arguments ended, Cadena flew back home to his teaching duties. Whether he was too conscientious to miss class or whether he had little choice, he did not stay to celebrate or bask in the glory of the momentous occasion. Herrera may have wanted to stay but a nasty fall on an icy sidewalk while wearing his high-heeled boots forced him back to Houston for examination and treatment. The other members of the party also returned home, except for Tony García. Tony accompanied Gus to New York City, although unlike Gus, he stayed only one day. But before he went to New York, Gus had already made his rounds in Washington, D.C., visiting senators and "prominent congressmen" to talk about the problems that Mexican Americans faced. It is difficult to know who accompanied Gus, though it probably included Herrera, Cadena, and Aldrete before the end of the oral arguments and possibly Tony García shortly after the court hearing.[1]

This small contingency of reformers pointed out to those who would listen that there was a "wetback" problem; there were virtually no Spanish-speaking persons in American embassies in Latin America; and no Latin Americans in the military mission to Spain, where Generalismo Franco now governed with an iron fist.[2] Gus had no high expectations that anyone would be swayed by this "very insignificant pressure group" but believed that it was their responsibility to "explain, suggest and protest" and not let things be "lost by default."[3] Gus, mostly by himself after García left, also visited the American Civil Liberties Union, the Anti-Defamation League of B'nai B'rith, the Japanese American Citizens League, the Rockefeller Foundation, the American Federation of Labor, the Marshall Trust Foundation, and the Congress of Industrial Organizations, as well as other organizations that had, in the past, shown an interest in the problems of Mexican Americans.[4]

From them he heard what he probably already knew; Mexican Americans had to establish national organizations with lobbyists in Washington, D.C., and in the state capitals where they constituted a sizeable population. In a sarcastic note, he pointed out that these unofficial advisors told him that it would be a simple matter of every person "of our ethnic group" contributing a pittance to the "cause" and this way the organization would "amass a great fund." "I smiled and told them that they didn't know Mexicans," he later wrote.[5] Gus felt the necessity of instructing his fellow reformers about organization building and the sacrifices it required to have a truly national entity. He already belonged to the two "national" organizations in the barrios of the Southwest, the American GI Forum and LULAC, but neither of them had ever "amass[ed] a great fund" nor had a national presence.

He again revealed his unease with the circumstances of his people and wondered out loud if his own people could ever assume their place in American society. He was not alone in this line of thinking. George Sánchez often wondered if his people would ever assume the responsibilities of American citizenship, and even Hector P. García, the most sensitive of the reformers of that generation to his people's problems, occasionally questioned his people's ability to "step up to the plate." He wrote to a friend, "Sometimes I feel like giving up knowing well that we need organizations . . . badly, but [our] people are not willing to contribute one dollar to get it moving." He added that "Negroes seem to be doing alright" and so were other groups, but he could not help but wonder "why in the Lord's name we can't organize our people."[6] This frustration usually revealed itself during the difficult moments for most reformers, but for Gus it always seemed to be just beneath the surface.

Mingling among the nation's most successful and best-funded civil rights and ethnic organizations highlighted for Gus the disparity between Mexican American reform activities and organizational abilities and those of the other major ethnic groups. As noted before, he was not the only Mexican American reformer to feel this way. Even Cadena seemed to feel the same frustration and he chastised Mexican American reformers for seeking to build a "cultural wall" to keep away from other ethnic groups, particularly "the ultra-progressive Negro-Americans."[7] Here, Cadena spoke to a contradiction present within many Mexican American reformers. They envied the progress of other ethnic groups and their acceptance—or perceived acceptance—by American society, yet they were not really interested in any close association with any of them. In essence, they saw no real benefit from creating such partnerships because most of the other minorities—by this time white ethnics were simply seen as Anglo Americans—were racially different. It seemed obvious to many Mexican American reformers that adding to their own racial dilemmas was not much of an advantage.

As practical reformers, few were interested in being part of a coalition of colored people. This would eventually change but in the early 1950s there was also little opportunity to do so. African American organizations and civil libertarians were not particularly interested in coalitions with those who had little influence and resources to bring to the civil rights battle. Individual African American leaders like W. E. B. Dubois and Marcus Garvey might have tried these coalitions around the world, but they had rarely ventured into the ethnic hinterlands of American society. Then, as it is today, the problem with sharing the struggle was that the piece of the American pie available to nonwhites did not grow much regardless of how many new advocacy groups arose. Another point to be made is that Mexican Americans and African Americans in Texas were usually found in different places and where they shared space they were usually competing for the same jobs and for the Anglo community's favor. This did not create the circumstances for alliances.

The other element to this discomfort with alliances grew from the fact that American liberals never really felt a great necessity in helping Mexican Americans in their civil rights struggles. The absence of Anglo names is noteworthy in the annals of Mexican American struggles to desegregate their schools, fight the Bracero Program, or argue for their inclusion in petit and grand juries. With the exception of Carey McWilliams in California and a few union leaders in the Southwest and some state agency heads in Texas, few Anglos ever became part of the struggle for Mexican American civil rights. This would lead Ed Idar Jr. of the American GI Forum to declare a few years later, "Latins have been taken for granted once too often by liberals." George Sánchez would add, "I personally no longer give a damn what the liberals think."[8] Given this attitude, it was quite natural for Mexican American reformers to go it alone and to often be suspicious of coalitions with other groups.

Gus, however, was of a different mindset because he saw this provinciality as detrimental to both the organizational development of Mexican Americans and to their integration. What Mexican Americans needed to do, he would write later, was to become familiar with the law of the land and their respective localities, keep "abreast of the times" and report any "violations or attempted circumvention of court rulings, laws, or constitutional provisions." In other words, Mexican Americans had to become vigilant and self-reliant in defending their rights. After all, he continued, most social crusaders were rapidly approaching middle age and found themselves "without any semblance of security," and could not be counted on continuing to "pull Mexican chestnuts out of the fire" forever.[9]

Gus believed that social discrimination was the least of the worries that faced Mexican Americans. "If little Adelita is not asked to pledge that exclusive sorority—worry not. She is probably a lot better off anyway. If we are denied service in one restaurant, we can always find another where the tinkling of coins means more than the teachings of *Mein Kampf*. Furthermore, I have no desire to go where I am not wanted." Gus did make exception for public places or facilities that were maintained through public taxes.[10] Mexican Americans were taxpayers and needed to be given the same rights and opportunities, and they needed to be ready to fight for them. Yet, it seemed to him an unfortunate circumstance that the "least important incidents" were those that got the biggest headlines and usually caused the "greatest amount of harm to Anglo-Latin relations."[11] These incidents were usually caused by Mexican Americans wanting to be where they were not wanted and where no law required them to be included. Gus accepted that there were limitations in society and found nothing particularly wrong with that unless these limitations really hampered the well-being and the rights of American citizenship. He wrote shortly after the case was settled,

> We are not passing through anything different from that endured
> at one time or another by other unassimilated population groups:
> the Irish in Boston (damned micks, they were derisively called);
> the Polish in the Detroit area (their designation was bohunks and
> polackers); the Italians in New York (referred to as stinking little
> wops, dagoes and guineas); the Germans in many sections of the
> country (called dumb square-heads and krauts); and our much
> maligned friends of the Jewish faith, who have been persecuted
> even here, in the land of the free, because to the bigoted they were
> just "lousy kikes."[12]

The thing to remember, continued Gus, was that they had managed to overcome the same problems to now be settled Mexican Americans. He acknowledged that the problem "is somewhat more difficult" because of the proximity of the border, but he saw the eventuality of Mexican Americans fully assimilating into American society. In essence, Gus saw the border as a problem because those of Mexican origin continued to keep connections—"the cultural umbilical cord has not yet been completely severed," he wrote.[13] For him, as with many other reformers of his period, this connection was a drawback. He also, however, blamed "nitwits" who delighted in reopening wounds continually by shouting "Remember the Alamo" and other divisive slogans.

Using presumption as demography, he predicted that by 1970 Mexican Americans would be the majority in Texas as well as in the other states that had a "heavy" Mexican population. "Thus," he argued, "in spite of infant diarrhea, tuberculosis, and other diseases which would seem to decimate our ranks, we are rapidly being swept forward to a position which will call for more responsible leadership and for more effective participation in the every day affairs of our society."[14] By this time, Gus was himself being "swept" by an exaggerated optimism that fifty years later would still be seen as extremely wishful thinking in some quarters. He did underscore, however, that education was a key to this transition and after at least a decade fighting school segregation, he revealed some apprehensions about whether much had been accomplished.

"If you pick out at random any day of the school year, and make a check of school attendance, you will discover that over one-half of school-aged children of Mexican descent will not be found in any grade in any school," he wrote. He continued, "We are producing generation after generation of illiterates, semi-illiterates and cotton pickers."[15] Here again, Gus expressed discomfort with his people's social circumstances. He was particularly embarrassed by the fact that a "disgraceful" number of Mexican Americans draftees had been rejected because of illiteracy during World War II. Still, he did put much of the responsibility on the government and educational institutions to correct the problem, but in doing so, he failed to point out the efforts of many Mexican Americans who wanted their children educated and created educational clubs and Spanish-language schools, or who simply homeschooled their children. After so many years of struggle, most Mexican Americans were still not finishing school, not attending college, and not improving their social status much, and this infuriated Gus, who seemed to believe passionately in reform and yet at the same time yearned for having a "normal" life to pursue personal goals and to acquire financial stability.

He cautioned those who would listen that reformers should not be placed on a pedestal. "Crusaders," he declared, "at best or at worst, depending on your point of view are simply ordinary folk with little quirks and an inflated social conscience—and, perhaps, a Messiah complex."[16] More important, their efforts could only accomplish so much. In the end, Mexican Americans could not simply depend on them demanding rights or creating a social status for their people. This had to be earned, he concluded. This little bit of advice, as he called it, firmly expressed Gus's view of the world. At a time when many reformers were moving toward making government and society more responsible for what happened to those left out of the benefits of American society, he clung on to an older LULAC code of the self-made man.[17] This older code, under attack by some of Gus's contemporaries, was class-conscious and served to distinguish the best and brightest in the barrio from the mass of brown souls whose lot seemed to be hard jobs, poor housing, bad health, and no political power. It spoke to the anxiety of being left behind in a "progressive" society. By promoting their talents, hard work, and "noble heritage" these older reformers hoped to overcome the disadvantages of their ethnicity, but yet they had to have an "other" within their midst to accomplish the task. For these older reformers the "other" was the uneducated and unassimilated laborer and his family, but to Gus's generation it was the "wetback" and the Bracero.

Neither Gus nor the older reformers were self-haters. They were genuinely concerned with what happened to their people but they had no philosophical foundation for creating either a critique of the society around them or a place for their own people. They saw American abundance, world prominence, and much opportunity for those in position to take advantage. In contrast, they saw many in their community who seemed to be out of step and on the road to nowhere. They understood the limitations and what role society and even government played in those limitations, but given their war experience, their loyalty to American ideals, and their limited voice, they chose to stress assimilation while protesting the most egregious part of white supremacy. They did not lack intellect as much as they lacked a larger perspective and mentors who could articulate a larger view of their situation in American society. So soon after the war, only a few leftists and old nationalists could argue alternatives and provide visions but they had so little influence and so little to show for their efforts that they came across as archaic.

Gus's writings then reflected optimism mixed with apprehension about a society that seemed both opened and closed at the same time, that invited and rejected, and that continued to be ambivalent about Mexican Americans. Gus must have seen himself and most Mexican Americans in the same situation as Moses of the Old Testament: up to the river's edge but unable to cross into the Promised Land. Arguing before the Supreme Court was as close to the American Promised Land as one could get, but it was still only the edge. He could see his people on the other side but he was not quite sure how they would make it. This then was the paradox of the Mexican

American community in the middle of the twentieth century. Or at least that is what was in Gus's mind because like most reformers, leaders, and heroes, he tended to see his own people through the prism of his own experiences and desires.

The end of his experience on the East Coast would begin with a relapse of an intestinal flu that he caught in San Antonio and which left him bedridden for three days in Washington, D. C. after his trip to New York City. Always one to attract loyal friends, he was "mothered" by Jaime Escobar of the Mexican delegation to the United Nations and Rafael Carvajal of the Voice of America while he ran up "room, doctor's, and drug bills."[18] Bemoaning the fact that he had no money to take a taxi or to catch a show, "not even the free television performances," he finally returned to San Antonio three weeks from the day he arrived in the nation's capital. "If the reader," he wrote, "will consider the cost of traveling, of lodging, cabs in Washington . . . tips . . . 'handouts', etc., he may well understand why civil rights lawyers don't get rich."[19]

Gus's lamentation reflected recognition that talent and accomplishment were not enough in a society that required economic stability and influence. Here he was, atop the legal world, just having argued before the Supreme Court, but he would have to return to the segregated world of Texas, where most of his clients lacked the means to pay for his services, and where many in the political and social establishment quietly if not openly condemned rather than praised his actions. He would get his fifteen minutes in the limelight but then he would be required to roll up his sleeves and jump into the next segregation or antidiscrimination crusade that awaited him and other reformers. His reflections seemed an effort both to prolong those few minutes and to try to stimulate a greater civil reform effort. Most important, whether he knew it or not, these were the opening moments of his swan song as within five years his name would be missing from most important civil rights events and in less than a decade he would be dead. That, however, was in the future and for the moment Gus was simply stretching his stay and delaying his return to that never-ending process of making money and fighting discrimination.

Given his lamentations, it is hard to know how aware or interested Gus was about the cases dealing with Mexican Americans that the Supreme Court had faced in the past and would concurrently face along with *Hernández*. On January 2, 1952, the Supreme Court had heard *Rochin v. California*, and on the same day as the *Hernández* oral arguments, the justices also heard *Galvan v. Press, Officer in Charge, Immigration and Naturalization Service*. The latter case was so complicated that they heard arguments for two days and decided it on May 24. These two cases involved individual rather than collective civil rights but were still rather significant because of the issues they dealt with and the impact of the rulings. In the first one, the Court reversed the lower court's decision, while in the second they affirmed it. Even though both of these cases would not be seen as "ethnic" cases, ethnicity may well have formed a basis for their existence, though in quite different ways.

Rochin, "a non-English speaker," was convicted of possession of morphine but he appealed his conviction on the grounds that police officers had violated his due process rights. Three deputy sheriffs of the county of Los Angeles had received "some information" that Rochin was selling drugs. On the morning of July 1, 1949, they came to the home where he lived with his mother, common-law wife, and some brothers and sisters, found the door open and entered without a search warrant. They found Rochin in his bedroom, along with his wife and two capsules of morphine on a nightstand. When they asked him "Whose stuff is this?" Rochin took the capsules and swallowed them despite efforts by the sheriffs to prevent it. He was then taken to the hospital where his stomach was forcibly pumped and he vomited out the capsules.[20]

In delivering the opinion, Justice Frankfurter, wrote,

> We are compelled to conclude that the proceedings by which this conviction was obtained do more than offend some fastidious squeamishness or private sentimentalism about combating crime too energetically. This is conduct that shocks the conscience. Illegally breaking into the privacy of the petitioner, the struggle to open his mouth and removal what was there, the forcible extraction of his stomach's content—this course of . . . methods are too close to the rack and screw to permit . . . constitutional differentiation. Coerced confessions offend the community's sense of fair play and decency.[21]

Justice Black wrote a concurring opinion in which he stated that states as well as the federal courts had the obligation to obey the Fifth Amendment's command that "no person . . . shall be compelled in any criminal case to be a witness against himself." "I think a person is compelled to be a witness against himself not only when he is compelled to testify, but also when as here, incriminating evidence is forcibly taken from him by a contrivance of modern science," he wrote.[22] Justice Douglas concurred but admitted that most states in the country would have allowed the evidence as was obtained. Only Arkansas, Iowa, Michigan, and Missouri would have excluded the evidence. While he agreed with the high court's decision, he expressed his disagreement with the majority's opinion that the other states were violating the "decencies of civilized conduct."[23]

Nowhere in the brief does it mention that Rochin was of Latin extraction or that the police officers acted with such brutality because he was a person of color or of another nationality. Yet, to most ordinary Mexican Americans and many reformers this kind of brutality was common in the barrios of the Southwest. The history of Texas, and most of the rest of the Southwest, reflected a usage of law enforcement muscle against Mexican Americans in indiscriminate ways. The whole notion of law enforcement as it applied to Mexican Americans was to keep them intimidated and regulated. It started with the way the law was applied against them—since there were few actual anti-Mexican laws—and continued with the way law enforcement officials administered it. The *Hernández* case also underscored how the law continued to work against them even after the charge and the arrest. Many Mexican Americans who participated little in the civic functions of their community, often because they were not allowed to, did not always understand the law and got in trouble because of that ignorance.

The cases dealing with jury discrimination also revealed another use of the law against Mexican Americans. In several of the cases, the authorities argued that the defendants had "confessed" to their crimes while the accused argued either that they had not or had been coerced or misunderstood. In every one of the cases, the confessions stood and they undermined the defense's arguments. What happened to Rochin was not uncommon for Mexican Americans who confronted the police or sheriff departments of the Southwest. They were often arrested without warrants as law enforcement officers counted on the individuals not knowing the law, not getting good legal representation, and on friendly judges allowing their illegal searches and arrests to stand in spite of their constitutional violations. They also often counted on having Mexican Americans "confess" and accept punishment, often to avoid even harsher punishment.[24] Needless to say, most Mexican Americans distrusted law enforcement officers because their experience with them usually was unpleasant.

Gus, whose law practice depended on who showed up to his door, was probably familiar with these cases. More important is that Mexican Americans tended to get in trouble with the law frequently because they did not understand it, they were falsely accused, or because of the high volume of alcohol consumed within many of the barrios of the Southwest. Many young men, who worked hard at menial jobs and who were often emasculated by their powerlessness in the job and their inability to escape poverty or provide a skill to their children, usually found solace in the local tavern. There, among other men in similar situations, their masculinity was affirmed through their macho role-playing, heavy drinking, and willingness to engage in violence to defend their honor. Tavern killings, alcohol-related homicides, and domestic violence were unfortunately more common than most reformers were willing to acknowledge publicly, though they often referred to them in their civic campaigns among the barrios of the Southwest.

There were many Rochins in the barrios of the Southwest and everyone knew one. Yet the story of the police's conduct against him was also just as familiar to most Mexican Americans. They could both loathe his action of selling drugs as well as empathize with him as a victim of police brutality. Few would have had any qualms that police acted the way they did because he was of Latino origin. This had been the case with Pete Hernández; people had been horrified by his crime but had felt that the state had given him a life sentence because of who he was, as well as whom he had killed. Pete, of course, had become embroiled in an important case, one that involved his whole community, but Rochin—whose case became much more significant in legal terms—would not be seen as fighting for the rights of Mexican Americans. Strangely, Rochin's case went to the heart of law enforcement's relationship with the citizen, but he would receive little support from Mexican American reformers. He simply did not fit the bill for a community anxious to integrate into American society.

One could argue that Pete should not have fit the bill for a community anxious to integrate into American society either, but he did because his case dealt with a fundamental constitutional issue, which had become a part of the Mexican American reform agenda. Probably just as important was the fact that most jury discrimination cases in the past had involved gruesome murders and the community may well have become used to these types of cases, but drugs were still something quite taboo, though surely not uncommon. Another reason may have simply been that Mexican American reformers in California were not pursuing jury discrimination as a civil rights issue as aggressively as their Texas counterparts. Whatever the reasons, Rochin simply did not garner any attention from reformers and his victory in the courts would not be greeted with much fanfare. And yet, his case would be more important legally and be the subject of more discussions in law schools across the country than the *Hernández* case ever would, although it is also certain that the *Rochin* decision had little impact on the civil rights struggle of Mexican American reformers in the way *Hernández* would.

The *Galvan* case also represented a very important legal case as it dealt with internal security at a time when the Cold War worried many political leaders. Galvan had lived in the United States thirty-six years after coming from Mexico in 1918 at the age of seven. He was married to an American citizen and had four American-born children as well as a stepson who served as a paratrooper in the U.S. Army. A laborer who worked at the Van Camp Seafood Company in San Diego, he had joined the Communist Party in 1944 at a time the party could still field candidates and when it was not a crime to be a member of such.[25] In March 1948 he was questioned by the INS and indicated to them that he had been a member of the Communist Party. Exactly one year later he was served with a deportation warrant for violating the Internal Security Act of 1950, which was a piece of legislation aimed at punishing anyone who was or had been a Communist, Socialist, or part of any other organization seen as subversive.[26]

This insidious piece of legislation had later been strengthened by the passage of the McCarran-Walter Act of 1952. Three provisions within that law made it particularly anti-immigrant. It provided a new and longer list of grounds for which aliens could be deported or excluded, included conditions under which naturalized citizens could be denaturalized, and expanded the powers of the Immigration and Naturalization Service to interrogate any alien about their legal status and to enter and search private lands within twenty-five miles of the border. These two pieces of legislation were a result of the harsh anticommunist mood of the nation in the mid-1950s. Anticommunism, of course, often targeted not only leftists, socialists, and radicals but also anyone who was not considered a mainstream American. Immigrants, particularly the undocumented ones who had been recruited by the Bracero Program or invited by the massive need for labor in this country, were particularly seen as a threat to the nation. President Truman's declarations about the threat of illegal aliens in the early 1950s had created the conditions for the backlash against those who had only years before been welcomed to do the labor that most Americans were not willing to do. A report issued by the president's office sounded a call to action that incited alarm. "The magnitude of the wetback traffic has reached entirely new levels in the past seven years . . . it is virtually an invasion," it concluded.[27]

Galvan sought to prevent his deportation by arguing that he had joined the Communist Party when it was not illegal to do so, that he had never known it to ever advocate the overthrow of the U.S. government, and that he had not been a member for nearly six years. He also argued that the act was only applicable to those aliens who joined the party fully conscious of its advocacy of violence.[28] The Court rejected his arguments and insisted that support or "even demonstrated knowledge of Communist advocacy of violence" was not intended to be a prerequisite to deportation. "It is enough that the alien joined the party," wrote Justice Frankfurter.[29] The justice underscored the "severe consequences" of the measure and even questioned the "wisdom" of Congress in dealing with the issue in such a way, but added that the Congress traditionally had the right to set such laws it deemed necessary to safeguard the nation. He admitted that, "we cannot say that this classification [of subversives] by Congress is so baseless as to be a violation of due process and therefore beyond the power of Congress."[30]

Two justices, however, dissented from the majority opinion. Justice Black argued that the defendant was being punished along with his job, his home, his friends, and even his children for joining a "lawful political group," an act that he "had no possible reason to believe would subject him to the slightest penalty." He continued,

> It is possible that this deportation order for engaging in political activities does not violate the First Amendment's clear ban against abridgement of political speech and assembly. Maybe it is not even a denial of due process and equal protection of the law. But . . . I am unwilling to say, however, that despite these constitutional safeguards this man may be driven from our land because he joined a political party that California and the Nation then recognized as perfectly legal.[31]

Douglas, in concurring, wrote that there was no constitutional basis for deporting someone for having engaged in an act (such as joining the Communist Party) that was legal when done. "I agree that there is, therefore," he wrote, "no constitutional basis for deportation, if aliens, as well as citizens, are to be the beneficiaries of due process of law."[32] He continued even more adamantly, "This action is hostile to our constitutional standards. Aliens who live here in peace, who do not abuse our hospitality, who are law-abiding members of our communities, have the right to due process of law. They too are 'persons' within the meaning of the Fifth Amendment. They can be molested by the Government in times of peace only when their presence here is hostile to the safety or welfare of the nation. If they are to be deported, it must be for what they *are and do*, not for what they once believed" (my italics).[33]

Ironically, Galvan's deportation case did not garner much support from Mexican American reformers like Sánchez who were anxious to promote American citizenship. In fact, in a letter to ACLU lawyer Al Wirin,

Sánchez wrote in reference to the deportation cases: "Frankly, I do not regard them as of great consequence to Mexican Americans. I think they are worthy as general civil liberties cases, but not in the same class with housing, jury, school, etc., where Mexicans are specifically singled out for discrimination."[34] As head of the American Council of Spanish-Speaking People, which was administering monies from the Marshall Civil Liberties Trust Fund for Mexican American civil rights struggles, Sánchez grudgingly agreed to "sweeten the pot for these (immigration) cases, but with very little sugar."[35] Sánchez, like Gus, Herrera, and possibly Cadena, was committed to fighting for Mexican American rights of citizenship, and saw immigration cases as peripheral to that struggle, as well as reminders that for Anglos the hyphen was all that separated Mexican Americans from being "foreign."

These reformers were not completely insensitive to immigrants and many often empathized with their plight of having no rights and no privileges, and being exploited. Nonetheless, the struggle for citizenship rights took precedence over the rights of the "wetback."[36] Yet, this lack of support by Mexican Americans reformers and advocacy organizations only added to the disdain with which immigrants, particularly undocumented ones, were seen by American society. As we will see later, the constant complaint against them that they took jobs away from Mexican Americans would help lead to blaming immigrants for the postwar economic stagnation and to a massive deportation campaign.

Nearly the same Court ruled quite differently in *Charles Rowoldt v. J. D. Perfetto, Acting Officer in Charge, Immigration and Naturalization Service* when it reversed an order of deportation for Rowoldt, who had been a member of the Communist Party. In that case, the Court took into consideration his stay in the country—forty-six years compared to Galvan's thirty-six—and his denial that he knew or supported the Communist Party's advocacy of violence. "From his own testimony in 1947," wrote Frankfurter, ". . . the dominating impulse to his 'affiliation' with the Communist Party may well have been wholly devoid of any 'political' implications."[37] Basically, the Court had rejected these pleas when they were presented by Galvan one year after Rowoldt's original testimony but accepted them when Rowoldt argued them later. It is important to note that Rowoldt had been charged earlier than Galvan but he and not the latter was given the "benefit" of changes in the Internal Security Act in 1951 that sought to clarify what constituted a "membership" in the Communist Party.

Why did Rowoldt find his arguments successful and not Galvan? There are probably many factors involved, most beyond the scope of this book, but one of them has to be the hysteria in the early 1950s against "illegal" immigration. As noted before, the McCarran-Walter Act was simply one of the manifestations of this hysteria. The most significant one would be the massive deportations carried out mostly against Mexicans that began the summer after the Court ruled on the *Hernández* case. Named Operation Wetback, this large-scale roundup of undocumented workers and their families would prove to be the most massive effort ever undertaken by the government to rid itself of those it saw as expandable and unwanted.[38] As noted earlier, this alarm had been sounded by the Truman Administration and was followed by discussions and sensationalist reporting such as that of the *New York Times*, which ran a five-part series on the growing undocumented labor force and on the growers in the West who recruited and then exploited these workers. Immigration officials added to the hysteria by proclaiming that nothing could stop all of Mexico's population from simply coming over across the border.[39]

In 1953, a retired military officer was named head of the Immigration and Naturalization Service to militarize the agency and make it more assertive in rounding up undocumented persons throughout the West and Midwest. Retired Lieutenant General Joseph M. Swing sought and got a massive increase in funding, began building walls and even set deportation quotas for the different regions of the border. In 1953, the INS deported nearly 900,000 Mexicans and in the process tore families apart and sent American-born children to live in a country many of them had never visited. In the five year period, 1950–1955, over 3,600,000 Mexicans were deported. Ironically, the hysteria quickly abated as the economy grew, starting in 1955 when deportations fell to 242,608 from a high of 1,075,000 in 1954. The following year deportations dropped to 72,442 and dropped even further during the rest of the decade, never going above 50,000 until 1965 when the Bracero Program was terminated.[40]

Operation Wetback lasted only a short time but it came to be known as one of the most traumatic experiences affecting Mexicans and Mexican Americans in the Southwest and Midwest. It would be years before those who experienced the roundups, family breakups, or the interrogations overcame their apprehensions about that period. For many Mexican Americans it signaled another instance in which the United States had betrayed their loyalty and had criminalized their existence. Those who had been here long enough had seen several instances of this before, though for many of them deportation or roundups were not the only forms of hostilities they encountered in American society. It was particularly galling to some that it came only a few years after many of them had served in the armed forces and fought in World War II. While those veterans tended to be American citizens or resident aliens, what most policymakers did not always know and Mexican American reformers failed to acknowledge, was that most Mexican Americans still had family members who did not have a green card, or they had relatives in Mexico who were making the trek to the United States to find jobs that were abundantly available in the agricultural fields and in the factories.

While a number of Mexican American reformers had supported Operation Wetback rather energetically, it eventually spurred them to undertake a profound re-evaluation of their border politics and led to the decline of the anti-immigrant rhetoric so common among them. It is important to note here that reformers in Texas, particularly those of the American GI Forum, as well as some in LULAC, had engaged in their own anti-immigrant activity, which culminated in the publication of a report titled, *What Price Wetbacks?* This report, which came out sometime in 1953, was a joint project of the American GI Forum and the Texas State Federation of Labor.[41] The purpose was to attract attention to the problems Mexican American laborers were facing with the growing number of undocumented Mexican workers coming across the border. It was a legitimate concern for reformers as they saw many of their fellow Mexican Americans forced to migrate to California, the Midwest, and the Northwest to find seasonal work because most Texas growers were hiring "illegals" whom they paid less and exploited without fear of legal reprisals.

The report was mostly written by Ed Idar Jr., who had been a journalist and was one of the most assertive of the GI Forum leaders. He usually pulled no punches and saw through both the agriculture industry's appreciation for the "good Mexican workers," and the subtle prejudices of Texas liberal politicians. Yet, Idar seemed unprepared to deal with the subtleties of working-class Mexican culture. Instead of trying to create a complex, nuanced narrative of the problem, Idar instead chose to scare politicians into dealing with the subject of "wetbacks." He made two specific arguments that would eventually come back to haunt the American GI Forum and its leaders. First, he wrote that "wetbacks" were a direct threat to the health, property, and culture of American society, and second, that the Border Patrol agents were unsung heroes who were simply overwhelmed by the masses of undocumented workers crossing the border.[42] While there were those working-class Mexican Americans who might have grudgingly accepted the first notion given the competition for jobs, it was much more difficult to swallow the second notion. Simply put, many Mexican-origin individuals, regardless of legal status, simply did not see anything heroic

Figure 4. The pamphlet *What Price Wetbacks?* created a firestorm of criticism for reformers who were seeking to distinguish Mexican Americans from those coming from Mexico to work in the fields.

about the Border Patrol that had earned its reputation as an indiscriminate police force that rarely distinguished between legal and illegal when it used its roughhouse methods.[43]

Idar took pictures, interviewed border patrolmen, businessmen, educators and visited migrant camps to see how undocumented Mexican farm laborers lived. He found abject poverty, children without schooling, and families with only cardboard walls for houses, and men who worked from sunup to sundown. Living on the periphery of society and at the edges of green fields full of crops, they accentuated the differences between those who hired the labor and those who performed it. Following his research, Idar was in an incredible position to critique America's voracious appetite for low-skilled labor and the exploitation of it, but he instead decided to go for Anglo sympathy and empathy and to do so he stereotyped and criticized the very people who were exploited. In doing so, he revealed the discomfort and disconnect that some Mexican Americans and many reformers felt toward those coming from Mexico. Possibly no earlier generation and none since has confronted the paradox of trying to be good citizens and finding acceptability at a time when the nation felt threatened by immigration to the extent that this generation did.

Mexicans and Mexican Americans before the 1940s and 1950s had simply been too alienated and isolated from American society to seek to divide themselves into legal and illegal, recent arrivals and native-born. Succeeding generations—after the 1950s—would be much more secure in their citizenship and their place in American society that by and large they would not give in to the nativist efforts to divide them. This should not imply that there have not existed throughout their history divisions between legals and illegals, recent arrivals and native-born, only that never had those divisions been played out in such a public manner, and never had Mexican American reformers felt so compelled to choose sides in that division. Mexican Americans in Texas and some other parts of the Southwest were making a very aggressive effort to be seen as full members of the American civic society, and they were not always thinking of the consequences of their actions, or if they were, they believed the gamble would work with limited consequences.

Idar started off by describing undocumented workers as "Guanajuato Joes" because many came from that state in Mexico, but also because it conjured up an image of a mass of people coming over the border instead of individuals seeking a better life for their families. He described them as "stoic" and philosophical in accepting their mistreatment, and he made them out to look like beasts of burden—much the way most growers saw them—and he depicted them as mostly worried about their immediate needs. "The [Mexican wetback] understands only his way of life: to work, to suffer, and to pray to the *Virgen de Guadalupe* for a better life in the hereafter," wrote Idar.[44] These "instant gratification, beasts of burden" were simply too many for the "hardworking, professional but overwhelmed Border Patrolman," to capture and deport. And American businesses were also suffering because these people were not spending their money locally but were simply sending it all back home, to a Mexico that wholeheartedly accepted its citizens going north so they could send back their dollars and expend their discontent somewhere else.[45]

Organized labor in Texas and some reformers like Idar had hoped the report or pamphlet would generate strong support for their fight against the Bracero Program and undocumented laborers in the field. The report, however, seems to have had little impact on the discussions about the issue of illegal immigration, though it certainly added to the paranoia already prevailing in many Southwestern and Midwestern states and in Congress. What they never expected was the backlash that it created among the Mexican and Mexican American communities, and the division it caused among the reformers themselves. Immediately, some American GI Forum members who were still smarting from an earlier Sánchez-supported report criticized Idar for undertaking the project without full organizational approval.[46] They felt the last report, which had done in academic jargon what this one did in journalistic style, had brought much criticism and this one was going to make things worse. Others simply resented the fact Idar was too sympathetic to the Border Patrol and had left most of American society off the hook for the exploitation and mistreatment of Mexicans, legal or illegal. One member, Salvador Paz, who published a small newspaper named *La Verdad* (The Truth), went further in his criticism and accused the Forum leaders of "taking food from the mouths of hungry people" by publishing such harsh and stereotypical information that encouraged mass deportation.[47]

The report brought out the deep divisions within the American GI Forum over the issue. While most understood that Mexican American laborers faced a disadvantage with the abundance of undocumented laborers from Mexico and even from the Bracero Program, there were those who believed that the growers and the state agencies were more to blame for the situation than the people who simply took a job that was offered. It was the unwillingness of growers to pay an appropriate wage and the reluctance of the state to force them to meet the minimum labor standards that caused many Mexican Americans to go to California or the Midwest to pick crops.

The undocumented Mexicans were willing to take the wage either because they did not plan to stay long in the country or because they had no other choice. If the growers paid the right wages, then Mexican Americans would stay in the state and "illegals" would have no jobs for which to come. Still other reformers and supporters of the Forum were uncomfortable with the friendly depictions of the border patrolmen.

The biggest casualty of the pamphlet, however, was the disappearance of Hector P. García, the American GI Forum founder, from the debate. He had been the leading advocate of getting rid of the Bracero Program and of the curtailing of illegal immigration. No one had documented better the impact that illegal immigration had on Mexican American farm workers, or the disastrous impact of northern migration on the children of those farm workers who chose to leave the state for seasonal work. Yet, Hector had always known who to blame and how to maintain sensitivity to the human tragedy. He was not callous to the difficulties of those caught in the vicious cycle of undocumented immigration. His advocacy for Mexican Americans had often been inclusive and he tried never to make distinctions between legal and illegal in those he served as a medical doctor and as a social reformer. He was not blind to the fact that many in his community were not citizens or legal residents.

Like many reformers, however, Hector García was not always conscious of what it would really take to stop illegal immigration and to deport the numbers already here. The trauma of Operation Wetback and harsh backlash from the pamphlet on "wetbacks" caused him to take a step back. He avoided making public statements on the subject and he avoided most of the Forum meetings called to resolve the split on the issue. Idar, in a letter written several months after the pamphlet appeared, told him that there was suspicion among Forum members that he was avoiding the issue. Idar even implied that he might have even encouraged some Forum members to actually criticize the report.[48] It was incredibly ironic to Idar that the man who had spearheaded the effort to deal with "wetbacks" and had made the end of the Bracero Program one of the cornerstones of the Forum's reform activities was engaged in a disappearing act, and, possibly worse, undermining the effort to finally deal with the issues.

Idar, although tenacious and capable, never had the knack of a reformer of the caliber of García, who understood that reform activities could be successful only as far as they maintained the loyalty of a large number of Mexicans and Mexican Americans. Yet, the reality was that by the late 1950s, the Mexican American Generation—as it has often been characterized by scholars—would soon reach its apex. This generation had been emotionally committed to assimilation and to the general belief that American society only needed to open its doors and the accessibility would solve most of the problems of the Mexican American barrios. Led, ironically, by García, they had begun to question that premise and to demand more than access; they wanted government action to help solve the deep problems of poverty and powerlessness.[49] By the end of Operation Wetback, they were beginning to conceptualize an agenda that called for not only accessibility but "recognition" and government action.[50]

By the beginning of the 1960s they would be in full throttle, demanding political appointments, New Deal programs for the Southwest, voting rights, protection for Mexican Americans, government-enforced desegregation, and support for their own candidates. The shift seemed dramatic from the outside but in reality it manifested the result of a contentious debate that had been playing itself out for years within Mexican American reform groups, and within the larger barrio communities. This debate had its roots in both the Mexican American community's alienation from the larger society and the desire by many within it to be seen as American citizens with full rights and accessibility. Many Mexican Americans wanted to be accepted as who they were but still be provided with the rights of citizenship. Many believed, somewhat naively, that other groups had been accepted as they were and given much of their rights by a benevolent federal government. In fact, this belief in a benevolent federal government would become the basis for the last phase of Mexican American Generation politics.

These politics sought to bypass intransigent state and local governments dominated by Anglo Americans who were prejudiced against Mexican Americans. There was a belief—a wishful thinking of sorts—that American national leaders were more sensitive to racial minorities and more liberal in their views of social policy. This view coincided with reformers'— particularly those in Texas—perceptions that American society, while often closed and hostile to minorities, was inherently fair and democratic. Their intense commitment to American foreign policy, their fear of being red-baited and their own obsession with being allowed full participation in American society allowed them to construct within their minds and politics a dichotomous criticism of the larger society. This critique defined Anglo Americans at the local and state level as "usually" prejudicial, overly conservative, and likely to limit Mexican American accessibility to the benefits of American society. On the other hand, national politicians, federal government officials, and American intellectuals were above those feelings and actually sought to create the kind of democracy that was inclusive and fundamentally fair. In essence, unlike their Mexican American counterparts on the Left, they believed in the institutions and the American creed despite the fact that they spent their time criticizing both.

The *Hernández* case thus stood as a critical transition to the new militancy that would come in the late 1950s and the early 1960s before this generation of reformers started fading and giving way to the Chicano Generation of the late 1960s and then the Hispanic Generation that followed. *Hernández* was a culmination of the argument that Anglos or whites at the federal level were much more sensitive and would act to counteract the prejudices at the state and local level. While the case was still about accessibility, it also spoke to intervention in that the high court's ruling would become the law of the land and effect change in the affairs of the state and local levels. It would also become proactive law by clearly identifying Mexican Americans as beneficiaries of the Equal Protection Clause of the Fourteenth Amendment. Gus, as he walked the streets of Washington, D.C. and went from advocacy offices to those of national politicians, hoped that the ruling would do what history books had not, and that was to make American society aware and conscious that Mexican Americans were as much a part of the nation as anyone else. To accomplish this would be the culmination of all the civil rights struggles of the past.

A Differentiated Class, Not a Class Apart

It is impossible to know what the justices thought of both the brief and the arguments of the *Hernández* defense team. No record exists of any journal entries, speeches given, or letters written from any of the justices on the case. Chief Justice Warren himself devoted two paragraphs to the case in his memoirs, but nothing on the lawyers, the strategy, or even the legal ramifications of the case.[1] This would be the first major civil rights case to be decided by the Warren Court but already it was framed by the discussion and debates on its much more famous cousin, *Brown v. Board of Education,* which had been heard twice before, one time with Chief Justice Fred M. Vinson at the helm and shortly before *Hernández* with the new chief justice presiding. Without a doubt, these circumstances made the justices particularly conscious of the issues of discrimination and exclusion.

By the time *Hernández v. Texas* arrived, the Vinson Court had already begun to move toward an expansion of civil rights for African Americans but had done so piecemeal, unable or unwilling to find consensus in making much more declarative rulings on behalf of minority rights.[2] Initially, no one expected the Warren Court to be any more aggressive in that direction as Earl Warren was seen as a moderate Republican who might continue the trends of the Court but who would take his cue from the man who appointed him, President Dwight Eisenhower. The former wartime leader had, in his short tenure, demonstrated the demeanor of someone who would be steady, govern in the mainstream, not incite racial tensions, but surely do little to advance the rights of minorities. Though a Texan by birth, he showed no particular knowledge or sensitivity to Mexican Americans, although thousands of them had served in his theater of war.

When Eisenhower chose Warren, he thought he had chosen a "safe" pick, one more political than judicial. Warren, once a presidential ticket possibility, was a former governor of California and state attorney general who was well known for his part in the Japanese American internment.[3] This was a part of his resume that he had begun to try to put behind him. Later, Mexican American reformers would point to his tenure as attorney general and governor in California to rationalize his "sensitivity" to their case. Japanese American legal scholars would be less sensitive and argue that his move toward civil rights was an effort to eliminate the worst parts of white supremacy in order to maintain white predominance.[4] It may well be said that Warren's actions were probably more practical than the afore-mentioned perceptions, although in his last days as governor he revealed a side only slightly known during his moderate years as governor. Warren, speaking at a good-bye party sponsored by reporters who had covered his administration, declared, "I am glad to be going to the Supreme Court because now I can help the less fortunate, the people in our society who suffer, the disadvantaged."[5]

Warren, whatever his judicial skills and accomplishments, was a moderate politician of the 1950s who understood that the nation faced critical racial tensions that had to be dealt with in the context of the Cold War, which at the time was in its most internally divisive stage. Much of American politics were in a state of paranoia with charges and countercharges between McCarthyites and liberals over the dangers of internal Communism.[6] At the same time, American diplomats were beside themselves with the racial conflicts—lynchings, beatings, segregation, riots—that were being played out in the international media, particularly in the Third World and in the Communist world. The world of propaganda was the first front in the Cold War and in the 1950s the United States was losing on that battlefield among people of color around the world. In India, Africa, and Asia, American diplomats faced a bombardment of hostile questions about American commitment to human rights every time there was a lynching and in every instance when an African American claimed a violation of his or her rights.[7]

The issue of rights, however, was not limited to those of African Americans. Latin American countries, particularly Mexico, were also concerned with the treatment of those of Latino origin. Only six years earlier, Latin American countries had energetically protested when a young Mexican American soldier had been refused the use of a funeral home chapel in a small rural community in Texas. Mexico had been particularly incensed over the treatment of its citizens who participated in the Bracero Program, and who came by the thousands to work in the agricultural fields of the Southwest. Their mistreatment, and the case of the deceased Mexican American soldier Felix Longoria, was widely described in the major Mexican newspapers.[8]

It is quite natural to assume that Warren, as a California politician, recognized the issues and had actually faced them as a government official, but again, nowhere in his memoirs or his writings does it appear that they were more than just a typical function of his office.[9] This may well have been best for Mexican Americans because they usually fared better when they did not become the focus of politicians, because that focus was usually hostile. Probably more to the benefit of the *Hernández* lawyers was a chief justice who could see Mexican Americans as just another part of the American mosaic. Regardless of Warren's familiarity with the situation of Mexican Americans, what really mattered was that he was neither hostile nor sorely indifferent. What Hernández needed was an impartial panel that could find a place for him in the legal system. The activist nature of this court was also an advantage for Hernández as it became involved in numerous civil right cases and was eventually credited with striking down many barriers to racial equality.

Warren's appointment, however, was not the only piece of good fortune for Pete's case. Unbeknownst to his lawyers, the bench memorandum, written by R. Dirk Flynn, strongly recommended a reversal, calling the lower court's two-class theory "fallacious" and arguing "if the Mexican Americans are the objects of discrimination as a class, they are entitled to the protection of the Fourteenth Amendment."[10] Warren's law clerk added that the record supported the contentions by Pete's lawyers. Interestingly, the memorandum also pointed out the procedural failings of the legal team: no printed papers had been submitted and the lawyers had failed to submit a "motion or an affidavit" asking permission to proceed with typewritten papers. But the memorandum also disputed the charge that the papers had been submitted late, noting that the Inauguration Day holiday had given them one extra day.

As soon as the discussion on the case began, two concerns arose over Warren's initial circulated draft of the ruling, which went out on April 29—ten days after the first draft by his clerk, R. Dirk Flynn. Those showing concern were Justices Sherman Minton, Clark, and Frankfurter, but we have notes only from the latter two. Clark's seemed to reveal overall indifference to the importance of the case. Speaking for Minton and himself he handwrote, "We have decided not to dissent on a factual basis. You have covered the law in the field so well that we go along with you . . . you mark me as agreeing. I'm sure that you will hear from Shay [i.e., Minton] likewise."[11] Yet, the letter began with a more ominous tone, with Clark, writing for both justices, stating that Warren's "facts" were setting up a "straw man."[12] Exactly what Clark and Minton were referring to can only be inferred as there are no other memos or letters expounding on the terminology Clark used. It is, however, impossible not to assume that Clark—and Minton—were troubled by the "reach" of the verdict, although it is difficult to know what that reach had to do with the evidence of discrimination, or the application of the ruling. Their concerns become clearer in looking at Frankfurter's comments. But before discussing Frankfurter, it is necessary to reflect on Clark's misgivings. It is important to note that Clark was much more exposed to Mexican American issues than he might have acknowledged.

As Harry Truman's attorney general, he had received correspondence from Mexican American reformers over the issue of "illegal" workers in Texas taking jobs away from American farm workers.[13] He had also been privy to the discussions and research conducted on the problems of the Mexican Americans in the Southwest before the publication of the president's Commission on Civil Rights in 1948. As a lifelong politician and jurist, Clark should have been aware of many of the issues that confronted Mexican Americans. Unfortunately no substantive work exists on Justice Clark that spells out his thinking on Mexican Americans and their legal struggles.

In the context of his knowledge of Mexican American issues and his own experience in the Lone Star State, a "straw man" would most likely refer to the exaggeration or overreach of the evidence. Clark probably shared the feelings of many of his fellow Texans that Mexican Americans were engaged in "much ado about nothing." It was common for Anglo-Texans to believe that Mexican Americans overreacted in their interactions with the mainstream population. In the famous Felix Longoria case, newspaper and veteran's groups accused both Mexican American reformers—led by Hector P. García—and Texas U.S. Senator Lyndon Baines Johnson, of blowing out of proportion a simple misunderstanding between the funeral director and Longoria's wife.[14] Even after Longoria was given an honorable burial in Arlington National Cemetery, a commission of Texas legislators declared, in a report that ran several hundred pages, that no evidence of discrimination had been found on the part of the funeral director or any other person in Three Rivers, Texas.[15] Ironically, on the first day of the hearings, a Mexican man was denied service by an Anglo barber in the same building, only a few doors away from where the legislators were listening to testimony.[16]

Continually, Mexican American complaints were treated as exaggerations, misunderstandings, or simple whining.

It is ironic that Shay and Clark could agree with the decision and its legal foundations while at the same time believing that the issues raised by the case formed part of the "straw man" line of reasoning concerning Mexican Americans in Texas and the rest of the Southwest. That this short memo appears to have been written in haste with little contemplation reinforces the perception that Mexican American civil rights litigation was of secondary importance. A memo written by Frankfurter sheds some more light on this indifference. Like Clark and Shay, he expressed support for the Chief Justice's "result" in *Hernández v. Texas*, but quickly expressed two concerns. The first, which he specified as the most important, was the ruling's discussion on the rejection of the "two-class" theory. "It [the ruling] is not restricted," wrote Frankfurter, "to equality of treatment in the administration of justice and more particularly, in ensuring an indiscriminating jury system."[17] In his comments he revealed himself to be the same justice who had expressed concern in the past that the Supreme Court could end up overreaching, "since the court is compelled to put meaning into the Constitution, not take it out."[18] He argued that the court needed to show restraint in its decisions.

Frankfurter seemed concerned by the scope of Warren's ruling, which clearly ruled as unconstitutional any laws or "their application" that "singled out [a] class for different treatment not based on some reasonable classification."[19] Warren had written that "community prejudices are not static," thus underscoring the changing nature of prejudices as well as the need for the law to keep up with such changes. Frankfurter was not particularly opposed to that interpretation, but he wondered if "it is not highly undesirable to make generalized pronouncements of that nature prior to the disposition of the segregation cases?"[20]

Here, Frankfurter revealed his priorities in terms of the two pending civil rights cases and the language that each should express. The case that came to be known as *Brown v. Board of Education* had taken time coming up the judicial ladder and had built on years of African American litigation. The case had been discussed the previous year and heard one week before the *Hernández* case, and was to be further discussed after it.[21]

The discussion on *Brown v. Board of Education* dwarfed any that *Hernández* could arouse. Simply put, African American educational segregation had been a point of litigation for much of the twentieth century, and the debates reached into the soul of American society in a way that few others did. The way it divided most Americans was the way that it divided the justices, with several favoring overturning *Plessy v. Ferguson,* and others favoring its maintenance. Warren's appointment as chief justice simply tipped the balance against segregation but initially did not end the divisions. Warren, understanding the passions that the case aroused, engaged in a marathon effort to get unanimous support for his views.[22] For Warren, *Plessy* rested on the "basic premise that the Negro race is inferior," and he believed that was the only way to sustain or accept "separate but equal." Yet, the "superb arguments of the Negro counsel" made that premise of inferiority ludicrous.[23] He also believed that "in this time and age" it was ridiculous to "set any group apart from the rest."[24]

The ongoing discussions went to the heart of what it meant to be American and to have civil rights. The whole history of the Constitution and the Fourteenth Amendment came under debate. These discussions sought to find a common ground and alleviate the internal philosophical conflicts within each justice. There were those who supported and saw segregation as constitutional but could see the rising political tide against it. There were those who saw segregation as constitutional but abhorrent, and there were those who saw it as unconstitutional but so entrenched as to make it difficult to strike down. Warren's persuasive discussion allowed each justice to work out his own conflicts and come to the conclusion that the decision needed to be unanimous. This unanimity did not mean solidarity or even a convergence of the judicial mind, but it did mean that they were buying into Warren's view that politics and social circumstances mattered in judicial decisionmaking.

This accommodation to what some had considered as an inevitable conclusion made the justices deeply aware of the issues of race in American society—but seemingly only those that dealt with black Americans. In seeking to accentuate the gravity of striking down segregation, Justice Clark reminded his colleagues on the bench that "the problem [of segregation in Texas] is as acute as anywhere. Texas also has the Mexican problem." He added that a "Mexican boy of fifteen" in a class "with a Negro girl of twelve" could spell "trouble"—meaning pregnancy.[25] Regardless of the insensitive implications of his remarks, Clark recognized that desegregation would impact others in addition to African Americans. It is also possible to read that in Clark's mind Mexican Americans remained segregated years after *Mendez v. Westminster,* and *Brown* would release them to join African Americans in creating new problems for his beloved Texas.

In the context of the larger debate on race, *Hernández* seemed like "small potatoes"—even for liberals like Frankfurter—to waste such potentially sweeping language. Yet, how could the court strike down de facto discrimination against Mexican Americans if the language rejecting the two-class theory did not create a legal umbrella against all kinds of extralegal practices in places like Texas? To wait for *Brown* would have crippled any ruling on behalf of *Hernández* and other groups who were treated differently. Still, Frankfurter recommended deleting the entire paragraph that declared as unconstitutional any laws or "their application . . . that singled out [a] class for different treatment not based on some reasonable classification."[26]

Frankfurter expressed further concern that the chief justice had unnecessarily "establish[ed] the existence of two definable groupings in the community," arguing that once proof was provided of the exclusion of Mexicans from juries, no further evidence was needed of discrimination in terms of school segregation or public facilities. "I should think that in these questions it is desirable to cover no more ground than is needed to establish an unequivocally inadmissible discrimination."[27] He continued,

> I suppose the fact that Mexicans are set apart in the community
> tends to show that they are in an inferior position in the eyes
> of non-Mexicans and therefore would carry that burden when
> judged exclusively by non-Mexican juries. But I should think that
> systematic exclusion of all members of a particular group, otherwise
> qualified, in the trial of a member of this excluded group, would
> constitute denial of equal protection of the law without the proof
> that they are otherwise disfavored because [of being] set apart in
> the community.[28]

Frankfurter's comments might have seemed logical and even as an expansion of the legal protection of the Fourteenth Amendment by simply including everyone. Why prove you are a "class apart," and not simply show evidence of "inadmissible" exclusion?

The problem with this logic was that it advertently dismissed the notion that Mexican Americans were in fact a disadvantaged or oppressed group. Being simply "inadmissible" denied that their exclusion was based on more than a whim. All the history of Mexican American maltreatment and marginalization was washed away by a simple ruling in their favor that recognized their "disfavor" in the local community. The designation of a "class apart," then, became one of the few weapons available to combat the strategy of whiteness used against Mexican Americans in Texas. After all, Mexican Americans had been claiming jury discrimination for nearly a quarter century in the courts and these had never ruled in their favor.

If prosecutors and judges could successfully argue that Mexican Americans were like any other whites in the community—as they had in the past—there would be little grounds for claiming exclusion. Furthermore, without conclusively proving exclusion as a class, Mexican American inclusion would always be hampered by the inclusion of an occasional member of their group, or even by the political predominance of Mexican Americans in such places where they were the majority population and held most political offices, but where they were still excluded from jury duty. This was not necessarily uncommon as whites continued to maintain a hold on the public institutions such as the schools and the courts even in places where their numbers might deprive them of complete political control.

Beyond the potential legal weakness of Frankfurter's suggestions, Mexican American reformers needed an articulation and an acceptance of the class-apart theory in order to make headway in their civil rights struggles. Two purposes would be served by the Court's acceptance of their theory. First, it would provide a protected "category" for Mexican Americans and thus provide them a legal strategy by which they could challenge not only exclusion from juries, but also attack the persistent segregation in the public schools and in public facilities. Very much like African Americans who had "their" Fourteenth Amendment, Mexican Americans would have "their" class-apart theory. Strengthening the concept with further actions and legal rulings would eventually codify it into law. This was a concept consistent with Sánchez's call for a "grand strategy" to combat segregation and discrimination.[29] And, of course, Sánchez had been claiming a "class-apart" status for Mexican Americans even before Carlos Cadena had been an undergraduate student in his classroom.[30]

In a letter to Hector P. García sixteen years after the case was decided, Sánchez sought to set the record straight on who came up with the "class-apart" theory. "I had long set forth, in my [university] class, that the Fourteenth Amendment protected against discrimination not only on the bases of 'race, creed, color' but also on the basis of recognition and differential treatment against a recognized 'class apart,'" wrote Sánchez. He added that then "it was a very ticklish argument" and not likely to work at the state level given the ruling that Mexicans were "white." But it was a different thing in the appeals process. Sánchez pointed out that in the "pre-Court of Criminal Appeals" phase of the *Hernández* case none of the lawyers had argued the class-apart theory. "So Carlos and I (and nobody else)," wrote Sánchez, "conceived of challenging the notion that because 'Mexicans' were legally 'white,' they couldn't complain that no 'Mexicans' were on the jury."[31] He continued, "Carlos and I outlined the brief, Carlos put it in legal lingo, and the GI Forum and others made it possible to send lawyers to Washington. All the lawyers except Gus were 'window dressing'. Gus argued Carlos's law and my factual findings brilliantly," he added.[32] Interestingly, the one lawyer who did not attend the Supreme Court hearing, but who was considered critical to the case—James De Anda—later questioned Sánchez's interpretation, and argued that it was his earlier brief that set the context for the *Hernández* challenge.[33]

The second purpose served by the class-apart theory was political unity in the ranks of Mexican American reformers. No other theory provided a potential win for both sides of the debate on whether Mexican Americans were white or racially different. The class-apart theory reaffirmed Mexican Americans' place in the category of white citizens while allowing those less comfortable with whiteness to maintain a sense of difference that came with the notion of being "apart." Mexican Americans could claim their racial, ethnic, cultural, and linguistic differences even as they proclaimed their Americanism. This allowed recognition of their oppression as well as their contribution to American society. Not all Mexican American reformers were comfortable with being identified as different, but eventually this strategy would become the dominant one in Mexican American reform activities. It is important to note the class-apart theory would ultimately be important in the creation of identity politics. Before the Chicano Movement and the affirmation of "race and class," the class-apart theory provided them the way to both distinguish themselves and yet be part of the whole, something that was important to Mexican Americans of that generation.[34]

Sánchez, as one of the older reformers and one of the few academicians and public intellectuals in the group, was in better position to develop and promote a conceptualization of the Mexican American experience. Six years after the *Hernández* case, and as part of the John F. Kennedy presidential campaign, he wrote a document he titled "The Americans of Mexican Descent: A Statement of Principles." The document outlines and expands on the class-apart theory even if it does not mention it. First, it declares that Mexican Americans had always "been here" by arguing that for many, "they did not cross the border but the border crossed them after the U.S.–Mexican War."[35] Second, they deserved to be "here" because of their loyalty in time of war. Third, they were a "forgotten" minority—"for whose well-being the United States has a special obligation . . . that has been . . . overlooked." Fourth, Mexican Americans were a valuable commodity to the nation; and finally that "only the *mexicano* can speak for the *mexicano*."[36]

These principles spoke to the class-apart theory by emphasizing Mexican American's native-born status, their loyalty, their worth, and their ability to speak for themselves. Only a people who were white or at least off-white and citizens could claim such a role. The document became part of the Viva Kennedy Club platform for the 1960 presidential campaign, and was used by Mexican American politicians and reformers as a way to distinguish their issues and concerns from those of other Kennedy supporters. By this time, Mexican Americans had begun moving away from seeking acceptance by society to demanding a greater integration into the political and social life of the nation. By reaffirming a native history and a profound loyalty, they went beyond simply being valuable laborers, and became citizens, with not only full rights but also full obligations. *Hernández*, after all, was not only about rights but also about duty. While some whites might attempt to avoid the obligation to serve on a jury, Mexican Americans were demanding the right to participate.

Being different, but not overly different—a class-apart—allowed them to enter American society as equal partners, even while maintaining a racial or ethnic difference that these reformers knew existed in the barrios. More important, by the 1950s most Mexican Americans reformers were moving toward emphasizing their uniqueness because within it, were found their contributions. They spoke a second language, valuable in an expanding world; they could relate to Latin America; and their community was extremely loyal and willing to fight for their country. Thus, being a class-apart provided them both the protection of the law and the elbowroom to accentuate their contributions and their uniqueness. The debates over jury selection had already shown that being "like everyone else" legally did not provide them any guarantees.

The official Supreme Court ruling did not particularly agree or promote this interpretation and did not use the defense lawyers' terminology, but it did recognize that Mexican Americans were treated as a "separate class." It is interesting to note that in the first memorandum circulated by the chief justice on April 19, 1954, there was a bit more discussion of the situation of Mexican Americans in Texas. Pete was identified as being of "Mexican descent," a descriptor omitted in the final ruling.[37] That memorandum also charged that Mexican Americans were "systematically, intentionally and deliberately excluded" from juries while the final ruling left it at "systematically" excluded. This is an important point because the memorandum implied, if not directly charged, that Mexican Americans were purposely discriminated against while the final ruling would leave enough room to consider discrimination as a byproduct of prejudices, biases, or insensitive administration of the law. While the final ruling would strongly condemn discrimination, it would hedge on specifically and forcibly condemning discrimination "on" Mexican Americans. In fact, while the memorandum would refer to discrimination "merely because of their racial origin," the final ruling would only use the word "race" in very general terms.[38]

The ruling was announced on May 3, two weeks before the more famous segregation case. After acknowledging Pete's allegation and the refusal of the Texas Court of Criminal Appeals to consider "the substantial federal question raised by the petitioner," the Court reiterated that "numerous [prior] decisions" made it a "denial of the equal protection of the law" to try an individual under indictment from a grand jury, or petit jury from which all persons of his race or color had been excluded. It specifically cited *Strauder v. West Virginia*, which declared that exclusion of a person on grounds other than race or color may also deprive that person of the constitutional guarantee of equal protection. The Texas Court had erred by ruling that there were only two classes "within the contemplation of the Fourteenth Amendment."[39] It reminded the Texas Court that the Supreme Court had never supported that view, and that the Texas courts themselves had taken a broader view of the issue in the past, citing in the notes *Juarez v. State* and *Clifton v. Puente*.[40]

Chief Justice Warren, who read the decision, then provided the context under which *Hernández v. Texas* would be decided. He pointed out that in the past "differences in race and color" had made it easy to identify groups who required the "aid of the courts in securing equal treatment under the laws."[41] Yet, the prejudices of a community, he continued, were far from static and "from time to time" new groups were seen as different from the community norm, and were likely to be discriminated against and thus "need the same protection."[42]

> Whether such a group exists within a community is a question of
> fact. When the existence of a distinct class is demonstrated, and it
> is further shown that the laws, as written or as applied single out
> that class for different treatment not based on some reasonable
> classification, the guarantees of the Constitution have been violated.
> The Fourteenth Amendment is not directed solely against discrimi-
> nation due to a "two-class theory"—that is, based upon differences
> between "white" and Negro.[43]

Here it is important to point out that the Court took no side on the issue of whether Mexican Americans were another race or not, nor did it specifically single them out as a "class apart." While it would go on to note the specifics of the alleged discrimination against Mexican Americans in Jackson County, it never fully acknowledged their existence as a distinct and particular class. Instead, it painted a broad picture of constitutional protections that would cover "all" groups. In this, it did not cover new ground, as numerous decisions already existed on the books covering discrimination of other racial and religious groups.[44]

If Pete's lawyers had been looking for the Court to affirm distinctively and without confusion that Mexican Americans were an identifiable racial or ethnic group, they might well have been disappointed. No record exists that they were, but it is important to note that yet again, Mexican Americans had been lumped together with other groups, and they had failed to merit their own classification as a growing and distinct ethnic group with particular problems. In essence, this reasoning by the Warren Court implied that given the community norms, Mexican Americans could slip in and out of public acceptance. Here, the Court revealed a complete lack of sophistication in dealing with a topic that Southwestern courts had ruled on continually in the first part of the twentieth century. It seemed to have ignored completely the social science literature presented, as well as to have missed the implications of the statistics provided in the defense brief.

Rather than taking the testimony, the statistics, and the literature as a foundation for understanding Mexican Americans as a group, they simply acknowledged the misdeeds against them without fully seeking to underscore the reasons for the problem. Rather than be seen as a group whose circumstances, history and differences were a challenge to the society at large, Mexican Americans were seen as just a group who happened at the time to be out of sync with a particular community. While the Court no doubt understood the dilemma of de facto discrimination, they seemed not to fully understand its impact on a community whose suffering was similar in many ways to that of African Americans but without the specific legal framework that codified discrimination into law.

"The exclusion of otherwise eligible persons from jury service," wrote Chief Justice Warren, "solely because of their ancestry or national origin is discrimination prohibited by the Fourteenth Amendment."[45] He added that the Texas statute was not discriminatory but that the petitioner alleged the administration of it was. The ruling then went on to argue that the petitioner had indeed proven that persons of Mexican descent were a "separate class in Jackson County, distinct from 'whites'."[46] But as the qualifier "in Jackson County" shows, the justices were willing to limit the discrimination to the circumstances of a violating of a "community norm." The ruling continued, "Here the testimony of responsible officials and citizens contained the admission that residents of the community distinguished between 'white' and 'Mexican' . . . Having established the existence of a class, petitioner was then charged with the burden of proving discrimination."[47] Here, the ruling repeated most of Cadena's brief on the number of Mexicans and Mexican Americans in Jackson County and how many might have been eligible for jury duty. The Court considered the burden of proof imposed by *Norris v. Alabama* as having been met, and rejected the state's rebuttal that the jury commissioners had testified that they did not discriminate against persons of Mexican descent.[48] Chief Justice Warren then declared, "Circumstances or chance may well dictate that no persons in a certain class will serve on a particular jury or during some particular period. But it taxes our credulity to say that mere chance resulted in there being no members of this class among the over six thousand jurors called in the past twenty-five years. The result bespeaks discrimination, whether or not it was a conscious decision on the part of any individual jury commissioner. The judgment of conviction must be reversed."[49]

This was the essence of the decision that Pete and his lawyers were looking for, but the Court felt the need to respond to the allegation that the petitioner was asking for proportional representation. Continued Warren, "The petitioner did not seek proportional representation, nor did he claim a right to have persons of Mexican descent sit on the particular juries which he faced."[50] His only claim, according to Warren, was the right of not having "members of his class" systematically excluded. "To this much, he is entitled by the Constitution," concluded Warren.[51]

Before assessing the reaction to the decision, it is important to note what the decision said and what it did not say. First, Pete's lawyers had established that Mexican Americans were a "separate class," that they were discriminated against according to the burden of proof imposed by *Norris v. Alabama*, and that they had been excluded from jury duty for twenty-five years—though the court did not venture to say whether it was intentional or not. It also reaffirmed that the Fourteenth Amendment did not provide for proportional representation. In meeting the criteria for a "separate group," the petitioners had succeeded in "qualifying" for the equal protection of the Constitution, as long as they remained outside the "norms" of their particular community. Finally, Pete had won the right to a jury that "might" (but was not required to) include someone of his "class." For Pete's lawyers and most Mexican American reformers of the era, this was a victory and a reaffirmation of their place in American society.

It is also important that we review what the Court did not do, and what it meant for Mexican Americans both legally and politically. First and foremost, the Court did not take sides on the debate of whether Mexican Americans were an identifiable racial or ethnic group. This would be the most important failure of *Hernández v. Texas*, and one that could be blamed on both Pete's lawyers and the justices: the lawyers for vacillating between racial and ethnic categorization, and the Court for failing to acknowledge that Mexican American discrimination was based on more than just "shifting" community standards. One could argue that the lawyers were simply trying to win the case for their client, but that would obscure the fact that their litigation strategy was a civil rights one and not a criminal one. That is, they were certain of their client's guilt and knew the best they could get was a retrial that would likely still mean a conviction. What they really wanted was to strike down jury discrimination and to guarantee Mexican Americans the protection of the Fourteenth Amendment.

Yet, they went into the appeal process without first resolving the issue over their identity. Whether Mexican Americans were a racial group, an ethnic group, or simply a minority remained a question unanswered. Each one of those categories had its supporters and retractors and without a real fundamental and intellectual discussion over the issue of identity, the lawyers were left with one legal strategy but not a philosophical one. This failure was particular to middle-class Mexican American reformers who were trapped in their "citizenship" strategy. Sánchez was the primary promoter of this strategy—using the concept of citizenship to both demand their constitutional rights from society in general, and to attract Mexican Americans to their civic obligations by arguing that citizenship did have its rewards. But citizenship in 1950s America was not colorblind and Mexican American reformers were conscious of that, yet they were never able to fully develop a strategy to deal with this dilemma. Sánchez, while a great promoter of the citizenship strategy, did not, however, ever seek to abandon his ethnic origins or to downplay them completely.

While he considered Mexicans "white" he never considered them as interchangeable with whites; only a few years after *Hernández v. Texas*, he would come close to making having Mexican American origins a prerequisite for political representation of that community. In 1961, while defending the newly established Political Association of Spanish-Speaking Organizations (PASO), he declared, "I may be wrong in saying that only the *mexicano* can speak for the *mexicano*. Up to now there hasn't been any evidence that the contrary is so . . . I can't help but take a completely cynical, pessimistic view of Anglo politics and Anglo politicians."[52]

There were simply too many debates inherent in finding racial identity among Mexican American reformers. As has been mentioned before, most Mexicans and Mexican Americans clung to the notion of being "Mexican," something akin to being racially different, although most would still have marked themselves as "white" in the census forms and in other government forms. This inherent contradiction made sense to the rank and file Mexican-origin person who had been brought up in Mexican schools, indoctrinated in barrio festivals, and admonished at countless kitchen tables that he or she was a *mestizo*, a mixture of Spanish and Indian. They had also been conditioned by the larger society to recognize that they were not really white, no matter the government document classifications. They did not feel the need to engage in nuances, something that Mexican American reformers, especially the lawyers and academicians, were steeped in.

If Mexican Americans were unsure, why should it be expected that the justices be any more educated on the issues of Mexican American identity? The answer would be that they did not need to be in order to provide greater and more expansive protection to Mexican Americans. They simply needed to reiterate what most, if not all, knew and that was that people of Mexican descent were numerous, were growing in numbers, and that they faced discrimination at present and had faced it for more than a century. Warren as governor and state attorney general surely understood this, and Clark, the Texas politician, was more than aware as his state had the largest number of Mexicans in the country and racial contentions were a common occurrence in the Lone Star State. At the same time, support was building during this period for a massive deportation effort. Both men had been in the public arena when the Mexican Repatriation had sent hundreds of thousands of Mexicans and Mexican Americans south of the border, and both were well aware that the Bracero Program was a key element of the economic explosion in the West, Southwest, and Midwest. The deportations and the Bracero Program were unmistakable evidence that people of Mexican ancestry were here to stay. To have thought otherwise was inconceivable and so was the notion that they would simply blend in. Yet, the justices had acted as if the issues brought up by the case were due to misapplication of the law or to community prejudices.

Whether they fully accepted Mexican American whiteness or found it the least problematic of the classifications to give them, the justices knew or should have known that Mexican Americans were neither going away nor were their problems going to evaporate by "localizing" the case. Instead of dealing with the legal dilemma that Mexican Americans presented, the Court chose instead to narrow the parameters of the case to Jackson County, notwithstanding efforts by Pete's lawyers to expand its effects to all Mexican Americans. In this, the Court received assistance from the inability of Pete's lawyers to present more evidence about jury discrimination across the West and Southwest. They would have done so if they had been well funded and had well-structured national organizations to help them accumulate such data. Gus had actually argued that this type of discrimination was constant in at least fifty counties in Texas and New Mexico, but he had no statistics, no witnesses, and no reports to back up that assertion. Had some reformers taken a step back from the euphoria that followed the ruling they would have understood that Mexican Americans—despite the Supreme Court ruling—remained both "invisible" and "forgotten" in American jurisprudence.

Interestingly, two days after the ruling but without benefit of the actual decision, Cadena expressed some concern with the language of the ruling. "According to the newspapers," he wrote Sánchez, "the opinion on the *Hernández* case took a dim view of 'different' treatment of minority groups. Whether Warren deliberately chose to use 'different' rather than 'unequal' is something that remains to be seen. Actually, this is not the first time the Supreme Court condemned 'different' treatment."[53] The newspaper accounts proved to be right, as the chief justice wrote, "When the existence of a distinct class is demonstrated, and it is further shown that the laws, as written or as applied, single out that class for *different* treatment not based on some reasonable classification, the guarantees of the Constitution have been violated" (my italics).[54] In fact, the ruling never mentions the word *unequal*, and mentions the word *discrimination* seven times, but only once directly in reference to Mexican Americans. This, when it declared that the absence of Mexican American jurors for twenty-five years "bespeaks discrimination whether or not it was a conscious decision on the part of any individual jury commissioner."[55]

Cadena did not elaborate on what the use of *different* treatment instead of *unequal* treatment might mean. Instead, he chose to "avoid creating confusion," and told Sánchez, "I will deliberately refrain from setting down any further thoughts on paper. Besides, any further cogitation on my part might necessitate getting down to the concrete, and concretization always involves the danger of cutting off all possibility of graceful retreat."[56] Without any other mention of the subject in the letter or any subsequent correspondence, it is hard to know exactly what Cadena meant. Was he concerned with misinterpreting the ruling before he had it in his hands? Or was he afraid that any criticism of the ruling might weaken its effect? It is quite possible that Cadena, much like Gus and Herrera, was as much a social reformer as he was a legal advocate, and he chose to take a political step forward rather than admit to an ideological back step.

Herrera was in his office when he heard the news from Texas Senator Price Daniels ten minutes after the ruling was announced at about 11:00

a.m. Houston time. He quickly closed shop and took his staff to celebrate.[57] No record exists of where Gus or Cadena were at the time of the ruling, though it is likely that the latter was attending to his teaching duties and the former was seeking new clients and new cases to strike at public school segregation. Their reaction was revealed several months later when they both wrote the pamphlet "Justice for a Cotton-Picker!" There, neither found fault with the ruling and saw it as a great victory for Mexican Americans not only in Texas but also across the nation. One could argue that given the strategy of Mexican American reformers their efforts had been completely successful. They got to the Supreme Court and they won. This was unprecedented and they expected to build on the case. In their minds, Mexican Americans were now part of the American legal mosaic.

The *San Antonio Light*'s night edition was the first newspaper to announce the decision with a bold, front-page headline: "High Court Rules Texas Biased." It simply retold the details of the case but did add that the opinion "did not state what steps Texas should take next in the case. It merely ordered reversal of the conviction."[58] The *Albuquerque Journal* declared that the "often-pronounced ban on barring Negroes from jury duty" extended to others, in this case Mexican Americans. But it pointed out that the Court never defined "reasonable classification," which it had implied was the only reason for differential treatment. It was, after all, wrote the *Journal* writer, the basis on which the Supreme Court had established the separate but equal doctrine.[59] On the same day, the *Corpus Christi Caller* presented its readers with a headline, "Latin American Jurors Barred; Verdict Upset" and emphasized that the Court had rejected the state's two-class theory based on the "differences between white and Negroes."[60] It also quoted district attorney Wayne Hartman of Cuero, Texas, who pointed out that double jeopardy did not apply to the *Hernández* case, and so he would recommend to his colleague, the county attorney, to reset the retrial at the earliest possible date.[61]

The county attorney told the newspaper that the next grand jury would meet in September, unless the district judge saw fit to call a special session. He added that since 1953, when he took over the county attorney's position, "Latin Americans had been serving on grand and petit, and on special venires."[62] The newspaper followed up with a separate article in which it pointed out that Texas district courts would have to give more "attention" to minority group participation in juries. It quoted a "Texas authority" who told the newspaper that "if a judge wants a trial to stand up on appeal, he is going to be forced to see that any minority group concerned is represented on the jury."[63] The *San Antonio Express* added that the ruling had the effect

Figure 5. A gathering of Who's Who in the Mexican American legal world in the 1950s to celebrate the *Hernández* victory at a banquet in Corpus Christi, Texas shortly after the Supreme Court decision. Standing left to right: John J. Herrera, Houston; Albert Peña Jr., San Antonio; Al Hernández, Houston; Frank M. Piñedo, Austin; Carlos Cadena (middle), San Antonio; David Longoria, Austin; Leo Duran, Corpus Christi; Gustavo "Gus" García, San Diego (at the time); and William Bonilla, Corpus Christi. Sitting from left to right: Hector de Peña, Corpus Christi; and Homero López, Kingsville. The only prominent person missing was James De Anda.

of "outlawing the excluding of Mexican Americans from juries not only in Jackson County but a number of other Texas and New Mexico counties where the practice has been prevalent."[64] It did point out, however, that the Court had not meant to require Mexican American jurors on the "specific jury" that would retry Hernández.[65]

The *Los Angeles Times* did not play up the decision, placing an article on it on the seventeenth page, but it did highlight that the Court had widened the ban on discrimination and gone beyond a two-classes interpretation.[66] The *Dallas Morning News* did place it on the front page, and declared that "Jackson County has been violating the Fourteenth Amendment by habitually excluding persons of Latin American descent from jury service."[67] The newspaper followed its front-page article the next day with an editorial in which it credited the Supreme Court with doing service to Texas "in correcting an error which has crept into the practice of picking juries in *Jackson County*" (my italics). It continued, "Obviously, the exclusion of such jurors has taken on the nature of a local custom and has been accepted unthinkingly for a number of years. But that is no reason why the practice should not be broken up and jury selection brought into line with even older Anglo-Saxon laws and traditions governing the selection of a jury of one's peers."[68]

Interestingly, the Dallas newspaper reduced the prejudices toward Mexican Americans in juries to that of a practice in one of the state's "historic areas." Nowhere did it expand or recognize the larger implication of the ruling, nor did it acknowledge that the practice was widespread in many areas, or that it was simply part of a larger problem of discrimination toward Mexican Americans in Texas. More important, it sought to cast the situation in Jackson County as an aberration in American society, completely ignoring the numerous Supreme Court rulings on this issue as it pertained not only to "Negroes" but also Asians, Catholics, Poles, and other groups.

The *San Antonio Express* seemed to take a slightly different attitude in praising the decision for overruling a "quarter-century's duration of that unconstitutional practice," and added that the "attorneys and . . . civic organizations that . . . were instrumental in getting the United States Supreme Court to start those wheels moving, have rendered their State's repute a distinct service."[69] It further pointed out that the high court had made "hash" of the State's contention that there was no systematic exclusion of Mexican Americans. It added,

> Not only the United States, but the Texas State Supreme Court
> goes its way—after some generations—undertaking to crush
> various discriminatory practices that offend against the fun-
> damental principle of "equality under the law." It is less than a
> month since the Texas Supreme Court reversed and remanded a
> Lubbock County civil case because attorneys had grossly humili-
> ated Negroes called as plaintiff witnesses—an affront so "highly
> inflammatory and prejudicial, such an appeal to race prejudice,
> that the case should be tried over."[70]

It continued, declaring that both the federal and state appeals "to simple justice" were going to have a "mighty impact."

The *Washington Post and Times Herald* also ran a front-page story declaring the Court's ruling as an expansion of the Fourteenth Amendment's provision to include more than black and white. It was a much more extensive article that quoted liberally from the ruling and explained slightly more the details of the case. It also noted that while not explicitly mentioning it, Chief Justice Warren had applied the same reasoning to *Hernández* as the *Scottsboro* case, which placed the burden on the prosecution to prove no discrimination existed when qualified individuals were excluded from jury duty.[71] The newspaper followed its news story with an editorial three days later, condemning the continual need to rule against jury discrimination. "It is strange that any citizen in this land—not to mention any court—should continue to think that individuals of a distinct minority group can be legally convicted of a crime when members of that group are systematically excluded from juries. Yet the Supreme Court has found it necessary once more to set aside such a conviction in Jackson County."[72]

The editorial took the Texas courts to task for seeking to "skirt around" the Fourteenth Amendment by using the "two-class theory" as some had used the "superior class" theory in the past. "If that conclusion [two-class theory] had been accepted," declared the editorial, "the great bulwark against discrimination would itself have become a source of discrimination."[73] It further added that the Court had "spoken plainly and forcefully" and now no state had an excuse to exclude any minority group from jury duty because the principle of inclusion had become a "matter of course."

The national press was not alone in its coverage of the *Hernández* decision, as the *Excelsior* from Mexico City also ran with the story. It first reprinted the Associated Press story on the day of the ruling, and then followed it up with another article six days later. The headline read, "One More Step Against Discrimination in Texas."[74] It quoted the American Civil Liberties Union as declaring that the ruling should "serve as warning to all southern states where racial exclusion exists." It also alluded to the opinion of several Puerto Rican lawyers, who in agreeing with the ACLU, argued that the Executive Branch needed to "order" a strict vigilance to prevent further exclusion in Texas as well as other states of members of minority groups. It further called the attitude of Jackson County officials as "cavernous and insulting."[75] Interestingly, the Mexican newspaper interpreted the ruling to mean that Hernández had to be tried by a jury whose members were of Mexican descent. There was also one other interpretation that was inconsistent with the ruling, and that was revealed in the subtitle of the article, which indicated that in cases against "foreigners" other foreigners had to participate.

The Mexican newspaper had fallen into the trap—perpetuated often by the American media—of calling Mexican Americans "foreigners." Nonetheless, the articles indicated that journalists and readers in Mexico were interested in what was happening to Mexicans in the United States. No doubt the Bracero Program and the growing deportation campaigns had heightened the Mexican public's interest in their countrymen and others of Mexican descent in the United States. They were also very aware that Mexicans and Mexican Americans were involved in a struggle for their civil rights. Cases like the Felix Longoria funeral conflict were often widely discussed in Mexican newspapers, and so were stories of Border Patrolmen's mistreatment of undocumented workers. Mexican American reformers often sought the assistance of the Mexican government in their struggles north of the border in order to put pressure on the U.S. government.[76]

A sampling of law journals indicates that the main lesson from *Hernández v. Texas* was the "expansion of the 'Norris rule'" and the inclusion of other groups under the protection of the Fourteenth Amendment. The *American Bar Association Journal* highlighted the refusal of the Court to accept the "two-classes" theory and pointed out that the petitioner had "met the initial burden of demonstrating that persons of Mexican descent constitute a separate class in the *county*" (my italics).[77] The journal seemed willing to accept the ruling that limited this "separateness" to the local community context. Harold T. Ackerman, in the *Alabama Law Review*, agreed that the emphasis on the notion of a "separate class" was explicit in the ruling and asserted that while the Court had rarely faced the issue of exclusion for reasons other than race or color, it had nonetheless in the past settled that question in favor of the discriminated group.[78] It added that in fact the Court had "liberalized" the rule of exclusion set out in *Norris* by not requiring that the petitioner provide "actual proof that a Mexican or Latin American had not served on a grand jury or petit jury."[79] In essence, the case of jury discrimination had relied on the word of the defense attorneys and the acquiescence of the prosecution, which had never really believed that the Court would give much credence to the "rule of exclusion" contention.

The *North Carolina Law Review* interpreted the ruling as being based on the state's misapplication of the Equal Protection Clause; a correct application of the "Norris" rule by the Supreme Court; and the state's failure to "rebut the prima facie showing of discrimination."[80] The journal pointed out that the Texas court had itself used language that implied a belief that "exclusion of citizens of a particular nationality from jury service" was a denial of equal protection of the laws when there was "proof" of actual discrimination.[81] "It appears," wrote Charles Kivett, the author of the piece, "that the Texas court has had no trouble applying the 'Norris' rule to classes other than white or Negro, except where the question presented involved the exclusion of persons of Mexican descent, and even there it intimated that the rule should be applied to the latter group if actual discrimination were shown against the defendant. No valid reason was given for the distinction."[82] In essence, the North Carolina journal agreed with the one from Alabama that "the decision in the principal case extends the 'Norris' rule for the first time." It further added that the "Court ruled correctly . . . [and] will continue to expand the application of the rule if the occasions arise."[83]

In the law journal discussions is best understood the contribution of *Hernández* to civil rights litigation, if not for all groups at least for Mexican Americans. The "expansion" of the Fourteenth Amendment alluded to by the journal writers was not something particularly new, but it was recent and it involved the largest ethnic group in the country and one that continued to grow. This meant that the case had the potential to play a part in other litigation dealing with either Mexican Americans or other ethnic and nationality groups that found themselves in a similar situation. More important, while the justices limited the ruling to "community standards" at the time, these journal writers had seen larger implications, and that was likely—to some extent—to be the case in the future. This meant that the Equal Protection Clause was expanded to cover more than "Negroes" in the minds of legal scholars—many of whom already believed that—and the serving justices. Whether *Hernández* was ever quoted again or not, the expansion had occurred and it would remain a part of constitutional law.

For Mexican Americans, *Hernández* had integrated them into the civil rights matrix that was taking shape in American society by the middle of the 1950s.

A Victory for
"Every Living Soul"

Initially, the person most impacted by the Supreme Court's ruling was Pete, who had now served nearly two and a half years in the State Penitentiary at Huntsville, Texas. He did not have much chance, however, to celebrate or even to taste freedom because three days after the ruling, Jackson County Justice of the Peace Joe Cherry issued a warrant for his arrest. The warrant was quickly forwarded to the prison so that he would remain there until the beginning of a new trial.[1] Three weeks after the ruling Gus visited Edna to request a change of venue. "I honestly don't think the boy (Hernández) can get a fair trial in Jackson County since there has been so much said and published on the case," he told an Edna reporter. He acknowledged that Pete had committed a "dastardly" crime and needed to be punished for it, but added that he had already been in jail for nearly three years, and needed to serve only a few more years "to pay for his crime."[2]

At the time, both the county and district attorneys were awaiting word from the state capital on how to proceed but both expressed certainty that he would be re-indicted by the September grand jury and subsequently retried.[3] On September 16 the county impaneled a grand jury and Pete headed the list of those whose cases were to be heard. Among those impaneled was a man by the name of Sesario Rodriguez.[4] Seven days later, Pete was re-indicted for murder and a trial date set for November 1.[5] Gus received his change of venue and the trial moved from Edna to nearby Refugio and the case came to trial on December 27. Because of a fire that occurred in the courthouse years later, no record exists of that trial either. All we have are some newspaper accounts, the most informative being the one from a Corpus Christi newspaper that reported Pete pleading guilty to shooting Espinoza and receiving a twenty-year sentence. Gus, according to the newspaper account, "expressed satisfaction with the verdict and [predicted] . . . that Hernández [would] be eligible for parole in six months because of time already served."[6] The newspaper account also had Gus providing a different spin on the details of the case. According to him, Pete had gotten into an argument with "some other persons" and had gone looking for them with the rifle but had run into Espinoza and shot him instead. This "new" version would only muddy the details that have survived from the case, given that the record of the first trial has been lost and what little testimony might have been given in the second trial is also missing. What really happened on that August day in 1951 will always be shrouded in controversy.

Pete had played a relatively small part in his own case and served as the forgotten man in this important affair. Shortly after the original trial, he became a name only and rarely appeared in the promotion of the case, in the fundraising, and even in the celebration of the victory. By the time of the retrial, Pete had served nearly forty months in the penitentiary. To his credit, Gus did not forget him and made every effort to get him paroled as soon as he became eligible. On February 12, 1960, he wrote a passionate letter to Jack Ross of the Board of Pardons and Paroles to inquire of Pete's circumstances. "It was with much chagrin," he wrote, "that I learned . . . that Pete Hernández . . . who served as a guinea pig for our appeal to the United States Supreme Court . . . is still in jail." He asked Ross to investigate Pete's circumstances and asked for a meeting to discuss Pete's record in prison, which he admitted he did not know much of. "I really feel conscience stricken, Jack," he wrote, "and I would like to do everything within my power to gain freedom for this boy who was willing to risk a potential death sentence upon the second trial . . . in order to help us establish a very important principle of law and civil rights for Latin Americans everywhere."[7]

On June 7, Gus received a letter from Ross informing him that the Board of Pardon and Paroles had recommended parole for Pete. A day later, a delighted Gus wrote to several friends: "while I do not wish to claim credit for the final successful conclusion of our historical issue, I have pestered Jack Ross for several months now via letters, long distance calls and two personal visits in Austin. I can now truthfully say that my conscience is clear in this matter."[8] But Gus did not leave things there. That same day, June 8, he wrote Pete, telling him of the letter from the parole board and expressing confidence that the governor would approve it and he would soon be a free man. "You probably thought that we had forgotten all about you," he wrote. "As a matter of fact, we have been in frequent communication with the Board . . . to discuss your case." The problem, added Gus, was that "your record was very bad in recent years. You know that you made no effort until recently to improve your [prison record]. You would not even go to Chapel, which was a simple way of getting additional points."[9]

In the letter we see a tender side of Gus that all his friends knew he had but which did not always come through in his lawyering and advocacy. Despite his shortcomings with alcohol and his flamboyance, Gus had a moralistic view of the world. "I am telling you these things because I do not want you to feel resentful towards anyone for your long imprisonment," he wrote. "We all make mistakes in this life, Pete, and yours was a terrible one. But I do not want you to think of the past. You are still young and your whole life is ahead of you. You will find that most people will be ready to show you kindness and understanding if you only give them a chance." He cautioned Pete about his temper and told him to think about his time in prison when he began to feel anger, and to "RUN, don't walk, away from trouble."[10] Gus then listed his home and office telephone numbers and told him to call whenever he felt he was getting into trouble. He asked him to come visit him before he fully situated himself. "I will be glad to give you any kind of assistance that I can possibly muster for you." He added that he never wanted to see him in jail again, but reminded him that "the Lord only helps those who help themselves." He then wished him a long and fruitful life as a "free man and useful citizen."[11] This ended the known contact between Pete and his lawyers. They would not refer to him again in their correspondence except to correct the historical record.

Pete did not disappear after his parole although he never again attracted public attention. He remained close to his family in Edna though he moved to Port Lavaca, near Corpus Christi, and got married and had one son. Later, he got sick; his family moved to Austin and he was interned in a long-term care unit there. He died sometime in the 1970s. His family remembered him as a loyal, quiet, and respectful man, though one possessing a quick temper. They never remembered him talking much about the case, nor showing any remorse. Pete was a temperamental young man who did not see himself responsible or guilty of the event that led to Espinoza's death. Beyond the guilty plea, no record or memory exists of him expressing regret. Like many other young men of his circumstances, he seemed to begrudge the world for his sufferings and his limitations.[12] The years he spent in prison hardened him, and probably contributed to his failing health. But possibly he remembered Gus's counsel and managed to stay away from serious trouble and jail.

The immediate impact of the Supreme Court ruling ended with Pete, though there was one man whose trial was delayed in order for the court to find a more suitable jury.[13] There might have been other cases but no record exists of them. One of the great handicaps of the Mexican American reform community was its lack of funds with which to pursue a retrial of other cases. Even if there had been funds, they most likely would have been spent trying to find out whose circumstances were similar to Pete's. There had simply been no research, no data gathered, and no other reformers coming forward with similar cases to provide any foundation for a strategy to overturn more cases. Because the Supreme Court provided no enforcement provisions in the ruling, no real strategy could be pursued without large amounts of money.

The most important aspect of the case, in legal terms, was that it served as one more piece of evidence against jury discrimination, though initially it was used mostly for African American jury discrimination cases—although there were efforts later to use the ruling as one that spoke to the treatment and to the segregation of Mexican American students. In fact, De Anda, one of the original lawyers in the *Hernández* case, attempted to use the case as a foundation for a desegregation case in Texas.[14] In the end, however, Mexican Americans would find justice mostly through *Brown v. Board of Education*, which over time bestowed upon them the one thing that *Hernández* did not—a racial/ethnic status. Mexican Americans became people of color and thus protected by the Fourteenth Amendment. This would occur in the late 1960s about the time when no real debate existed anymore within the Mexican American community about whether its members were white or not. They were now people of color—brown, Chicano, or Mexican American.[15]

The actions of the three lawyers with the partial acquiescence of the Supreme Court had spurred a Mexican American odyssey toward an accentuation of their differences, their ethnicity, and their "color." While much of this action would be promoted by more militant Chicano activists, Mexican American reformers contributed their share to the building of a new Mexican American or Chicano identity. It is important to note that while not all Mexican American reformers became Chicanos—in fact, few did—they did construct an "experience" that was racialized. Instead of simply seeking entrance into American society, they demanded an acceptance of their existence as an identifiable minority group. The entrance would have to be collective and not just individual. While Mexican American reformers had always advocated on behalf of their community, they often accepted the notion that assimilation and integration would come individually and the end result would be an Americanization of their community.[16] They never sought a total subsuming of their culture and ideals but did see a gradual and substantive change in them as Mexican-origin people became more American. It would have been difficult for the originators of LULAC and the other Mexican American organizations to see themselves demanding a collective integration of their community with many of its Mexican trappings intact. Yet, this is precisely what happened by the time the 1960s rolled around.

This collective search for identity and its trappings was a direct result of the actions of numerous reformers and their hodgepodge of ideas. Among those were, of course, Gus, Herrera, and Cadena. Herrera was a leader of LULAC—he served as its president during the time of the *Hernández* appeal (1952–1953)—and other Mexican American organizations and his position always, particularly in the 1960s, made him conscious of the need for a collective identity. He would remain a strong institutional reformer, organizing twelve unions and fifty-three new LULAC councils throughout the Southwest, and serving in the Viva Kennedy and Viva Johnson political campaigns, where he strongly promoted Mexican American issues. As more and more Mexican Americans became more concerned about their place in American society, the greater the need arose to maintain a collective identity. LULAC and other Mexican American organizations became less groupings of elites in the barrio, and more representatives of the masses of those barrios. Herrera proved to be a leader in those efforts.[17]

Cadena, from the beginning, saw the *Hernández* case as a way to create coalitions with other groups to combat racism and segregation. He defended Mexican Americans but also African Americans, and he saw civil rights as the domain of all. His efforts were consistent in trying to underscore the collective identity that Mexican Americans had developed given their experiences in fighting for their rights and in their loyalty toward American society. This viewpoint would lead to a tenacious legal career in civil rights that eventually got him appointed to the Texas Fourth Court of Criminal Appeals in 1965, where he would acquire the reputation of a man who saw beyond color and circumstances. In 1977 he became the chief justice of the court.[18] Cadena, through his civil rights work and his tenure in the court of appeals, became the most successful Mexican American lawyer of his time and possibly of all time with four major victories, including three in the Supreme Court. Aside from *Hernández*, he argued *Clifton v. Puente* in the appellate court, which set aside restrictive clauses that prohibited selling land to people of Mexican descent; *Delgado v. Colorado School District*, which struck down the segregation of Mexican Americans in the public schools; and *Harvey v. the State of Texas*, which declared unconstitutional the prohibition of mixed fights in boxing.[19] No lawyer of his generation could claim such a judicial record, and only Reynaldo G. Garza, who became a federal judge in 1961, would rise as high in the profession.[20]

Gus, of course, had been the one who put life into the concept of being Mexican American before the Supreme Court. Through his own family, he provided Mexican Americans historicity, he acknowledged them as both good and bad, and he expected them to both take responsibility for their own actions and to demand that government assume responsibility for their civil rights. While he believed in the "melting pot" concept of American society, he did not believe that it would occur until Mexican Americans first came into their own as a distinct group that could demand and merit its place in society. Gus died before the advent of the Chicano Movement and so we can only speculate on what his reactions would have been to this angry collective cry for cultural identity and separatism. It is likely that like other reformers of his generation, he would have followed part of the way, resisted its more radical aspects, and defended his generation's contribution to its creation.

Interestingly, Gus, the one who seemed most to represent the Mexican American reformer-types who took advantage of their advocacy to establish profitable law practices, get appointed to government posts, or find other remunerated positions, became the one who least profited from his experience at the Supreme Court. By 1955, his alcoholism had become a major obstacle to his law practice and it made him a difficult friend and colleague. Two years after the *Hernández* case, invitations to LULAC or GI Forum conventions became infrequent as many of his former friends moved away from him, embarrassed or simply exhausted from defending his outrageous behavior. He moved out of San Antonio to friendlier south Texas but his fortunes did not improve. His health problems and his erratic behavior eventually got him into trouble. He committed fraud by issuing bad checks and he lost his right to litigate for two years (1961–63).[21]

On June 3, 1964, Gus died of a seizure when he was taking refuge in an office in the Old Farmer's Market in San Antonio, where a friend had given him a place to stay to dry out from his drinking bouts. His death ended a roller coaster last few years in which he tried to quit drinking, went to rehabilitation, and tried to rebuild his law practice, but to no avail. He lost his third wife and most contact with his two children from a second marriage. He would have been totally alone had it not been for Herrera, who always stood ready to provide him a few dollars, visit him in the hospital, take him in as a law partner, and even read him the "riot act."[22] In the end, the friendship was not enough to save Gus. In an undated, untitled obituary in the Herrera Collection files, an unknown writer remarked, "Maybe Gus loved the bright lights too much, or maybe he drew so many honors in his early life that they began to pall. Whatever the cause, he lived it up at night, took it easier during the day, and spent the last years of his life in a state of declining fortune."[23] In the same obituary, Cadena expressed the feelings that Gus simply did not believe that conventions applied to him, but he added, "With all his faults and all of the things he did, or was accused of doing, Gus García was a pretty good guy and he did some pretty great things for the Mexican people."[24] Gus died less than two months before his forty-ninth birthday.

Some would blame his alcoholism on the fact that he never garnered the recognition that other reformers received and that he never found monetary compensation for his hard work in civil rights. Most of his colleagues in the profession and even those in the *Hernández* team went on to do well in their professions and attained economic stability. It is more likely that his alcoholism was partly inherited from an alcoholic father, and was compounded by his early brilliance, which promised much but could not deliver in a segregated society where limitations were rampant even for a brilliant Mexican American. Today, we are more likely to be sensitive to someone with a drinking problem, and much better able to medically treat the problem, and the individual is likely to have better opportunities to make "something" of his or her life. Gus was a giant of a man in the legal and political sense, but he never seemed satisfied with the accolades that the community for which he labored could give him. He loved his people but he probably believed himself as deserving more than simple gratitude from his constituency. He wanted more and he wanted it quickly. Had he lived a longer and much more stable life, he likely would have gotten more material compensation out of his life, but whether it would have been enough for a man whose dreams were majestical is unknown.

This same Gus, who believed that the ruling had been a highlight of Mexican American lawyering history, would surely have been disappointed if not devastated by the United States Commission on Civil Rights' report titled "Mexican Americans and the administration of justice in the Southwest" issued on March 1970. The commission "found serious and widespread under representation of Mexican Americans on grand and petit juries in state courts in many areas of the Southwest."[25] Citing extensive "field investigations" in 1967 and 1968, and the assistance of three state advisory committee meetings and one commission hearing in 1968, the report concluded that widespread evidence existed that "equal protection of the law in the administration of justice is being withheld from Mexican Americans."[26] The report itself dealt not only with juries but also with law enforcement treatment, bail and bond services, legal representation, and even employment opportunities in law enforcement agencies. In all the areas, they found that Mexican Americans simply did not receive fair treatment.

Quoting and citing Mexican American lawyers and other prominent members of the Mexican American community, the report provided facts and an overall picture that Gus, Cadena, and Herrera would have loved to have had for their case before the Supreme Court, and that might have strengthened their argument of a "class apart." The report clearly showed that jury discrimination was not an isolated incident in one or several counties in Texas or that it depended on "community norms" to rear its ugly head. In Texas, lawyers testified that they had tried hundreds of cases in county after county without ever seeing one Mexican American in a petit jury. In Phoenix, Arizona, a probation officer stated that in 95 percent of all trials, not one single Mexican American served on the jury. This testimony was bolstered by two attorneys and a city councilman who agreed that few Mexican Americans were called for jury duty. In Colorado, Mexican American advocates claimed the same situation, and in Fort Summer, New Mexico—where Mexican Americans made up 60 percent of the population—residents told the commission that Mexican Americans simply did not serve on juries. In Los Angeles, a public defender was quoted as saying, "I recall very few Mexican Americans on any jury I have tried in a period of fifteen years."[27] Sixteen years after *Hernández*, jury commissioners were still excluding Mexican Americans from the jury box. This vividly underscored the weakness of the justices' ruling when it failed to recognize Mexican Americans as a community treated "unequally" rather than "differently," and when it defined discrimination against them within the context of "community norms."

Compounding the problem of jury exclusion, said the report, was the use of peremptory challenges to eliminate those Mexican Americans who did get on the jury venires. Matt García told the commission in San Antonio that the small number of Mexican Americans on the venire were "often placed at the end—'so far down that you are not going to get to them'— and the use of peremptory challenges made it possible for the prosecution to assure that there are no Mexican Americans on the jury." He added, "And I'm speaking of areas where the percentage of Mexican Americans exceeds fifty."[28] Another San Antonio attorney recounted a case in which he requested and got three venires, and saw the number of Mexican Americans included go from one to five but then all five were peremptorily challenged. In Arizona, Mexican Americans complained about the same thing, while Manuel Aranda, a Los Angeles lawyer, described it this way: "It turns out to be a game trying to get your Mexican American juror on as the district attorney tries to get him off."[29]

The report would go on to cite other problems not only in the petit but also the grand jury system. Then it concluded with what it called the "effects of exclusion," an indictment of corrosive effects that jury discrimination had on Mexican American confidence in the judicial system, and on the actual application of the law. It cited a case in which a Mexican American chose to plead guilty rather than face a jury of whites who were not likely to give him a "fair shake." It referred to several lawyers who argued that Mexican Americans charged with a narcotics violation were likely to be convicted because white jurors believed that even if their client had not committed the present crime, he had probably violated the narcotics law at one time or another. In civil suits, said the report, the lack of Mexican American jurors often led to bias. It documented several cases in which Mexican Americans with solid suits against insurance companies had either lost or been awarded a pitifully small amount in damages. In one case a hung jury occurred because one of the jurors believed that "no Mexican is worth ten thousand dollars."[30] Said one lawyer: "I mean this is typical of these situations. You are not going to get what you are entitled to, because your life is worthless."[31]

The commission's report did not describe or uncover anything that Gus, Cadena, and Herrera did not know. They had been involved in discrimination litigation for too long not to know the tricks used by prosecutors and officers of the court to disadvantage Mexican Americans in the jury system. They would have been the first to underscore something that the report brought out that perhaps its writers did not completely understand—that Mexican American civil rights victories were usually temporary and just as usually undermined by a stubborn resistance by Anglos in the Southwest, who refused to treat them as equal. It may well have been accepted that they were *white*, but they surely were not *equal*.

Yet, the Civil Rights Commission Report was actually a victory for Mexican American reformers and proof that they continued to battle discrimination and segregation strongly. Hector P. García, a strong supporter of the *Hernández* case was the chief instigator in getting the commission to look into the problems of Mexican Americans in the Southwest. Lyndon Baines Johnson had appointed him to the commission and his promptings moved them toward looking at the problems of others even as he solidified

Mexican American support for the black civil rights movement. He also managed to work the other side of the hearing tables by publicizing the hearings and encouraging Mexican American reformers, Chicano activists and others to testify. While Richard Nixon would replace him on the commission before the actual report came out, García's handprint is clearly apparent in the report.[32]

Just as important, many of those who testified were simply following in the footsteps of men like Gus, Herrera, and Cadena. Their work inspired many Mexican Americans to engage more fully in advocacy for their people and in the civic life of the nation. *Hernández v. Texas* had solidified, in many of them, the desire to serve their communities, as well as given them confidence that change could actually come about. The fact that the case would fade from the public and scholarly view is not proof of failure by the lawyers but rather an indication of the difficulty that Mexican Americans and other Latinos continue to face in acquiring the full rights of citizenship, and in finding a niche in the American narrative. So often Mexican Americans' legal, social, and civil rights victories have been marginalized and ignored, but they cannot be stripped of their significance. As more Mexican Americans and other Latinos continue to uncover their victories, and their struggles, the more they will realize that their communities have not stood idly by against discrimination or racism.

Maury Maverick, whose name was on the Supreme Court brief but whose participation was actually minimal, saw *Hernández* as one of those events in history that are truly significant. He wrote:

> The *Hernández* case is such a mile post, and represents a climax of
> long years of struggle of Mexican American people for their first-
> class citizenship. It is not boastful to say that this case is even of
> world importance. . . . These attorneys made a substantial, dignified
> and creditable showing . . . before the Highest Court of our land.
> The unanimous decision upheld these lawyers' viewpoint, and it was
> a victory for dignity and equality for *every living soul* in the United
> States. (my italics)[33]

Maverick recognized that the ruling, notwithstanding its limitations, had expanded the notion of civil rights and equal protection beyond the simple white/black binary of traditional American jurisprudence. Now, all Americans regardless of their color or ethnicity could claim their rights, even if it would take years before they fully gained those rights.

Referring even more specifically to Gus, Herrera, and Cadena, Maverick said, "Their pleas have reached the ears of responsible and great men in high places. They have fought like sensible men, not like *toreros* (bullfighters), and they will be remembered long after wealthier and more powerful men have been forgotten."[34] What Gus, Herrera, and Cadena had done was rewrite American legal history by winning recognition and protection for their people and in doing so shed light on those obscure cases that had come before that already affirmed the rights of other groups within the American mosaic.

Cadena could not have agreed more with Maverick that the decision was more than just a victory for Mexican Americans. "The rejection of the 'two classes' theory," he wrote shortly after the decision, "guarantees that all ethnic groups in our nation are assured of equality before the law and are protected against discrimination because of their ancestry or national origins."[35] He particularly pointed out that the case could surely work against the exclusion of women from jury duty in places like Texas, which still barred them from serving on juries. After all he argued, women—as opposed to men—were [really] a "distinct class." "Is such different treatment (against women) based on some 'reasonable classification?'" he asked. "*Quien Sabe?* (Who knows?)," he replied, probably with a mischievous wink as he wrote. And women did win the right to jury duty that same year as the efforts of women activists combined with the ruling on *Hernández* made their exclusion indefensible.[36]

Today, as Mexican Americans and Latinos continue their struggle for inclusion, acceptance, and a more profound understanding of their rights, the story of *Hernández v. Texas* offers hope, a hope that American jurisprudence will continue to expand and learn to accommodate the diversity of its citizens. Twenty-first century America brings the challenges of language, mixed ancestry, new religious forms, immigration status, gender rights, new abortion battles, and probably many others to the court system. Gus, Herrera, and Cadena simply took a small step—but a gigantic step to Mexican Americans—toward making the highest court in the land relevant to its citizens regardless of their unique character.

Notes

Introduction

1. The term "Anglo" is often used instead of "white" in this work as it better reflects the terminology used in Chicano or Mexican American scholarship. Quite early in the twentieth century, white Americans—regardless of ethnicity or nationality—came to be referred to as "Anglos" by English-speaking Mexican Americans.

2. See Montejano, *Anglos and Mexicans*.

3. See Dudziak, *Cold War Civil Rights*.

Chapter 1. Pete, His Lawyers, and "the Town" That Discriminated

1. U.S. Bureau of the Census, Fifteenth Census of the United States: 1930, Population Schedule, Jackson County, Texas, Precinct 1, District 3. Bureau of the Census (Washington, D.C, 1931).

2. For general histories of Jackson County and its communities, see "Corpus Christi: 100 Years" (*Corpus Christi Caller-Times*, 1952), and I.T. Taylor, *The Cavalcade of Jackson County*. For information on east central Texas, see De León, *Ethnicity in the Sunbelt: Mexican Americans in Houston* and Foley, *The White Scourge*.

3. See "Bond is Denied Edna Youth Charged in Rifle Slaying" the *Edna Herald*, August 9, 1951; "Edna Picks Cotton But Needs More Help," *Victoria Advocate*, August 12, 1951; also, see Gus García letter to Garza and Hector P. García, October 18, 1950, in the Hector P. García Papers in the Special Collections and Archives at Texas A&M University, Corpus Christi.

4. See U.S. Bureau of the Census, *1930*.

5. Ibid.

6. Manuel, *Education of Mexican and Spanish-Speaking Children in Texas*, 92. Also,

see Sánchez, "Concerning Segregation of Spanish-Speaking Children in the Public Schools."

7. P. S. Taylor, *An American-Mexican Frontier.*

8. I. T. Taylor, *The Cavalcade of Jackson County,* 106. See also, "Edna, Texas," *The Handbook of Texas Online.* The population of Edna in 1896 was 1,000; in 1929, 2,500; and in 1958, 6,500.

9. Ibid.

10. Ibid.

11. For Progressivism in Texas, see Gould, *Progressives and Prohibitionists;* and Anders, *Boss Rule in South Texas.* For white primaries in Jackson County see I. T. Taylor, *The Cavalcade of Jackson County,* 49–50.

12. I. T. Taylor, *The Cavalcade of Jackson County,* 49–50.

13. See Anders, *Boss Rule in South Texas* for a discussion of Mexican American political machines and their relationship to Anglo political bosses during the Progressive Era. Also, see Montejano, *Race, Labor Repression, and Capitalist Agriculture,* and his *Anglos and Mexicans.*

14. For a discussion of labor control, see Montejano, *Anglos and Mexicans,* 197–219.

15. Ibid.

16. For a discussion of these Mexican schools, see San Miguel, *"Let All of Them Take Heed."*

17. For more on Mexican American children, see Manuel, *Education,* and *Spanish-Speaking Children of the Southwest;* Little, *Spanish-Speaking Children in Texas;* and Burma, *Spanish-Speaking Groups,* 72–81.

18. For a discussion of the breakdown of the rigid labor segregation that affected Mexican and Mexican American labor, see Montejano, *Anglos and Mexicans,* 262–287.

19. See Foley's *White Scourge* for a discussion on this change in the labor market.

20. Burma, *Spanish-Speaking Groups,* 35–71.

21. See San Miguel, *"Let All of Them Take Heed."*

22. For a discussion of Mexican American legal victories in the battle over segregation, see San Miguel, *"Let All of Them Take Heed."*

23. Author's interview with retired farm worker "Fidel" in Edna, Texas, during the summer of 2004.

24. Victor Rodríguez, interview by Carlos Sandoval, summer of 2006, transcript in author's possession, 7.

25. Ibid., 6.

26. Ibid., 28.

27. Ibid., 38.

28. This information comes from a roundtable conversation with three of Pete's nephews and the wife of one of them. The conversation took place in Edna, Texas, in the summer of 2004. Tape recording is in possession of the author.

29. See the "Transcript of Record, Supreme Court of the United States, October Term, 1953, No. 406, Pete Hernández, Petitioner, v. The State of Texas, on Writ of Certiorari to the Court of Criminal Appeals of the State of Texas," which reports the day of the killing as August 4, although most of the newspapers report it as August 7.

30. "Bond is Denied Edna Youth Charged in Rifle Slaying," 1.

31. See Rodríguez interview, 16. Victor remembers working with him and described him as "frail" but a hard worker who liked to compete at his work. He was known in the fields as *Pedro el Chueco*, which means "Pete the Cripple."

32. Oralia Espinoza, interview by Carlos Sandoval, June 28, 2006, 9–10.

33. See "Transcript of Record," 8–15; also reported in "Jury to Get Hernández Slaying Case," *Victoria Advocate*, October 11, 1951; "Edna Laborer Draws Life in Slaying," *Victoria Advocate*, October 12, 1951.

34. See "Slaying Leads Edna Grand Jury List," *Victoria Advocate*, September 16, 1951, and "Jackson County Grand Jury Indictments Include Charge of Murder," *Victoria Advocate*, September 20, 1951; also, see trial story in the September 9 issue, no title available.

35. Nephews' roundtable discussion. See note 28.

36. See "Transcript of Record," 11; also, reported in "Jury to Get Hernández Slaying Cases," *Victoria Advocate*, October 11, 1951; "Edna Laborer Draws Life in Slaying," *Victoria Advocate*, October 12, 1951.

37. Nephews' roundtable discussion. See note 28.

38. See Rosales, ¡*Pobre Raza!*, especially chaps. 4 and 7; and Handman, "Preliminary Report on Nationality and Delinquency," 258; see also Kibbe, *Latin Americans in Texas*, 230.

39. Nephews' roundtable discussion. See note 28.

40. James De Anda interview with author, April 2003. No specific day is available for the tape.

41. Ed Idar Jr., interview by author, April 29, 2003.

42. Mike Herrera, interview by Carlos Sandoval, summer 2006, 18–19.

43. Gustavo C. García, "An Informal Report to the People, A Cotton Picker Finds Justice! The Saga of the Hernández Case," compiled by Ruben Munguia, published by Munguia Printers, 1954. This is a pamphlet put out shortly after the Supreme Court decision by a local print shop owned by the Munguia family, who were much involved in Mexican American reforms. There is no specific publication date and the pamphlet has no page numbers.

44. Gustavo García came to be known to fellow reformers and historians as simply "Gus," and this is the way I refer to him in this book. No disrespect is intended.

45. See De Anda interview.

46. G. C. García, "A Cotton Picker Finds Justice!" 8.

47. Rodríguez interview, 26.

48. Ibid., 27.

49. Ibid.

50. This story came to the author from a high school teacher who interviewed Herrera shortly before his death, and who swears that as the old reformer told it, he laughed and shook his head, still, after so many years, unable to believe the foolhardiness of his partner.

51. G. C. García, "A Cotton Picker Finds Justice!" 10.

52. Oralia Espinoza interview, 6.

53. Ibid., 28.

54. Ibid., 7, 14, 28.

55. Ibid.

56. Nephews' roundtable discussion. See note 28.

57. "Fidel" interview with author.

58. Oralia Espinoza interview.

59. See the *Edna Herald*, August 9, 1951; *Victoria Advocate*, September 16, 17, and 20, 1951. These were all front-page news items.

60. See *Victoria Advocate*, October 10, 1951, and "Jury to get Hernández Slaying," *Victoria Advocate*, October 11, 1951.

61. See "Transcript of Record," 16–18; "Edna Laborer Draws Life in Slaying," *Victoria Advocate*, October 12, 1951; "Hernández Life Term Appealed," the *Edna Herald*, October 18, 1951; and G. C. García, "A Cotton Picker Finds Justice!"

62. De Anda interview.

63. "Transcript of Record," 2–4.

64. Ibid.

65. G. C. García, "A Cotton Picker Finds Justice!" 10.

66. "Transcript of Record," 26–27.

67. Ibid., 28–29.

68. Ibid., 30.

69. Ibid., 31–32.

70. Ibid., 31.

71. See *Westminster School District v. Mendez*, 161 F. 2nd 774 (1947); see also I. M. García, *Hector P. García*, 143–144.

72. "Transcript of Record," 32–33.

73. Ibid., 35–37.

74. This notion of "whiteness" in this region is discussed in Foley's *The White Scourge*. For a more in-depth discussion of "whiteness" and its parameters, see López, *White by Law*.

75. "Transcript of Record," 37–43.

76. In the 1940s Mexican Americans complained to Texas Governor Coke Stevenson about discrimination in public facilities. In response to signs posted by small businesses that read "No Mexicans," Stevenson declared, "[B]usinesses are free to establish their own standards." Despite the governor's insistence that discrimination was rare, in 1943 the Mexican government decided to

discontinue the practice of sending *braceros* across the border to Texas, citing racism and discrimination as the reasons. See Green, *The Establishment in Texas Politics*, 80–81. See also "No Mexicans Allowed," 8; and Kibbe, *Latin Americans in Texas*, 208–211. On the day that Hernández was indicted—September 20, 1951—Hector P. García, head of the American GI Forum, received a letter from a person by the name of Molina, regarding a "No Mexicans Served" sign in Edna. The letter is in the García Papers, Texas A&M University, Corpus Christi.

77. Kibbe, *Latin Americans in Texas*, 222.

78. I. M. García, *Hector P. García*, 125.

79. "Transcript of Record," 44.

80. Ibid., 44–45.

81. Ibid., 46–47.

82. Ibid., 48.

83. Ibid., 48–49.

84. Ibid., 49.

85. Ibid.

86. This discussion on "language deficiencies" and segregation are best discussed in San Miguel's *"Let All of Them Take Heed."*

87. "Transcript of Record," 56.

88. Ibid., 56–57.

89. Ibid., 57–60.

90. Ibid., 60–61.

91. Ibid., 63–71.

92. Ibid.

93. Ibid., 73–75.

94. "Transcript of Record," 75–76. Herrera claimed he "accidentally discovered" the restroom sign. See also G. C. García, "A Cotton Picker Finds Justice!"

95. Ibid., 77–79.

96. Ibid., 81–84

97. See "Jury Picking Continues in Murder Trial," *Victoria Advocate*, October 9, 1951; and "Testimony to Begin at Edna Trial," *Victoria Advocate*, October 10, 1951.

98. "Transcript of Record," 84–85.

99. Ibid., 85–86.

100. Ibid., 86–87.

101. Ibid., 88.

102. Ibid., 89.

103. Ibid.

104. Ibid.

Chapter 2. "The Mexican People Are of the Same Race"

1. G. C. García, "A Cotton Picker Finds Justice!" 10–11.

2. Ibid., 9.

3. The courts banned school segregation in numerous cases before the 1950s. See San Miguel's *"Let All of Them Take Heed."* School districts in particular, often responded to continuing segregation by showing that students attended the same schools, played on the same varsity teams and participated in the same extracurricular activities. For an example of this kind of logic, see I. M. García, *Hector P. García,* 125–130.

4. See *Sánchez v. State,* 243 S.W. 2d 700. The main author of that brief was James De Anda, who was working with Herrera at the time. For more on De Anda, see Nick Jimenez, "A forgotten hero; James De Anda helped to lead the fight for Mexican Americans to sit on juries in Texas," *Corpus Christi Caller-Times,* October 31, 2004, A15.

5. For short biographies on Herrera, see De León, *Ethnicity in the Sunbelt: Mexican Americans in Houston,* 130–133; *The New Handbook of Texas,* Vol. 3, 575.

6. Ibid. Also see Marquez, "Politics of Race and Class," and San Miguel, "The Struggle Against Separate and Unequal Schools."

7. See G. C. García, "A Cotton Picker Finds Justice!" 10.

8. Ibid.

9. Ibid., 11.

10. De Anda phone interview with the author.

11. Mike Herrera interview, 3–9.

12. Ibid., 4.

13. San Miguel, *"Let All of Them Take Heed,"* 117–118.

14. See "Herrera, John J." in *The Handbook of Texas Online.*

15. See "García, Gustavo C." in *The Handbook of Texas Online.*

16. Ibid.

17. Ed Idar Jr. phone interview with author, April 29, 2003. Tape recording in possession of the author.

18. For Gus's comments, see G. C. García, "A Cotton Picker Finds Justice!" 10. For short bios on Carlos Cadena, see *Los Angeles Times,* January 19, 2001, Obituary section P.B.6; "Justice for Justice," *San Antonio Express-News,* June 22, 1975, 2-B.

19. See Ramos, "The Educational Legacy of Racially Restrictive Covenants," 149–184, 159–166. For the case itself, see *Clifton v. Puente,* 218 S.W. 2d 272.

20. See "Let the Games Begin," *The Society Page,* Vol. 2, Issue 1, Fall 2005, 4. This is a publication of the University of Texas law school Office of Student Life.

21. See De Anda phone interview with author.

22. Not much has been written on Aldrete, but see I. M. García, *Hector P. García,* 163–164, 184.

23. For information on Maverick's involvement in the case and his take on it, see the introduction of G. C. García, "A Cotton Picker Finds Justice!"

24. San Miguel, *"Let All of Them Take Heed,"* 133.

25. For a discussion of hardball politics that some Mexican American reformers were promoting, see I. M. García, *Hector P. García.*

26. Ibid.

27. For a further discussion of this approach, see M. T. García's *Mexican Americans*, the chapter on LULAC, 25–61; also, see I. M. García, *Viva Kennedy*, 60–84. A more recent work on this generation's politics is Quiroz's *Claiming Citizenship.*

28. In this context I describe "Barrio Americanism" as the practice of a politics of integration that emphasized citizenship, loyalty to Cold War America, the learning of English over that of the Spanish language and the moving away from a concern with Mexico. This Americanism was "Barrio" because it was practiced within the confines of the Mexican barrio, and because it remained suspect outside its confines. Simply put, these reformers were expressing their Cold War Americanism in the only place they were allowed.

29. See note 28 above.

30. Two recent books on Mexican Americans and the military expand on this notion. See Oropeza, *¡Raza Sí! ¡Guerra No!;* Rivas-Rodriquez, ed., *Mexican Americans and World War II.*

31. R. A. García, *Rise of the Mexican American Middle Class*, 302–310; he speaks of a change in identity, strategy, and leadership, and of the Americanization of the Mexican American in the 1940s.

32. G. C. García, "A Cotton Picker Finds Justice!" 9; and the *San Antonio Light*, October 1951.

33. See letter from Alfredo Guerrero Jr. to Hector P. García, October 17, 1949, García Papers, Texas A&M University, Corpus Christi.

34. There were numerous court cases involving jury discrimination against African Americans in Texas and other parts of the South in the 1940s and 1950s. See *Akins v. State of Texas*, 65 S.Ct. 1276, U.S. Tex., 1945; *Cassell v. State*, 216 S.W. 2d 813, Tex. Crim. App., 1948; *Smith v. Texas*, 238 S.W. 2d 649, Ark. 1951; *State v. Green*, 60 So. 2d 208, La. 1952.

35. I. T. Taylor, *The Cavalcade of Jackson County*, 49–50.

36. See Brand, "The Supreme Court, Equal Protection, and Jury Selection." For its impact on Texas, see "Important Orders by General Griffins—Jurors in Texas" *New York Times*, May 8, 1967.

37. See Civil Rights Act 18 U.S.C.5, 243 (1988).

38. See Schmidt, "Juries, Jurisdiction, and Race Discrimination."

39. See "The Supreme Court, Equal Protection and Jury Selection," 59; also *Strauder v. West Virginia*, 110 U.S. 308–309 (1880). Other cases thereafter established that the exclusion of jurors based on "race or color" was unlawful and a violation of the Equal Protection Clause under the Fourteenth Amend-

ment. See *Green v. State*, 73 Ala. 26 (1882); *Binyon v. U.S.*, 76 S.W. 265, Indian Terr. (1903); *Bonaparte v. State*, 61 So. 633, Fla. (1913); *State v. Cook*, 95 S.E. 792 W. Va. (1918); *State v. Walls*, 191 S.E. 232, N.C. (1937).

40. *Norris v. Alabama*, 294 U.S. 587 (1935).

41. Ibid.

42. See *Strauder v. West Virginia*, 303; *Virginia v. Rives*, 100 U.S. 313 (1880); *Neal v. Delaware*, 103 U.S. (1881); and *Carter v. Texas*, 177 U.S. 442 (1900).

43. See note 19 above.

44. See *Akins v. State*, 1276; and *Cassell v. State*, 813.

45. Ibid.

46. For a more detailed explanation of the treaty and its legacy, see Griswold del Castillo, *The Treaty of Guadalupe Hidalgo*.

47. López, *White by Law*, 61–62, 242.

48. Ibid.

49. Ibid.

50. *People v. de la Garza*.

51. Lopez, *White by Law*.

52. See Sheridan, "'Another White Race.'"

53. Kibbe, *Latin Americans in Texas*, 229.

54. Montejano, *Anglos and Mexicans*, particularly chap. 12, titled "The Demise of 'Jim Crow.'"

55. See *Ramirez v. State*, 112 Tex. Crim. 332, 16 S.W. 2d 814 (1929), and *Ramirez v. State*, 119 Tex. Crim. 362, 40 S.W. 2d 138 (1931).

56. See second *Ramirez* case (1931).

57. Ibid.

58. See first *Ramirez* case, 814 (1929).

59. Ibid. During the trial, a special prosecutor had "vigorously assailed appellant for not putting his wife on the witness stand to testify to his innocence." Since she had been convicted for the same crime, under Texas law she was "incompetent as a witness" to testify on his behalf. Since the judge failed to clarify that point to the jury, the appeals court reversed the decision.

60. See second *Ramirez* case (1931).

61. Ibid.

62. Ibid.

63. Ibid.

64. Ibid. (1931).

65. See Montejano, *Anglos and Mexicans*, 220–234. Other works that reveal these attitudes in Anglo Americans are Tuck, *Not With the Fist*; and Servín, *The Mexican Americans*.

66. Second *Ramirez* ruling (1931).

67. Ibid., 141.

68. See *Carrasco v. State*, 95 S.W. 2d 433 (1936).

69. Ibid., 434.

70. Ibid.

71. Ibid. Also see *Honda v. People* (1943), when the appeals court ruled in a similar manner.

72. Ibid., 434–435.

73. See *Lugo v. State*, 124 S.W. 2d 346 (1938).

74. For more on González, see M. T. García, *Mexican Americans*, 27, 29–31, 36, 40–45, 55; and also Márquez's *LULAC*, 24–28, 36, 44. The court records refer to M. C. Gonzáles but he was actually González with a z.

75. See M. T. García, *Mexican Americans*, 25–61; Marquez, "The Politics of Race and Class," 84–101; Sandoval, *Our Legacy*.

76. *Lugo v. State*, Appellant's Motion for a Re-Hearing (No. 19,994), 2.

77. See note 15.

78. Appellant's Motion for a Re-Hearing, 2.

79. Ibid., 5.

80. See Motion for Re-Hearing, 5–8.

81. Ibid.

82. Ibid.

83. *Lugo v. State*, 346.

84. Ibid.

85. Ibid., 347.

86. Ibid.

87. See *Sanchez v. State*, 181 S.W. 2d 88 (1944).

88. Ibid., 89.

89. Ibid.

90. Ibid., 90–91.

91. See *Salazar v. State*, 193 S.W. 2d 211 (1946).

92. Ibid., 212.

93. For a discussion of this postwar concern with "whiteness," see I. M. García, *Hector P. García*, 96–97.

94. For a discussion of this shift toward dependence on government support, see Kaplowitz, *LULAC*.

95. *Salazar v. State*, 193 S.W. 2d 212 (1946).

96. For one scholar's personal discussion about the duality of identity for many Mexican Americans, see the preface in Ruiz Urueta, *Memories of a Hyphenated Man*.

97. See Oropeza, *¡Raza Sí! ¡Guerra No!*, for the "Americanist" views of Mexican American reformers' anger over discrimination.

98. See the chapter, "Barrio Americanism: Constructing a Veterans' Movement," in I. M. García, *Hector P. García*, 74–103.

99. More will be said about Sánchez in the next chapter.

100. See the introductory chapter in M. T. García, *Mexican Americans*, for a further discussion of this generation's collective mindset.

101. See *Bustillos v. State* 213 S.W. 2d 837, 839–840.

102. It is important to note from the aforementioned cases that Mexican Americans and their advocates keenly understood that the courtroom reflected Anglo-Texan prejudices and thus were anything but hospitable to them. Having few Mexican American lawyers to represent them, and even fewer judges and prosecutors who could understand their plight, they pinned their hopes on impartial juries. These, however, were rarely encountered and so they fought to have at least "their kind" in the jury box. For an extensive look at the legal campaign against educational inequality in Texas, see San Miguel, *"Let All of Them Take Heed."*

Chapter 3. Caucasian Cloak

1. De Anda phone interview with author. The case would be known as *Sanchez v. Texas* (1951).

2. For more on Mexican Americans and World War II, see Rivas-Rodriguez, *Mexican Americans and World War II;* also Morin, *Among the Valiant.*

3. I. M. García, *Hector P. García,* includes a discussion of the development of the politics of the war experience.

4. Ibid.

5. I. M. García, *Hector P. García,* 96.

6. For an excellent discussion of this generation's mindset, see M. T. García's *Mexican Americans,* especially the introduction and the first chapter; also R. A. García, *The Mexican American Middle Class.*

7. Vasconcelos, *The Cosmic Race / La raza cosmica (Race in the Americas),* trans. Jaén; and Paz, *El laberinto de la soledad.*

8. See Perea, "Ethnicity and the Constitution," for a discussion of the white/black binary in law.

9. For a discussion of this re-emergence in the 1960s of the debate over the racial identity of Mexican Americans, see I. M. García, *Chicanismo.*

10. See M. T. García, *Mexican Americans;* also Kaplowitz, *LULAC.*

11. See brief for *Salazar v. Texas,* 193 S.W. 2d 211 (1946).

12. See *Glasser v. Texas,* U.S. 315 60 (1942).

13. See *Salazar v. Texas.*

14. See *Akin v. Texas* (1945).

15. Ibid.

16. See "Record of Inquests" for Fort Bend County, Texas, dated April 23, 1950, reproduced from the Holdings of the Texas State Archives in the *State of Texas v. Aniceto Sanchez,* no. 7103.

17. See "Statement of Facts," *State of Texas v. Aniceto Sanchez,* no. 7103.

18. Ibid.

19. See "George I. Sanchez Lecture," by Judge James De Anda, Institute for Higher Education Law and Governance, University of Houston Law Cen-

ter, November 19, 2004, at http://utopia.utexas.edu/explore/clark/Hernández
.html, 1.

20. Ibid., 2.

21. Ibid.

22. De Anda phone interview.

23. De Anda lecture, 6.

24. Ibid., 7.

25. See Kaplowitz, *LULAC*, for a more explicit discussion on this point.

26. See I. M. García, *Viva Kennedy*, for a discussion of González's complex use of ethnic politics to remain popular with both Mexican Americans and Anglos.

27. I. M. García, "Latinos in the Politics of the West."

28. See I. M. García, *Hector P. García*, 201–203, for a discussion of this conflict over the "wetback."

29. See http://www.maldef.org/webpages/tributes/ to access several tributes and obituaries on Judge De Anda. This is the official Web site of the Mexican American Legal Defense and Educational Fund. This specific information comes from the "UT Law School Tribute On-Line."

30. For a discussion of one reformer who did, see the chapter on Carlos Castañeda in M. T. García, *Mexican Americans*, 231–251. It should be noted that Castañeda was of the earlier generation but lived long enough to experience the veteran generation as well.

31. De Anda lecture, 2.

32. "Bill of Exception No. 1" *State of Texas v. Aniceto Sanchez*, no. 7103, Holdings of the Texas State Archives, 2.

33. Ibid., 4.

34. Ibid., 6.

35. Ibid., 3.

36. Ibid., 3–4.

37. Ibid.

38. "Defendant's Motion to Quash" *State of Texas v. Aniceto Sanchez*, no. 7103, Holdings of the Texas State Archives, 34.

39. Ibid. See *Patton v. State of Mississippi*, 332 U.S. 463 68 S. Ct. 184.

40. Ibid.

41. Ibid., 36.

42. Ibid., 37.

43. Ibid., 38.

44. See "Bill of Exception," 8.

45. De Anda lecture, 2. De Anda vaguely remembers this in speaking of a possible Supreme Court appeal, but it is likely that the reluctance extended to the first appeal also.

46. See "Appellant Brief," *Aniceto Sanchez v. The State of Texas*, no. 25, 496, in the Holdings of the Texas State Archives, 3.

47. Ibid., 3. Also, see *Patton v. State of Mississippi*, 184.

48. Ibid., 4.

49. Ibid., 5–6.

50. Ibid., 5. See also, *Cassell v. State of Texas*, 282.

51. Ibid., 6. See also, *Hill v. State of Texas*, 316 U.S. 400, 404; 62 S. Ct. 1159, 1161.

52. Ibid. See *Smith v. Texas*, 311 U.S. 128, 61 S. Ct. 164 (1940).

53. Ibid., 7.

54. Ibid. See also *Sanchez v. State*, 181 S.W. 2d 87.

55. Ibid., 8. Also, see *Patton v. State of Mississippi*, 463.

56. Ibid., 8–9. Cases referred to were *Peña v. State*, 24 S.W. 2d 24; *Carrasco v. State*, 130 Tex. Cr. R. 659, 95 S.W. 2d 433; *Ramirez v. State*, 40 S.W. 2d 138; *Rodriquez v. State*, 58 Tex Cr. R. 275, 125 S.W. 403.

57. See "Opinion," *Aniceto Sanchez v. The State of Texas*, no. 25, 496 from the Holdings of the Texas State Archives.

58. De Anda phone interview.

59. This is not a legal term, but rather an attempt to explain the Anglo lawyers' efforts, given that they provided very little in terms of legal scholarship in their briefs.

60. Ibid.

61. See Ed Idar Jr. phone interview with author.

62. See *Hill v. Texas* (1942), 406.

63. See "Appellant's Brief" in the Court of Criminal Appeals, No. 25, 816 in folder 25 of the John Herrera Collection at the Houston Metropolitan Public Library Special Collections. Also see *Ross v. Texas*, 233 S.W. 2d 126 (1950).

64. "Appellant's Brief," 6.

65. Ibid., 7. See also *Ramirez v. Texas* and *Hill v. Texas*.

66. Ibid., 7–8. See also, *Norris v. Alabama*; and *Smith v. Texas*.

67. Ibid. See also *Cassell v. Texas*, 282–289; and *Smith v. Texas*, 132.

68. Ibid. See *Hill v. Texas*, 403–405.

69. Ibid., 8–9.

70. Ibid., 9.

71. See *Sanchez v. Texas*, 90–91.

72. Ibid., 10. See *Hirababyashi v. United States*, 12 Am. Jur., 129.

73. See *Gibson v. Mississippi* (1896), 162 U.S. 567.

74. Ibid., 10.

75. Ibid., 12–13. See also *Yick Wo v. Hopkins*, 118 U.S 356, 369; *American Sugar Refining Co. v. Louisiana*, 179 U.S. 82–89, and *Truaz v. Raich*, 239 U.S. 33.

76. Ibid., 13.

77. Ibid., 14. Also see *Mendez v. Westminster School District*, 161 F. 2d 774, *Lopez v. Seccombe*, U.S. D.C., Cal., 1944, 71 F. Supp. and *Gonzales v. Sheely*, U.S. D.C., Arizona 1951, 96 F. Supp. 1004.

78. Ibid., 14. See *Clifton v. Puente*, Tex. Civ. App. 1948, err. Dism. N. r.c., 218 S.W. 2d 272.

79. Ibid. See *Juarez v. Texas*, 102 Tex. Cr. R. 297, 277 S.W.1091.

80. Ibid., 15.

81. Ibid. See also *Gibson v. Mississippi*, supra, 162 U.S. at 580–581.

82. Ibid., 15.

83. Ibid.

Chapter 4. "May God Permit You Triumph in This Most Grand of Campaigns"

1. *Hernández v. State*, 160 Tex. Crim. 72, 251 S.W. 2d 531, 2.

2. Ibid., 3.

3. *Sanchez v. State*, 87, 90.

4. See *Smith v. Texas*, L.Ed 84; *Hill v. Texas*, L.Ed. 1559; *Cassell v. Texas*, L.Ed. 839; and *Ross v. Texas*, L.Ed. 1352.

5. *Hernández v. State*, 3.

6. Ibid.

7. Ibid., 4.

8. The court cited several cases in which the higher court had taken issue with the concept of proportional representation. See *Thomas v. Texas*, 212 U.S. 278, 29 S.Ct. 393, 53 L.Ed. 512; *Martin v. Texas*, 200 U.S. 316, 26 S.Ct. 338, 50 L.Ed. 497; and *Carter v. Texas*, 177 U.S. 442, 20 S.Ct. 687, 44 L.Ed. 839.

9. *Hernández v. State*, 5.

10. Ibid., 4.

11. For a very good overview of the legal cases that Mexican Americans won pertaining to segregation and educational discrimination, see San Miguel, "*Let All of Them Take Heed.*"

12. See the *San Antonio Light*, October 1951, page number and exact date unavailable.

13. I. M. García, *Hector P. García*, 75–88.

14. Ibid., 156–162.

15. For more information on the Bracero Program, see Craig, *The Bracero Program*; Galarza, *Merchants of Labor*; McBride, *Vanishing Bracero*; and Scruggs, "Texas and the Bracero Program."

16. I. M. García, *Hector P. García*, 156–162.

17. See letter to Robert K. Carr from Carlos E. Castañeda, May 9, 1947, in the President's Committee on Civil Rights papers in the Harry S. Truman Library.

18. Ibid., 5.

19. See note 17.

20. Ibid.

21. Ibid., 6.

22. Ibid., 8.

23. See "The 'Wetback' Problem of the Southwest," in the files of Philleo Nash in the Harry S. Truman Papers of the Harry S. Truman Library, 1.

24. Ibid.

25. For a more in-depth discussion of Sánchez's political and educational views, see M. T. García, *Mexican Americans*, 252–272.

26. "The 'Wetback' Problem," 2.

27. Ibid., 3.

28. Ibid., 4.

29. Ibid., 5.

30. See I. M. García, *Hector P. García*, for Sánchez study and the pamphlet *What Price Wetbacks?* 198–201.

31. For a discussion of segregation in Texas, see Montejano, *Anglos and Mexicans*, 220–234.

32. See Acuña's *Occupied America*, 148–174, for a look at Mexican unionism in the Southwest.

33. I. M. García, *Viva Kennedy*, 97.

34. I. M. García, *Hector P. García*, 200.

35. See J. R. García, *Operation Wetback*.

36. Real border vigilance arose in the late 1920s and it is likely that Franciso came before it did, given that he had several American-born children by the census of 1930.

37. Hector García and R. A. Cortez were both organizational leaders and Sánchez was a well-respected educator and civil libertarian of long standing. In one form or another they worked the grass roots and were considered leaders in the Mexican American community. Gus García's erratic behavior, lack of economic stability, and aloofness kept him from ever achieving a high position or the kind of respect that Sánchez had. He was, however, well respected as an excellent courtroom lawyer among most reformers, even if they did not always trust him with their money.

38. For a discussion of the slow demise of segregation, see Klarman, *From Jim Crow to Civil Rights*, 236–292.

39. Ibid. For a more in-depth discussion of civil rights during the Cold War, see Dudziak, *Cold War Civil Rights*.

40. For a Mexican American view of this invisibility, see Samora, ed., *La Raza*.

41. See *Nebraska Law Review*, Vol. 32, No. 1, November 1952, 621–623.

42. The case is cited in Kibbe, *Latin Americans in Texas*, 229.

43. This story comes from Tuck, *Not With the Fist*, 211–212.

44. *Nebraska Law Review*, 623.

45. See *Temple Law Quarterly*, Vol. 26, No. 4, 1952–1953, 446.

46. Ibid.

47. See *Washington University Law Quarterly*, Vo. 1953, 214.

48. 332 U.S. 261, 283, *rehearing denied,* 332 U.S. 784 (1947); see footnote 16 on page 215 of law article.

49. *Washington University Law Quarterly,* 215; for naturalization rulings see *Ex parte* Shahid, 205 Fed. 812 (E.D.S.C. 1913), and in *re Rodriguez,* 81 Fed. 337 (N.D. Tex. 1897).

50. See *Virginia Law Review,* Vol. XXXIX, 1953, 374.

51. See *Texas Law Review,* Vol. 31, 1952–1953, 583.

52. Ibid.

53. See *Baylor Law Review,* Vol. V, 1952–1953, 298.

54. Ibid., 299–300.

55. Ibid. See *Mendez v. Westminster School Dist.* (1946); *Mendez v. Westminster School Dist.* (1947); and *Gonzales v. Sheely* (1951).

56. *Baylor Law Review,* 301.

57. Ibid., 303.

58. I. M. García, *Viva Kennedy,* 13–15, includes a short discussion on the lack of Anglo support.

59. The author found no articles in either paper that covered the case as it made its way to the Supreme Court, nor many articles from the period following the decision.

60. See "Miscellaneous Docket Sheet, Case no. 2, Pete Hernández v. State of Texas" in the Tom C. Clark Papers, Box C 70, folder 6 at Tarlton Law Library, University of Texas at Austin.

61. G. C. García, "A Cotton Picker Finds Justice!" 12.

62. See letter dated October 12, 1953, from Harold B. Willey, Clerk, to Carlos C. Cadena, Esquire. The letter is located in the Clark Papers in Tarlton Law Library, University of Texas at Austin. No box or folder number available.

63. G. C. García, "A Cotton Picker Finds Justice!" 12.

64. See "Conference List for Week of October 5, 1953, List 1, Sheet 15" in Clark Papers, Box A26, Folder no. 10.

65. See "Miscellaneous Docket Sheet, Case no. 2, Pete Hernández v. State of Texas".

66. See "'Giveaways' to Get High Court Hearing" the *Washington Post,* October 13, 1953, 13.

67. See letter from Harold B. Willey to Carlos C. Cadena on October 26, 1953, in the Clark Papers in the Tarlton Library at the University of Texas at Austin.

68. See letter from Ed Idar Jr. to Albert Armendariz, October 27, 1953, in the García Papers in Special Collections at Texas A&M University, Corpus Christi.

69. See Carlos Cadena letter to George I. Sánchez, dated only "Sunday," found in the George Sánchez Papers in the Benson Latin American Collection at the University of Texas at Austin, Box 9, Folder 2.

70. Ibid.

71. See Blanton, "George I. Sánchez, Ideology, and Whiteness," 588. This money was part of a larger donation of fifty thousand dollars spread out over a period of six years (1951–1957) that went to both civil rights and immigration cases. The specific five thousand dollar donation is mentioned in Olivas, ed. *"Colored Men" and "Hombres Aqui,"* xvi.

72. See letter from Ed Idar Jr. to Carlos Cadena, October 27, 1953, in García Papers.

73. See letter from Ed Idar Jr. to Albert Armendariz, November 23, 1953, in García Papers.

74. See letter from Hector P. García to Chris Aldrete, November 18, 1953, in García Papers.

75. Ibid.

76. See Idar letter to Cadena, October 27, 1953.

77. See Idar letter to Gus García, December 4, 1952. The date should read "1953."

78. See Idar letter to Cadena, December 4, 1952, in García Papers. The date on this letter should also read "1953" rather than "1952."

79. See letter from Idar to Carlos Cadena, February 15, 1954, in García Papers.

80. See undated letter from Hector P. García to "Appreciable Amigo," in García Papers.

81. Ibid.

82. See undated, untitled ledger page in the *Hernández* folder in the García Papers that shows the names of thirty-six contributors and the amounts of their contributions.

83. See letter from A. V. Gutiérrez to Hector P. García in García Papers.

84. See letter from Simon Moya Sr. to Hector P. García, December 14, 1953, in the García Papers.

85. See Francisco and Alfredo Martinez to García, undated, in García Papers.

86. Pablo Renaud to Hector P. García, December 20, 1953, in García Papers.

87. Juan Montiel to García, December 15, 1953, in García Papers.

88. See letters from Manuel García (December 17), and Octabiano Canul (undated) to García, in García Papers.

89. See letter from Jesse F. Castillo (December 21), to García, in García Papers.

90. Manuel Castilla Jr. to Hector P. García, December 22, 1953, in García Papers.

91. See Abel G. Acosts (probably Acosta), to Dr. H. García, January 7, 1954 in García Papers.

92. See "Chicago Groups Contribute to Hernández Case" Forum News Bulletin, February 1954, 4.

93. See press release, undated, found in the *Hernández* files of the García Papers.

94. Ed Idar Jr. to Hector P. García, January 15, 1954, in García Papers.

95. Idar to Cadena, January 22, 1954, in García Papers.

96. Idar to Cadena, February 15, 1954, in García Papers.

97. G. C. García, "A Cotton Picker Finds Justice!" 12.

98. Ibid.

99. Ibid.

Chapter 5. "There Must Be a White Man in the Wood Pile"

1. This was told to the author by documentary filmmaker Carlos Sandoval who learned firsthand of it from one of Cadena's daughters during a conversation at their home. This conversation between Sandoval and Cadena's daughter occurred in the early summer of 2006.

2. See letter from Carlos Cadena to George I. Sánchez at the Sánchez Collection at the University of Texas Benson Collection. The letter has no date, except "Sunday," and is found in the "Hernández folder."

3. See Cadena letter to Sánchez, undated except for "Thursday" in Sánchez Collection.

4. G. C. García, "A Cotton Picker Finds Justice!" 13. For a discussion of Spanish-language radio, see Gutierrez, *Spanish Language Radio.*

5. Ibid., 14.

6. Ibid.

7. Ibid.

8. See "Thursday" Cadena to Sánchez letter for Cadena's lamentation to Sánchez about Gus's grandiose plans.

9. See "Sunday" letter from Cadena to Sánchez.

10. Ibid.

11. See "Thursday" letter from Cadena.

12. Ibid.

13. For a discussion on the changing nature of the court, see Klarman, *From Jim Crow to Civil Rights,* 290–312.

14. See Salinas, "Gus García and Thurgood Marshall: Two Legal Giants Fighting for Justice," 28 *T. Marshall L. Rev. 145* (section III).

15. Ibid.

16. See Pete Hernández, *Petitioner v. The State of Texas, Respondent,* Brief for Petitioner On Writ of Certiorari to the Court of Criminal Appeals of the State of Texas, 7.

17. See *Strauder v. West Virginia,* 303, 308 (1879).

18. See *Yick Wo v. Hopkins,* 336, 369 (1886).

19. See *Juarez v. Texas* (1925).

20. See Pete Hernández, *Petitioner.*

21. Ibid., 10.

22. See *Gonzalez v. Sheely.* (1951); *Mendez v. Westminster School Dist.* (1946),and (9th Cir., 1947); and *Del Rio Independent School District v. Salvatierra,* 33 S.W. 2d 790 (Tex. Civ. App., 1930).

23. See *Clifton v. Puente* (Tex. Civ. App. 1949, err Ref.).

24. See Pete Hernández, *Petitioner.*

25. Ibid., 12.

26. Ibid., 13.

27. Ibid., 13–14.

28. Ibid., 14–15.

29. Ibid., 117.

30. Montejano, *Anglos and Mexicans.*

31. See Pete Hernández, *Petitioner,* 24.

32. Ibid., 25.

33. Ibid. Also see *Oyama v. California,* 332 U.S. 633 (1948), and *Buchanan v. Warley,* 245 U.S. 360 (1917).

34. *Petitioner,* 27.

35. Ibid., 8.

36. Ibid., 29.

37. Ibid., 30–31. See also *Hirabayashi v. United States* (1943).

38. See Appendix Status of Persons of Mexican Descent in Texas found in *Petitioner,* 37–41.

39. Ibid., 40–41.

40. G. C. García, "A Cotton Picker Finds Justice!" 24.

41. See "Brief in Opposition."

42. Ibid., 2.

43. Ibid.

44. Ibid., 2–3.

45. Ibid., 4–5.

46. Ibid., 14.

47. I first heard this story from Tom Kreneck, director of Special Collections at Texas A&M University in Corpus Christi, Texas, who was a friend of John Herrera, and conducted several interviews with him.

48. See "Jury Bias Put to High Court," *San Antonio Light,* January 12, 1954, 1.

49. Ibid.

50. Ibid.

51. See G. C. García, "A Cotton Picker Finds Justice!" 15.

52. Ibid.

53. See "Jury Bias Put to High Court," *San Antonio Light,* January 12, 1954, 1.

54. Ibid.

55. Ibid.

56. Ibid.

57. See Herrera letter to the editor of the "Sound Off" column in the *Houston*

Post, dated February 22, 1972, as one example of the celebratory nature of the repetition of the story.

58. Ibid.

59. Ibid.

60. Ibid.

61. See G. C. García, "A Cotton Picker Finds Justice!" 15.

62. Gus García and John J. Herrera were interviewed by KLBL-Radio Morales, a radio station in Houston (although the actual taping took place in a studio in San Antonio). No transcripts exist of the radio interview but there is a copy of the tape in the Houston Metropolitan Public Library, in the John J. Herrera Papers.

63. Ibid.

64. See next chapter for a discussion of Gus's correspondence with the Truman Administration.

65. By "groomed in a traditional manner," I mean offered a position in a major firm, granted a federal judgeship, and then moved to the appeals court.

Chapter 6. Lamentation, Deportation, and Integration for "Mexicans"

1. See G. C. García, "A Cotton Picker Finds Justice!" 15.

2. Gus was playing on the fact that Franco's Spain was very militaristic and would appreciate a military man who could speak Spanish.

3. See G. C. García, "A Cotton Picker Finds Justice!" 15.

4. Ibid., 16.

5. Ibid., 17.

6. See letter from Hector P. García to Manuel Ávila, September 18, 1961, in García Papers, Special Collection and Archives, Bell Library, Texas A&M University, Corpus Christi.

7. See G. C. García, "A Cotton Picker Finds Justice!" 24.

8. I. M. García, *Viva Kennedy*, 132–134.

9. G. C. García, "A Cotton Picker Finds Justice!" 18.

10. Ibid., 19.

11. Ibid.

12. Ibid.

13. Ibid., 20.

14. Ibid.

15. Ibid.

16. Ibid., 21.

17. For a good discussion of this LULAC ideal, see M. T. García, *Mexican Americans*, 25–61.

18. G. C. García, "A Cotton Picker Finds Justice!" 16.

19. Ibid., 17.

20. See *Rochin v. California* 342 U.S. 165, 1, 6–7.

21. Ibid., 5–6.

22. Ibid., 8.

23. Ibid., 9.

24. For a more detailed discussion of law enforcement violence and coercion, see Mirandé, *Gringo Justice;* Julian Samora, et al., *Gunpowder Justice;* and Rosales, *¡Pobre Raza!.*

25. See *Galvan v. Press, Officer in Charge, Immigration and Naturalization Service,* 347 U.S. 522 74 S. Ct. 737: 98 L.Ed. 911; 1954 U.S. LEXIS 2660, 14–15.

26. See Navarro, *Mexicano Political Experience in Occupied America,* 241–246.

27. For a further discussion of the McCarran-Walter Act, see Navarro, *Mexicano Political Experience,* 245–246; and Acuña, *Occupied America,* 301.

28. See Navarro, *Mexicano Political Experience,* 247.

29. See *Galvan v. Press,* 4.

30. Ibid., 12.

31. Ibid., 13–14.

32. Ibid., 15.

33. Ibid.

34. Ibid., 16.

35. This quote is found in Blanton, "George I. Sánchez, Ideology, and Whiteness," 588.

36. Ibid.

37. Ibid., 586–587.

38. See *Charles Rowoldt v. J. D. Perfetto, Acting Officer in Charge, Immigration and Naturalization Service,* Department of Justice, St. Paul, Minnesota, 78 S. Ct. 180.

39. For an outstanding discussion of this massive deportation campaign, see J. R. García, *Operation Wetback.* Also, see Navarro, *Mexicano Political Experience,* 246–250.

40. Ibid., 247.

41. Ibid., 248–249.

42. For further discussion on the pamphlet and the fallout from it, see I. M. García, *Hector P. García,* 198–202.

43. Ibid., 199–203.

44. See Hernández, *Racial Profiling,* for an in-depth work on the border patrol.

45. I. M. García, *Hector P. García,* 200.

46. Ibid., 200–201.

47. I. M. García, *Hector P. García,* 196–197, includes a discussion of the report "The Wetback in the Lower Rio Grande" by Lyle Sanders and Olen Leonard. Particularly objectionable to some reformers were the interviews conducted by the authors with several Anglo growers who made disparaging remarks about Mexicans. The report was published by the University of Texas in 1951 as an

Inter-American Occasional Paper, and funded by the American Council of Spanish-Speaking People, which Sánchez headed.

48. Ibid., 201–202.

49. See Ed Idar Jr. letter to Hector P. García, Dec. 21, 1954, in the Hector P. García Papers, Special Collections and Archives, Bell Library, Texas A&M University, Corpus Christi.

50. For a more extensive discussion of these points, see I. M. García, *Viva Kennedy*, 123–159.

Chapter 7. A Differentiated Class, Not a Class Apart

1. See Warren, *Memoirs of Earl Warren*, 299. The chief justice simply retold some of the facts of the case and reported that the Court reversed the lower court ruling because the Fourteenth Amendment applied to any "delineated class."

2. See Johnson, "The Vinson Court and Racial Segregation, 1946–1953," 220–230.

3. A limited sampling of works on Earl Warren include White, *Earl Warren: A Public Life*; Pollack, *Earl Warren: The Judge Who Changed America*; Katcher, *Earl Warren: A Political Biography*; Schwartz, *Super Chief*; Bozell, *The Warren Revolution*; and more recently, Newton, *Justice For All*.

4. For an Asian American critique of Earl Warren and his efforts to "redeem whiteness," see Cho, "Redeeming Whiteness." Cho argues that Warren went through a period of "racial redemption" that involved "repudiating white supremacy's 'old' regime; burying historical memories of racial subordination; and transforming white supremacy into a viable contemporary regime." In other words, Cho argues that Warren sought to "clean up" white supremacy in order to maintain whites' superior asymmetric relationship with other racial and ethnic groups.

5. Cray, *Chief Justice*.

6. Whitfield, *The Culture of the Cold War*; Caute, *The Great Fear*.

7. Dudziak, *Cold War Civil Rights*; Skrentmy, "The Effects of the Cold War on African-American Civil Rights," 237–285.

8. See Carroll, *Felix Longoria's Wake*, 167–170, for a discussion of the incident and its impact on the efforts to negotiate a foreigner workers agreement between the United States and Mexico. Also, see Guglielmo, "Fighting for Caucasian Rights," 1212–1237.

9. For a view that he was sensitive to Mexican American concerns, see Salinas, "Gus García and Thurgood Marshall."

10. See "Bench Memorandum—Cert to the Court of Criminal Appeals of Texas," in the Mexican American Civil Rights File in Clark Papers.

11. See handwritten memo from Tom C. Clark to Earl Warren, dated April

30, 1954, in Clark Papers, Box A32, Folder #6. There is also a typed version of the letter in the same location. "Shay" was a nickname for Justice Minton.

12. Ibid.

13. See letter from R. A. Cortez to Tom Clark, November 4, 1948; and letter from Clark to Cortez, dated December 1, 1948. Both letters are found in the Truman Papers. The same file also contains a letter from Watson B. Miller, Commissioner of Immigration and Naturalization Service, dated October 26, 1948, which indicates that Clark had requested a response to Mexican American reformers' concerns of issues of illegal immigration.

14. See Carroll's *Felix Longeria* and I. M. García, *Hector P. García*.

15. Ibid. It is interesting to note that Gus García served as the Longoria family's attorney during the legislative hearing.

16. I. M. García, *Hector P. García*, 135.

17. See letter, Felix Frankfurter to Earl Warren, April 29, 1954, in the Hernández File, Earl Warren Papers, Library of Congress.

18. Baker, *Felix Frankfurter*, 261–263. Also, see Lash, *From the Diaries of Felix Frankfurter*, for a discussion of Frankfurter's dilemma in seeking to reconcile his need to be sensitive to the "times" while maintaining "judicial independence."

19. Ibid.

20. Ibid.

21. The Court had heard the case before Warren joined it and would rehear it once he became chief justice.

22. For an excellent discussion of the process that finally brought a unanimous decision, see Newman, *Hugo Black: A Biography*, 432–487.

23. Klarman, *From Jim Crow to Civil Rights*, 302.

24. Schwartz, *Inside the Warren Court*, 82–83.

25. Klarman, *From Jim Crow to Civil Rights*, 297.

26. Frankfurter letter to Warren.

27. Ibid.

28. Ibid.

29. I. M. García, *Hector P. García*, 145–146.

30. Ibid., 191–192.

31. See George I. Sánchez letter to Hector P. García, July 23, 1970, in Hector P. García Collection at Texas A&M University, Corpus Christi.

32. Ibid. Also, in a now unavailable recording conducted by Professor Martha Tewe, Carlos Cadena is said to have confirmed this version. Also see Ricardo Romo, "George I. Sanchez and the Civil Rights Movement: 1940–1960," *La Raza Law Journal* Vol. 1, No. 3 (Fall 1986), 357.

33. See De Anda interview.

34. See I. M. García, *Chicanismo*, 68–85, for a discussion of the Chicano Movement's racial and class differentiation from mainstream America.

35. See I. M. García, *Viva Kennedy*, 74–83, for the only available discussion of the Statement of Principles.

36. Ibid.

37. See Memorandum by the Chief Justice, No. 406—*Pete Hernández v. State of Texas*, April 19, 1954, Hernández File, Warren Papers.

38. Ibid., 2.

39. See Supreme Court ruling.

40. Ibid., 3.; The Texas Court had ruled in the Juarez case that Roman Catholics could not be systematically excluded from jury duty; and in the Puente case, the same court had struck down restrictive covenants prohibiting the sale of land to persons of Mexican descent.

41. *Hernández v. Texas*, 3.

42. Ibid.

43. Ibid.

44. For an example of these rulings, see Cadena's brief and those of M. C. González and James De Anda.

45. Ibid., 4.

46. Ibid.

47. Ibid., 4–5.

48. Ibid., 6.

49. Ibid., 7.

50. Ibid.

51. Ibid.

52. See "Political Interests of Latins United," the *Texas Observer* (September 15, 1961), for a discussion and reaction to Sánchez' comments.

53. See letter from Carlos Cadena to George I. Sánchez, May 6, 1954, in the Sanchez Collection, Box 19, Folder 5.

54. See page 3 of the ruling.

55. See page 6 of the ruling.

56. See letter to Sánchez, May 6, 1954.

57. See letter from John J. Herrera to the *LULAC News* on the twenty-fifth anniversary of LULAC's founding (1954). The letter is undated but can be found in the García Collection at the Texas A&M University, Corpus Christi Special Collections as part of a stapled pamphlet titled, "50 Years of Serving Hispanic, Golden Anniversary, 1929–1979."

58. See the *San Antonio Light* of May 3, 1954, front page.

59. See "High Court Rules Hernández Case In Texas Is Void," *Albuquerque Journal*, May 4, 1954, no page number available.

60. See *Corpus Christi Caller*, May 4, 1950.

61. Ibid.

62. Ibid.

63. See "Texas Jury Selection Methods May Be Altered."

64. See "Latin Americans Ordered Allowed Jury Duty Rights," front-page article on May 4, 1954.

65. Ibid., 2.

66. "Court Widens Ban on Discrimination," *Los Angeles Times*, May 4, 1954.

67. "Texas Case Reversed in High Court," the *Dallas Morning News*, May 4, 1954.

68. "Jackson County Juries," the *Dallas Morning News*, May 5, 1954.

69. "The Mills of Justice Also Grind Slowly," *San Antonio Express*, May 5, 1954.

70. Ibid.

71. "Bar to Mexican Americans on Jury Illegal, Says Supreme Court Ruling," the *Washington Post and Times Herald*, May 4, 1954, 1.

72. See "Lopsided Juries," May 7, 1954, 28.

73. Ibid.

74. "La Suprema Corte de E.U. Condena los Distingos Raciales en Texas," *Excelsior*, Mayo 4, 1954; and "Un Paso más Contra la Discriminación en Texas," Mayo 10, 1954.

75. Ibid.

76. See note 8 above, "Fighting for Caucasian Rights." No extensive work on Mexican newspaper coverage of Mexican American issues is available and so it is difficult to assess the amount and reach of the coverage of *Hernández* and other civil rights cases.

77. "Exclusion of Persons of Mexican Descent from Jury Service," 619–620.

78. "Constitutional Law—Discrimination in Selection of Jurors," 131.

79. Ibid., 133.

80. "Constitutional Law—Equal Protection Clause—Exclusion of a Class from Jury Service," 263.

81. Ibid., 266. The journal cited *Sánchez v. Texas; Carrasco v. State*, and *Ramirez v. State*, and provided a slightly different interpretation on them than did the Texas court.

82. Ibid. The journal specifically cited *Juarez v. Texas* as proof of previous Texas court rulings that acknowledged other groups besides whites and Negroes as being protected by the Equal Protection Clause of the Fourteenth Amendment.

83. Ibid.

Chapter 8. A Victory for "Every Living Soul"

1. See "County Puts 'Hold' on Hernández," the *Edna Herald*, May 6, 1954, no page number available.

2. See "García Will Ask For Venue Change In Pete Hernández Murder Trial," the *Edna Herald*, May 27, 1954, page unavailable.

3. Ibid.

4. See "Grand Jury Will Be Impaneled, To Hear 33 Cases," the *Edna Herald*, September 16, 1954, page unavailable.

5. See "Pete Hernández Is Re-Indicted By Jury," the *Edna Herald*, September 23, 1954; also, "Jury Returns Indictment On Hernández," *Victoria Advocate*, September 23, 1954.

6. See "Retrial in '51 Killing Brings Reduced Sentence," *Corpus Christi Caller*, December 28, 1954.

7. See letter from Gus García to Jack Ross, February 12, 1960, George I. Sánchez Collection, Folder 20.

8. See Gus García letter dated June 8, 1960, which was not addressed to anyone but was carbon copied to several individuals including Herrera, Sánchez, De Anda, Hector P. García, and his friend Anthony "Tony" García. This is also found in the Sánchez Collection.

9. See Gus García letter to Pete Hernández, June 8, 1950, in Sánchez Collection, Folder 20.

10. Ibid.

11. Ibid.

12. Much of the information regarding Pete's whereabouts came from his extended family, who seemed to know isolated details about many aspects of his life.

13. This occurred in Williamson County, Texas, one year after the *Hernández* ruling. The delay brought Mexican Americans to the jury commission and one served on the petit jury. The name of the defendant is not given in the GI Forum newsletter where it appeared in the "Marching Along" section on January 3, 1955.

14. See De Anda interview.

15. By the late 1960s Chicano activists, intellectuals, and politicians had racialized the term Mexican American and fully accepted their ethnic, if not racial, "otherness."

16. For a good discussion on this topic, see M. T. García, *Mexican Americans*, 25–61.

17. See "Herrera, John J." in *The New Handbook of Texas*, 575.

18. See column "Justice for justice" by Veronica Salazar in the *San Antonio Express-News*, June 22, 1975, 2-B; also, "Remembering Cadena, Former Appeals Court Justice, Civil Rights Lawyer Laid to Rest" *San Antonio Express-News*, January 16, 2001, no page number available.

19. See "Justice for Justice," supra 15.

20. See I. M. García, *Viva Kennedy*, p. 112 and p. 119, for a discussion of how Garza got his appointment.

21. See "García, Gustavo C." on *The Handbook of Texas Online*, dated March 30, 2004.

22. There are numerous letters between Gus and Herrera in Folders 21 and 22 in the John J. Herrera Collection in the Special Collections of the Metropolitan Public Library of the City of Houston that shed light on Gus's declining fortunes, and that reveal the closeness of the two men. There are also

some letters between Eleanor, one of Gus's wives, and Herrera within which they discuss the estrangement and Gus's two daughters.

23. This obituary is found in Folder 21 of the John J. Herrera Collection.

24. Ibid.

25. See "Mexican Americans and the Administration of Justice in the Southwest," A Report of the United States Commission on Civil Rights, March 1970, 36.

26. Ibid., iii.

27. Ibid., 37–38.

28. Ibid.

29. Ibid., 38–39.

30. Ibid., 45–46.

31. Ibid., 46.

32. For more on García's involvement, see I. M. García, *Hector P. García*, 282–287.

33. G. C. García, "A Cotton Picker Finds Justice!" 2.

34. Ibid., 6.

35. Ibid., 24.

36. No work exists yet on that connection, but it is quite logical to conclude that Texas legislators understood that when the Supreme Court struck down any perceived exclusion of Mexican Americans and African Americans from jury duty, that it would not be long before they would do the same to the exclusion of women.

Bibliography

Acuña, Rodolfo. *Occupied America: A History of Chicanos*. 5th ed. New York: Pearson Longman, 2004.

Anders, Evan. *Boss Rule in South Texas: The Progressive Era*. Austin: University of Texas Press, 1982.

Baker, Liva. *Felix Frankfurter*. New York: Coward-McCann, Inc., 1969.

Blanton, Carlos K. "George I. Sánchez, Ideology, and Whiteness in the Making of the Mexican American Civil Rights Movement, 1930–1960." *Journal of Southern History* 72, no. 3 (August 2006): 588.

Bozell, L. Brent. *The Warren Revolution: Reflections on the Consensus Society*. New Rochelle: Arlington House, 1966.

Brand, Jeffrey S. "The Supreme Court, Equal Protection, and Jury Selection: Denying that Race Still Matters." *Wisconsin Law Review* (1994).

Burma, John H. *Spanish-Speaking Groups in the United States*. Durham: Duke University Press, 1954.

Carroll, Patrick J. *Felix Longoria's Wake: Bereavement, Racism, and the Rise of Mexican American Activism*. Austin: University of Texas Press, 2003.

Caute, David. *The Great Fear: The Anti-Communist Purges under Truman and Eisenhower*. New York: Simon & Schuster, 1978.

Cho, Sumi. "Redeeming Whiteness in the Shadow of Internment: Earl Warren, Brown, and A Theory of Racial Redemption." *Boston College Law Review* 40 (1998): 73.

Clark, Tom C. Papers. Tartlon Library, University of Texas at Austin.

"Constitutional Law—Discrimination in Selection of Jurors." *Alabama Law Review* 7 (1954–55): 131.

"Constitutional Law—Equal Protection Clause—Exclusion of a Class from Jury Service." *North Carolina Law Review* 33 (1954–55): 263.

Craig, Richard B. *The Bracero Program: Interest Groups and Foreign Policy.* Austin: University of Texas Press, 1971.

Cray, Ed. *Chief Justice: A Biography of Earl Warren.* New York: Simon & Schuster, 1997.

De León, Arnoldo. *Ethnicity in the Sunbelt: A History of Mexican Americans in Houston.* Monograph Series no. 7. Houston: University of Houston, 1989.

———. *Ethnicity in the Sunbelt: Mexican Americans in Houston.* University of Houston Series in Mexican American Studies no. 4. College Station: Texas A&M University Press, 2001.

Dudziak, Mary L. *Cold War Civil Rights: Race and the Image of American Democracy.* Princeton: Princeton University Press, 2002.

"Exclusion of Persons of Mexican Descent from Jury Service." *American Bar Association Journal* 40 (July 1954): 619–620.

Foley, Neil. *The White Scourge: Mexicans, Blacks and Poor Whites in Texas Cotton Culture.* Berkeley: University of California Press, 1997.

Galarza, Ernesto. *Merchants of Labor: The Mexican Bracero Story: An Account of the Managed Migration of Mexican Farm Workers in California, 1942–1960.* Charlotte, Calif.: McNally and Loftin, 1964.

García, Hector P. Papers. Special Collections and Archives. Texas A&M University, Corpus Christi.

García, Ignacio M. *Chicanismo: The Forging of a Militant Ethos among Mexican Americans.* Tucson: University of Arizona Press, 1997.

———. *Hector P. García: In Relentless Pursuit of Justice.* Houston: Arte Público Press, 2003.

———. "Latinos in the Politics of the West." In *Politics in the West.* Lawrence: University of Kansas Press, 2008. forthcoming.

———. *Viva Kennedy: Mexican Americans in Search of Camelot.* College Station: Texas A&M University Press, 2000.

García, Juan Ramon. *Operation Wetback: The Mass Deportation of Mexican Undocumented Workers in 1954.* Westport, Conn.: Greenwood Press, 1980.

García, Mario T. "In Search of America." In *Mexican Americans.* New Haven: Yale University Press, 1989.

———. *Mexican Americans: Leadership, Ideology, and Identity, 1930–1960.* New Haven: Yale University Press, 1991.

García, Richard A. *Rise of the Mexican American Middle Class: San Antonio, 1929–1941.* College Station: Texas A&M University Press, 1991.

Gould, Lewis L. *Progressives and Prohibitionists: Texas Democrats in the Wilson Era.* Austin: University of Texas Press, 1973.

Green, George Norris. *The Establishment in Texas Politics: The Primitive Years, 1938–1957*. Westport, Conn.: Greenwood Press, 1979.

Griswold del Castillo, Richard. *The Treaty of Guadalupe Hidalgo: A Legacy of Conflict*. Norman: University of Oklahoma Press, 1990.

Guglielmo, Thomas A. "Fighting for Caucasian Rights: Mexicans, Mexican Americans, and the Transnational Struggle for Civil Rights in World War II Texas." *Journal of American History* 92, no. 4 (March 2006): 1212–1237.

Gutierrez, Felix F. *Spanish Language Radio in the Southwestern United States*. Austin: University of Texas Press, 1979.

The Handbook of Texas Online. Austin: Texas State Historical Association, 2005. http://www.tshaonline.org/handbook/online/

Handman, Max. "Preliminary Report on Nationality and Delinquency: The Mexicans in Texas." In *The Mexican and the Law*. New York: Arno Press, 1974.

Hernández, Kathleen Anne Lytle. *Racial Profiling and the United States Border Patrol, 1924–1955*. UMI Dissertation Service, 2002.

Herrera, John. Papers. Houston Metropolitan Public Library.

Johnson, Whittington B. "The Vinson Court and Racial Segregation, 1946–1953." *Journal of Negro History* 63, no. 3 (July 1978): 220–230.

Kaplowitz, Craig A. *LULAC: Mexican Americans and National Policy*. College Station: Texas A&M University Press, 2005.

Katcher, Leo. *Earl Warren: A Political Biography*. New York: McGraw-Hill, 1967.

Kibbe, Pauline R. *Latin Americans in Texas*. Albuquerque: University of New Mexico Press, 1946.

Klarman, Michael J. *From Jim Crow to Civil Rights: The Supreme Court and the Struggle for Racial Equality*. New York: Oxford University Press, 2004.

Lash, Joseph P. *From the Diaries of Felix Frankfurter*. New York: W. W. Norton & Co., 1975.

Little, Wilson. *Spanish-Speaking Children in Texas*. Austin: University of Texas Press, 1944.

López, Ian F. Haney. *White by Law: The Legal Construction of Race Critical America*. New York: New York University Press, 1996.

Manuel, Herschel T. *The Education of Mexican and Spanish-Speaking Children in Texas*. Austin: University of Texas Press, 1930.

———. *Spanish-Speaking Children of the Southwest: Their Education and the Public Welfare*. Austin: University of Texas Press, 1965.

Márquez, Benjamin. *LULAC: The Evolution of a Mexican American Political Organization*. Austin: University of Texas Press, 1993.

————. "Politics of Race and Class: The League of United Latin American Citizens in the Post-World War II Period." *Social Science Quarterly* 68 (March 1987).

McBride, John. *Vanishing Bracero: Valley Revolution.* San Antonio: Naylor, 1963.

Mirandé, Alfredo. *Gringo Justice.* Notre Dame: University of Notre Dame Press, 1990.

Montejano, David. *Anglos and Mexicans in the Making of Texas, 1836–1986.* Austin: University of Texas Press, 1987.

————. *Race, Labor Repression, and Capitalist Agriculture: Notes from South Texas, 1920–1930.* Berkeley: Institute for the Study of Social Change, University of California, 1977.

Morin, Raul. *Among the Valiant: Mexican-Americans in World War II and Korea.* Alhambra, Calif.: Borden Publishing Company, 1963.

Navarro, Armando. *Mexicano Political Experience in Occupied Aztlán: Struggles and Change.* Walnut Creek, Calif.: Altamira Press, 2005.

The New Handbook of Texas. Vol. 3. Austin: Texas State Historical Association, 1996.

Newman, Roger K. *Hugo Black: A Biography.* New York: Fordham University Press, 1997.

Newton, Jim. *Justice for All: Earl Warren and the Nation He Made.* New York: Riverhead Books, 2006.

"No Mexicans Allowed." *Inter-Americans* (Sept. 1943): 8.

Olivas, Michael A., ed. *"Colored Men" and "Hombres Aqui": Hernández v. Texas and the Emergence of Mexican-American Lawyering.* Houston: Arte Público Press, 2000.

Oropeza, Lorena. *¡Raza Sí! Guerra No!: Chicano Protest and Patriotism during the Viet Nam War Era.* Berkeley: University of California Press, 2005.

Paz, Octavio. *El laberinto de la soledad y otras obras.* New York: Penguin Books, 1993.

Perea, Juan F. "Ethnicity and the Constitution: Beyond the Black and White Binary Constitution." *William & Mary Law Review* 36, 571.

Pollack, Jack Harrison. *Earl Warren: The Judge Who Changed America.* Englewood Cliffs, N.J.: Prentice-Hall, 1979.

Quiroz, Anthony. *Claiming Citizenship: Mexican Americans in Victoria, Texas.* College Station: Texas A&M University Press, 2005.

Ramos, Christopher. "The Educational Legacy of Racially Restrictive Covenants: Their Long Term Impact on Mexican Americans." *4 Scholars: St. Mary's Law Review* (Fall 2001): 149–184, 159–166.

Rivas-Rodriguez, Maggie, ed. *Mexican Americans and World War II*. Austin: University of Texas Press, 2005.

Rosales, Arturo. *¡Pobre Raza! Violence, Justice and Mobilization among México Lindo Immigrants, 1900–1936*. Austin: University of Texas Press, 1999.

Ruiz Urueta, Ramón Eduardo. *Memories of a Hyphenated Man*. Tucson: University of Arizona Press, 2003.

Salinas, Lupe S. "Gus García and Thurgood Marshall: Two Legal Giants Fighting for Justice." *Thurgood Marshall Law Review* 28 (Spring 2003): 145.

Samora, Julian., ed. *La Raza: Forgotten Americans*. Notre Dame: University of Notre Dame, 1966.

Samora, Julian, Joe Bernal, and Albert Peña. *Gunpowder Justice: A Reassessment of the Texas Rangers*. Notre Dame: University of Notre Dame Press, 1979.

Sánchez, George I. "Concerning Segregation of Spanish-Speaking Children in the Public Schools." *Inter-American Educational Occasional Papers*, no. 9. Austin: University of Texas Press, 1951.

Sánchez, George I. Papers. Benson Latin American Collection. University of Texas at Austin.

San Miguel, Guadalupe, Jr. *"Let All of Them Take Heed": Mexican Americans and the Campaign for Education Equality in Texas, 1910–1981*. Austin: University of Texas Press, 1987.

———. "The Struggle against Separate and Unequal Schools: Middle Class Mexican Americans and the Desegregation Campaign in Texas, 1929–1957." *History of Education Quarterly* 23 (Fall 1983).

Sandoval, Moises. *Our Legacy: The First Fifty Years*. Washington, D.C.: LULAC, 1979.

Schmidt, Benno C. "Juries, Jurisdiction, and Race Discrimination: The Last Promise of *Strauder v. West Virginia*." *Texas Law Review* 61 (1983): 1401–1409.

Schwartz, Bernard. *Inside the Warren Court*. New York: Doubleday & Co., 1983.

———. *Super Chief: Earl Warren and His Supreme Court: A Judicial Biography*. New York: New York University Press, 1983.

Scruggs, M. Otey. "Texas and the Bracero Program, 1942–1947." *Pacific Historical Review* 32 (1963).

Servín, Manuel P. *The Mexican-Americans: An Awakening Minority*. Beverly Hills: Glencoe Press, 1970.

Sheridan, Clare. "'Another White Race': Mexican Americans and the Paradox of Whiteness in Jury Selection." *Law and History Review* 21 (2003): 109.

Skrentmy, John David. "The Effect of the Cold War on African-American Civil Rights: America and the World Audience, 1945–68." *Theory and Society* 27 (1998): 237–285.

Taylor, Ira Thomas. *The Cavalcade of Jackson County.* San Antonio: The Naylor Company, 1938.

Taylor, Paul Schuster. *An American-Mexican Frontier: Nueces County, Texas.* Chapel Hill: University of North Carolina Press, 1934.

Truman, Harry S. Papers. Philleo Nash files, Harry S. Truman papers. Harry S. Truman Library, Independence, MO.

Tuck, Ruth. *Not With the Fist.* New York: Harcourt, Brace and Company, 1946.

U.S. Bureau of the Census. *Fifteenth Census of the United States: 1930.* Washington, D.C.: Bureau of the Census, 1930.

Vasconcelos, José. *The Cosmic Race / La raza cosmica (Race in the Americas).* Trans. Didier T. Jaén. Baltimore: John Hopkins University, 1997.

Warren, Earl. Papers. Library of Congress. Washington, D.C.

Warren, Earl. *The Memoirs of Earl Warren.* Garden City: Doubleday & Co., 1977.

White, G. Edward. *Earl Warren: A Public Life.* New York: Oxford University Press, 1982.

Whitfield, Stephen J. *The Culture of the Cold War.* 2nd ed. Baltimore: John Hopkins University Press, 1996.

Index

Maverick, Maury, 57, 201–2
McCarran-Walter Internal Security Act,
    118, 159, 162
Menard County, Texas, 65–58
Mendez v. Westminster School District, 99, 126,
    131, 175
Mexican American civil rights: and equality,
    11, 65, 79, 88, 172, 202; halting expan-
    sion of, 104; history of, 2–6, 9–15, 175;
    importance of *Hernández*, 1–16, 169,
    191–202; and labor, 6, 17, 21–23; lack of
    finances for, 116–24; lack of help with,
    151; and other national advocacy groups,
    117, 149–51; pride in, 146–47; reformers,
    32, 53–56, 82–90, 112, 123–24; and
    Texas, 133–35; and veterans, 4, 7, 71,
    76–77, 79–81, 96, 128, 162–63; victories
    of, 57–58; views of, 153–55. *See also*
    American GI Forum; black/white binary;
    discrimination; Equal Protection Clause;
    Hernández v. Texas; immigration; jury
    selection; LULAC; Supreme Court
Mexican American identity: as bilingual, 82;
    and Chicano movement, 197; as a "class
    apart," 8–9, 65, 77, 82, 96, 170–91; debat-
    ing, 77, 81, 91, 101; desire for acceptance
    of, 112, 126; and other ethnicities, 87;
    proud of, 4, 108; questions about, 3-8, 11,
    86, 128–29, 195–96; as seen by Mexican
    Americans, 77–78. *See also* black/white
    binary
"Mexican Americans and the administration
    of justice in the Southwest," 198–200
Minton, Sherman, 172–74. *See also* Supreme
    Court

naturalization, 3, 8, 58, 64–65, 77, 115, 159.
    See also immigration
Neal v. Delaware, 76
New York City, 149, 155
Norris v. Alabama, 62–63, 69, 75, 98, 115,
    136, 182, 190–91

Oyama v. California, 137

Pan American Union, 11
Partido Liberal Mexicano(PLM) clubs, 12–13
Patton v. State of Mississippi, 92–94, 97
People v. de la Garza, 64
Perales, Alonso S. 11
Plessy v. Ferguson, 174–75
political ideologies: communism, 12–13,
    118, 159–61, 171; nationalism, 13, 123,
154; progressivism, 20; socialism, 4,
    12–13, 154, 159. *See also* veteranism

Ramirez v. State, 65–69, 72, 95, 97
Reed, Stanley F., 63, 94, 118. *See also*
    Supreme Court
re Rodriguez, 64–65
Rochin v. Califonia, 155–58
Rodriguez, Sesario, 192
Rodriguez, Victor, 25–26, 34
Rosas, Mrs. Chris, 49–51
Rosenberg, Harvey, 130
Ross, Jack, 193
Ross v. Texas, 97

Salazar v. State, 75–76, 83–86, 91
Sánchez, Chico, 28–29, 36
Sánchez, George I.: ideas of, 108–9, 150–51,
    177–78; letters of, 118–20, 126, 128–30,
    183, 185; as reformer, 10, 58–59, 77, 112,
    124, 160–61, 166, 177–78
Sánchez v. State, 74–76, 102–3
Sánchez v. Texas, 37, 78, 84–86, 90–95, 98,
    103
San Patricio County, Texas, 71–72
school segregation: challenges to, 4, 11,
    128, 151; in "class" argument, 11, 134,
    137, 176–77; in Edna, Texas, 19, 35,
    38–50; lawyers expertise in, 54–57, 60,
    153, 186; litigation history, 37, 71, 95,
    99, 104, 116, 131, 196–97; pressures on,
    22–25, 53, 57; as unconstitutional, 24–27
Smith v. Texas, 63, 94, 98, 103
Spanish Americans. *See* Mexican Americans
Spanish-language newspapers, 189–90
Spanish-language radio, 121–22, 127
Spanish-speaking people. *See* Mexican
    Americans
St. Mary's University Law School, 56–57,
    96
Strauder v. West Virginia, 62–63, 132, 180
Supreme Court: arguments in, 125–48,
    154–55; case chosen by, 117–18; deci-
    sion of, 1, 8–9, 117, 170–91; expecta-
    tions about, 33–34, 53, 59–60, 104,
    119–20; *Hernández* opening brief,
    132–38; leanings of, 131; and other
    cases, 57, 62–63, 75, 83, 92–99, 102–3,
    114–15, 155; decisions of, reviewed by
    media, 186–91; preparing for, 128–30;
    questioning decision of, 132–33; and
    significance of *Hernández*, 1–16, 157–58,
    169, 192–202; as symbol, 123–25

About the Author

Ignacio M. García is the Lemuel Hardison Redd Jr. Professor of Western and Latino History at Brigham Young University. He is the author of four books on Mexican American civil rights in addition to this one and is currently expanding his expertise to civil rights in the West. His first two books, *United We Win* and *Chicanismo*, both published by the University of Arizona Press, are considered classic works on the Chicano Movement, while his third book, *Viva Kennedy*, won the Coral H. Tullis award for the best book on Texas history in 2000. He is currently working on a series of letters that interprets Mexican American history for a new generation of scholars.

CPSIA information can be obtained at www.ICGtesting.com
Printed in the USA
LVOW060007110213

319488LV00003B/5/P